CLARENDON LAW SERIES

Edited by

PETER BIRKS

CLARENDON LAW SERIES

Introduction to Roman Law
By BARRY NICHOLAS

Legal Reasoning and Legal Theory
By NEIL MCCORMICK

Natural Law and Natural Rights
By JOHN G. FINNIS

The Concept of Law (2nd edition)
By H. L. A. HART

An Introduction to the Law of Contract (5th edition)
By P. S. ATIYAH

Principles of Criminal Law (2nd edition)
By ANDREW ASHWORTH

Playing by the Rules
By FREDERICK SCHAUER

Precedent in English Law (4th edition)
By SIR RUPERT CROSS AND JIM HARRIS

An Introduction to Administrative Law (3rd edition)
By PETER CANE

Policies and Perceptions of Insurance
By MALCOLM CLARKE

An Introduction to Family Law
By GILLIAN DOUGLAS

Discrimination Law
By SANDRA FREDMAN

The Conflict of Laws
By ADRIAN BRIGGS

The Law of Property (3rd edition)
By F. H. LAWSON AND BERNARD RUDDEN

Introduction to Company Law
By PAUL L. DAVIES

Tort Law
By TONY WEIR

PERSONAL PROPERTY LAW

PROFESSOR M.G. BRIDGE

LLB (London) LLM (London) Barrister, Middle Temple
Professor of Commercial Law and Dean of the Faculty of Laws,
University College London
Director of Research, Norton Rose

OXFORD
UNIVERSITY PRESS

OXFORD
UNIVERSITY PRESS

Great Clarendon Street, Oxford OX2 6DP

Oxford University Press is a department of the University of Oxford.
It furthers the University's objective of excellence in research, scholarship,
and education by publishing worldwide in

Oxford New York

Auckland Bangkok Buenos Aires Cape Town Chennai
Dar es Salaam Delhi Hong Kong Istanbul Karachi Kolkata
Kuala Lumpur Madrid Melbourne Mexico City Mumbai Nairobi
São Paulo Shanghai Singapore Taipei Tokyo Toronto

Oxford is a registered trade mark of Oxford University Press
in the UK and in certain other countries

Published in the United States
by Oxford University Press Inc., New York

First and second editions published by Blackstone Press

British Library Cataloguing in Publication Data

Data available

Library of Congress Cataloging in Publication Data

Data available

ISBN 0–19–925476–1

Typeset in Ehrhardt
by RefineCatch Limited, Bungay, Suffolk
Printed in Great Britain by
Biddles Ltd., Guildford and King's Lynn

'[M]y guiding-star always is, Get hold of portable property.'
(Wemmick, in Charles Dickens, *Great Expectations*, chapter 24)

Preface

The union of Oxford University Press and Blackstone Press has resulted in the adoption of this third edition by the Clarendon Law series, though the agnatic bond with Blackstone Press survives in the enduring form of the first and second editions. The book remains an introductory, but by no means a rudimentary, text. As stated in the first edition, my aim in writing this book was to define the subject of Personal Property for curricular purposes by focusing on the acquisition, loss, transfer and protection of interests in personal property. Some of this material may already be picked up in courses on tort, land law, restitution and trusts, though often in an incomplete or unsystematic way. This book is intended to do three things: first, to provide the personal property component of a general property course; secondly, to serve as a text for a free-standing course on personal property law; and thirdly, to lay a foundation for later Commercial Law studies.

There are numerous changes in this third edition. The text has been rewritten and extended in a number of areas, particularly those parts dealing with tracing and resulting trusts. There has also been a significant amount of new case law to assimilate. Without listing the major cases, let it be said that they concern subjects like conversion, assignment, charges, forfeiture, insolvency, body parts, finding, gift, sale or return and mixtures. Personal Property is a diverse subject.

I wish to record the debt I owe for past assistance to Heather Saward and her colleagues at Blackstone Press. I have also been greatly assisted in preparing the present edition by Sheila Parrington, and by Sophie Rogers of Oxford University Press who was particularly kind in allowing me to introduce at a very late stage text based upon the decision of the House of Lords in *Kuwait Airways Corpn v Iraqi Airways Co* [2002] UKHL 19.

University College London
5 June 2002

Contents

Preface   vii
Table of Cases   xi
Table of Statutes   xxvii

1. **The meaning of personal property**   I
   Types of property   I
   What is a property right?   12

2. **Interests in chattels**   14
   Introduction   14
   Possession   16
   Ownership   28
   Bailment   33
   Transferring possession   43

3. **The protection of property interests**   47
   Introduction   47
   Trespass to chattels   48
   Liability in conversion   52
   Entitlement to sue in conversion   62
   Remedies issues   72

4. **The conveyance**   80
   Introduction   80
   Consensual transfers: sale   80
   Gratuitous consensual transfers   93
   Transfers by operation of law   103
   Failed transfers and resulting trusts   111

5. **Transfer of title**   115
   Introduction   115
   Overriding legal property interests   115
   Overriding equitable property interests   137
   Tracing   138

6. **Transfer of intangible property**   144
   Introduction   144
   Assignment of things (or choses) in action   145
   Negotiability   165

7. **Security interests in personal property**   169
   Introduction   169
   Possessory security   170
   Non-possessory security   178

   Index   197

Table of Cases

(1957) 42 Cornell LQ 168 53

Agip (Africa) Ltd v Jackson [1990] Ch 265; [1991] Ch547...140, 141, 142
Agnew v Commissioner of Inland Revenue [2001] 2 BCLC
   188 (PC)..183, 188, 189, 190, 191
Agra Bank, Ex p (1868) LR 3 Ch App 555.....................................162
Akbar Khan v Attar Singh [1936] 1 All ER 545 167
Akron Tyre Co v Kittson (1951) 82 CLR 477 108
Albazero, The [1974] AC 774..92
Albemarle Supply Co v Hind [1928] 1 KB 307........................172, 174
Aldridge v Johnson (1857) 7 E & B 885 90
Alexander v Southey (1821) 5 B & Ald 247 57
Aliakmon, The [1986] AC 785 93
Alicia Hosiery Ltd v Brown Shipley Ltd [1970] 1 QB 195 56
Aluminium Industrie Vaasen BV v Romalpa Aluminium Ltd
   [1976] 1 WLR 676 ....82, 83, 91
Anchor Line Ltd, Re [1937] Ch 1 82
Ancona v Rogers (1876) 1 Ex D 285..19
Anglo–Maltese Dry Dock Co Ltd, Re (1885) 54 LJ Ch 730...............172
Anthony v Haney (1832) 8 Bing 186...78
Appleby v Myers (1867) LR 2 CP 651 108
Arab Bank v Ross [1952] 2 QB 216...165
Aramis, The [1989] 1 Lloyd's Rep 213 168
Armory v Delamirie (1722) 1 Stra 505 ....24, 66, 72
Armour v Thyssen Edelstahlwerke AG [1991] 2 AC 339.............83, 184
Arpad, The [1934] P 189...56
Arrow Shipping Co Ltd v Tyne Improvement Commissioners
   (The Crystal) [1894] AC 508 ....22, 23
Ashby v Tolhurst [1937] 2 KB 242..35
Astley Industrial Trust v Miller [1968] 2 All ER 36 126
Atari Corpn (UK) Ltd v Electronic Boutique Stores Ltd [1998]
   1 All ER 1010 (CA)...86
Atlantic Computers Ltd, Re [1992] Ch 505 (CA)..............................190
Attorney-General v Guardian Newspapers Ltd [1987] 1 WLR
   1248 6

Attorney-General v Trustees of the British Museum [1903] 2
   Ch 598..26
Attorney-General of Hong Kong v Reid [1994] 1 AC 324 (PC) 11
Automatic Bottle Makers Ltd, Re [1926] Ch 412 138
Aveling Barford Ltd, Re [1989] 1 WLR 360.......................................172

Bailey v Barnes [1894] 1 Ch 25...138
Bailiffs of Dunwich v Sterry (1831) 1 B & Ad 831 52
Bain v Brand (1876) 1 App Cas 762...104
Bank of Credit and Commerce International SA (No.8), Re
   [1998] AC 214 (HL)..191
Banque Belge pour l'Etranger v Hambrouck [1921] 1 KB 321............140
Barclays Bank plc v Willowbrook International Ltd [1987]
   1 FTLR 386..160
Barker v Cox (1876) 4 Ch D 464..195
Barker v Furlong [1891] 2 Ch 172 ....52, 58
Barlow Clowes International Ltd v Vaughan [1992] 4 All ER 22 143
BBMB Finance (Hong Kong) Ltd v Eda Holdings Ltd [1991] 2
   All ER 129..72
Beale v Taylor [1967] 1 WLR 1193 82
Belsize Motor Supply Co v Cox [1914] 1 KB 244 73
Belvoir Finance Co v Harold G Cole & Co [1969] 1 WLR 1877.........125
Bence v Shearman [1898] 2 Ch 582 148
Berchtold, Re [1923] 1 Ch 192 10
Biddle v Bond (1865) 6 B & S 225...65
Bim Kemi v Blackburn Chemicals Ltd [2001] 2 Lloyd's Rep 93
   (CA) 157
Birch v Treasury Solicitor [1950] 2 All ER 1198 103
Bird v Town of Fort Frances [1949] 2 DLR 791 (Ontario)..................66
Bishopsgate Motor Finance Corpn v Transport Brakes Ltd [1949]
   1 KB 322...116
Blades v Higgs (1861) 10 CB (NS) 713..77
Boardman v Phipps [1967] 2 AC 46 6
Bond Worth Ltd, Re [1980] Ch 228....................................113, 181, 190
Borden (UK) Ltd v Scottish Timber Products Ltd [1981]
   Ch 25..109
Boscawen v Bajwa [1996] 1 WLR 328 ....139, 142
Bowmaker Ltd v Wycombe Motors Ltd [1946] KB 505 174
Bowmakers Ltd v Barnet Instruments Ltd [1945] KB 65 81
Brandon v Leckie (1972) 29 DLR (3d) 633 (Alberta) 135

Brandt v Liverpool Brazil and River Plate Steam Navigation Co
  [1924] 1 KB 575 168
Brandt's Sons & Co v Dunlop Rubber Co [1905] AC 454 148
Brice v Bannister (1878) 3 QBD 569 159
Bridge v Campbell Discount Co Ltd [1962] AC 600, 626 27
Bridges v Hawksworth (1851) 21 LJQB 75 25
Brightlife Ltd, Re [1987] Ch 200 190
Brinsmead v Harrison (1872) LR 7 CP 547 ....68, 72
Bristol Airport plc v Powdrill [1990] Ch 744 171
Broadwood v Granara (1854) 10 Ex 417 174
Brown v Mallett (1848) 5 CB 599 18
Buckley v Gross (1863) 3 B & S 566 66
Burdick v Sewell (1884) 13 QBD 159 ....178, 183
Burnett (1960) 76 LQR 364 61
Burroughes v Bayne (1860) 5 H & N 296 53
Business Computers Ltd v Anglo-African Leasing Co [1977] 2
  All ER 241 157

Cahn v Pockett's Bristol Channel Co [1899] 1 QB 643 126
Cain v Moon [1896] 2 QB 283 103
Canadian Laboratory Supplies Ltd v Englehard Industries Ltd
  [1980] 2 SCR 450 119
Capital Finance Co v Bray [1964] 1 WLR 323 57
Car and Universal Finance Co v Caldwell [1965] 1 QB 525 ....123, 127
Carlos Federspiel & Co v Charles Twigg & Co [1957] 1
  Lloyd's Rep 240 90
Carlos v Fancourt (1794) 5 TR 482 166
Carreras Rothman v Freeman Mathews Treasure Ltd [1985]
  Ch 207 181
Carter v Wake (1877) 4 Ch D 605 ....176, 178, 179
Cartwright v Green (1803) 8 Ves Jun 405 21
Case of Swans (1592) 7 Co Rep 15b 108
Castell & Brown Ltd, Re [1898] 1 Ch 315 138
Caxton Publishing Co v Sutherland Publishing Co [1939]
  AC 178 56
Celtic Extraction Ltd, Re [1999] 4 All ER 684 (CA) 7
Central Newbury Car Auctions Ltd v Unity Finance Ltd [1957] 1
  QB 371 120
Chaigley Farms Ltd v Crawford, Kaye & Grayshire Ltd [1996]
  BCC 957 108

Chapman Bros v Verco Bros & Co (1933) 49 CLR 306 39
Charge Card Services Ltd, Re [1987] Ch 150 ....152, 191
Charles v Blackwell (1876) 1 CPD 48 167
Charlesworth v Mills (1892) AC 231..192
Chase Manhatten Bank v Israel-British Bank [1981] 1 Ch 105 113,
    114, 142
Chelsea Yacht and Boat Co Ltd v Pope [2001] 2 All ER 409...............105
Chettiar v Chettiar [1962] AC 294..101
Choithram (T) International SA v Pagarini [2001] 1 WLR 1 (PC)......98,
    102
City Fur Manufacturing Co v Fureenbond Ltd [1937] 1 All ER
    799..130
City of London Corpn v Appleyard [1963] 2 All ER 843 25
Clarke v West Ham Corporation [1909] 2 KB 858 37
Clarke, Re (1887) 36 Ch D 348..180
Claydon v Bradley [1987] 1 WLR 521 167
Clayton v Le Roy [1911] 2 KB 1031 57
Clayton v Ramsden [1943] AC 320..99
Clayton's Case (1816) 1 Mer 572 143
Clough Mill Ltd v Martin [1985] 1 WLR 111 ....109, 184
Cochrane v Moore (1890) 25 QBD 57..81, 94
Coggs v Bernard (1703) 2 Ld Raym 909 ....35, 36, 37, 175
Cohen v Roche [1927] 1 KB 169 76
Colbeck v Diamanta Ltd [2002] EWHC 616 (QB)............................72
Coldman v Hill [1919] 1 KB 443 38
Cole v North Western Bank (1875) LR 10 CP 354......................125, 126
Cole, Re [1964] Ch 175...95, 100
Colonial Bank v Cady (1890) 15 App Cas 257 118
Colonial Bank v Whinney (1885) 30 Ch D 261 3
Colonial Central Mutual Insurance Co Ltd v ANZ Banking
    Group (New Zealand) Ltd [1995] 3 All ER 987 162
Commonwealth Trust Ltd v Akotey [1926] AC 72...........................120
Compaq Computers Ltd v Abercorn Group Ltd [1991] BCC 484 164
Consolidated Co v Curtis [1892] 1 QB 495...60
Cooper v Bill (1865) 3 H & C 722 43
Cosslett (Contractors) Ltd, Re (1997) 11 JIBFL 530; [1998]
    Ch 495 (CA)..27, 183, 188, 190
Costello v Chief Constable of Derbyshire [2001] 3 All ER 150
    (CA)..66, 67
Craven's Estate, Re [1937] Ch 423...103

Crawford v Kingston [1952] OR 714 (Ontario) 39
Cremer v General Carriers [1973] 2 Lloyd's Rep 366.........................168
Cryne v Barclays Bank [1987] BCLC 548 187
Crystal, The *see* Arrow Shipping Co Ltd v Tyne Improvement
  Commissioners
Cundy v Lindsay (1878) 3 App Cas 459..122

Dallas, Re [1904] 2 Ch 385..162, 163
Daly v Sydney Stock Exchange Ltd (1986) 160 CLR 371 114
Dansk Syndikat v Snell [1908] 2 Ch 127..195
David Allester Ltd, Re [1922] 2 Ch 211..178
De Gorter v Attenborough and Son (1904) 19 TLR 19.......................128
De Mattos v Gibson (1858) 4 D & J 276 ....32, 33
Dear v Reeves [2001] EWCA Civ 277 8
Dearle v Hall (1828) 3 Russ 1 ....138, 162, 163, 164
Delgoffe v Fader [1939] Ch 922 ....102, 103
Dennant v Skinner [1948] 2 KB 164..83
Devereux v Barclay (1819) 2 B & Ald 702...62
Deverges v Sandeman Clark & Co [1902] 1 Ch 579 187
Diamond Alkali Export Corpn v Fl Bourgeois [1923] 3 KB 443...........46
Diplock, Re [1948] Ch 465; [1951] AC 251..............................137, 143
Dixon v London Small Arms Co (1876) 1 App Cas 632.......................40
Dobson v North Tyneside Health Authority [1997] 1 WLR 596...........4
Don King Productions Inc v Warren [1998] 2 All ER 608;
  [1999] 2 All ER 218 (CA) 161
Donald v Suckling (1866) LR 1 QB 585 ....30, 58, 172, 176, 177
Douglas v Hello! Ltd [2001] 2 All ER 289..5
Douglas Valley Finance Co v S Hughes (Hirers) Ltd [1969]
  1 QB 738 55
DTC (CNC) Ltd v Gary Sargent & Co [1996] 1 WLR 797................172
Du Jardin v Beadman Bros [1952] 2 QB 712.....................................126
Dublin City Distillery v Doherty [1914] AC 823 43
Durham Bros v Robertson [1898] 1 QB 765 ....151, 153

Eastern Distributors Ltd v Goldring [1957] 2 QB 600 118
Eastgate, Re [1905] 1 KB 465...114, 123
Edwards v Newland & Co [1950] 2 KB 534 38
Eide UK Ltd v Lowndes Lambert Group Ltd [1998] 1 All ER
  946 (CA) 171
Elafi, The [1982] 1 All ER 208 87
Elitestone Ltd v Morris [1997] 2 All ER 513 105

Elliott v Bishop (1855) 11 Ex 113...3, 105
Elvin and Powell Ltd v Plummer Roddis Ltd (1933) 50 TLR 158........61
Elwin v O'Regan [1971] NZLR 1124...135
England v Cowley (1873) LR 8 Ex 126 ....34, 54
Entick v Carrington (1765) 2 Wils KB 275 49
Erichsen v Barkworth (1858) 3 H & N 601 9
Evans v Rival Granite Quarries Ltd [1910] 2 KB 979 189
Everitt v Martin [1953] NZLR 29 48

Farina v Home (1846) 16 M & W 119..46
Farquarson Bros and Co v King and Co [1902] AC 325 119
Farrant v Thompson (1822) 5 B & Ald 826 58
Federal Commissioner of Taxation v United Aircraft Corpn
    (1944) 68 CLR 525 6
Fenn v Bittleston (1851) 7 Ex 152 ....70, 177
Fitzroy v Cave [1905] 2 KB 364 146
Fletcher v Ashburner (1779) 1 Bro CC 497 11
Florence Land and Public Works Co, Re (1878) 10 Ch D 530 190
Flory v Denny (1852) 7 Ex 581..181
Foamcrete (UK) Ltd v Thrust Engineering Ltd (CA, unreported
    21 December 2000) 162
Foley v Hill (1848) 2 HLC 28..9, 38
Folkes v King [1923] 1 KB 282 ....125, 126
Forsyth International (UK) Ltd v Silver Shipping Co Ltd
    [1994] 1 WLR 1334 ....133, 134
Forthright Finance Ltd v Carlyle Finance Ltd [1997] 4 All ER
    90 (CA) 42, 136
Foskett v McKeown [2000] 3 All ER 97; 2 WLR 1299...............111, 139,
    140, 142
Fouldes v Willoughby (1841) 8 M & W 540..............................48, 50, 54
Four Point Garage Ltd v Carter [1985] 3 All ER 12...........................134
Fowler v Hollins (1872) LR 7 QB 616 54
Fowler v Lanning [1959] 1 QB 426..50
Franklin v Neate (1844) 13 M & W 481 ....27, 176
Freightline One, The [1986] 1 Lloyd's Rep 266 171
Freke v Carberry (1873) LR 16 Eq 461...10
Future Express, The [1992] 2 Lloyd's Rep 79 46

G W K Ltd v Dunlop Rubber Co (1926) 42 TLR 593 48
Gamer's Motor Centre Ltd v Natwest Whole Australia Ltd
    (1987) 163 CLR 236..133

Garfitt v Allen (1887) 37 Ch D 48 184
Garnett v M'Kewan (1872) LR 8 Ex 10...156
General & Finance Facilities v Cooks Cars (Romford) Ltd [1963]
    1 WLR 644 ....72, 76
George Barker Ltd v Eynon [1974] 1 WLR 462...............................172
Gilbert-Ash (Northern) Ltd v Modern Engineering (Bristol)
    Ltd [1974] AC 689 155
Gilchrist Watt & Sanderson Pty Ltd v York Products Pty Ltd
    [1970] 3 All ER 825 ....24, 34
Glencore International AG v Metro Trading Inc [2001] 1
    Lloyd's Rep 284...109, 111
Glyn, Mills & Co v East and West India Dock Co (1882) 7
    App Cas 591 9
Godfrey Philips Ltd v Investment Trust Corpn Ltd [1953] Ch 449.......9
Goldcorp Exchange Ltd, Re [1995] 1 AC 74..................................86, 89
Goodhart (1929) 3 CLJ 195...25
Gordon v Harper (1796) 7 TR 9 63
Gorringe v Irwell India Rubber Works (1886) 34 Ch D 128........148, 163
Government of Newfoundland v Newfoundland Railway
    Co (1888) 13 App Cas 199...155, 157
Government Stock Investment Co v Manila Railway Co
    [1897] AC 81..189
Great Eastern Railway Co v Lord's Trustee [1909] AC 109 19
Greenwood v Bennett [1973] QB 195 ....75, 76
Greer v Downs Supply Co [1927] 2 KB 28.......................................137
Gunn v Bolckow, Vaughan & Co (1875) LR 10 Ch App 451..............45

Haig v Aitken [2000] 3 All ER 80...8
Hallet's Estate, Re (1880) 13 Ch D 696..142
Halliday v Holgate (1868) LR 3 Ex 299....................................176, 177
Hamilton Young & Co, Re [1905] 2 KB 772.....................................194
Hamps v Darby [1948] 2 KB 311 48
Hanak v Green [1958] 2 QB 9 157
Hannah v Peel [1945] KB 509 25
Harding v Commissioner of Inland Revenue [1977] 1 NZLR 337 39
Harrington v Price (1832) 3 B & Ad 170 3
Harrold v Plenty [1901] 2 Ch 314..178
Hatton v Car Maintenance [1915] 1 Ch 621 ....171, 172
Haynes's Case (1614) 12 Co Rep 113...22
Heap v Motorists' Advisory Agency [1923] 1 KB 577 129

Helby v Matthews [1895] AC 471 ....41, 135
Hellawell v Eastwood (1851) 6 Ex 295 104
Helstan Securities Ltd v Hertfordshire County Council [1978]
    3 All ER 262 ....159, 160
Henderson & Co v Williams [1895] 1 QB 521 119
Hendy Lennox Ltd v Grahame Puttick Ltd [1984] 2 All ER 152 108
Herbert Morris Ltd v Saxelby [1916] 1 AC 688 6
Hewett v Court (1983) 57 ALJR 211 194
Heyman v Flewker (1863) 15 CB(NS) 519 126
Highway Foods International Ltd, Re [1995] BCC 271 133
Hiort v Bott (1874) LR 9 Ex 86 61
Hiort v London and North Western Railway Co (1879) 4 Ex D 188.....73
Hobson v Gorringe [1897] 1 Ch 182 106
Holland v Hodgson (1872) LR 7 CP 328 105
Hollins v Fowler (1875) LR 7 HL 757 ....54, 55, 58, 60
Holroyd v Marshall (1862) 10 HLC 191 181
Holt v Heatherfield Trust [1942] 2 KB 1 ....150, 151, 154
Houghland v R. R. Low (Luxury Coaches) Ltd [1962] 1 QB 694.........37
Howard Perry & Co v British Railways Board [1980] 1 WLR
    1375 ....56, 77
Howard v Harris (1884) Cab & El 253 55
Hoyles, Re [1911] 1 Ch 179 10
Hubbard, Ex p (1886) 17 QBD 699 ....176, 193
Hudson v Shogun Finance Ltd [2001] EWCA Civ 1000 122
Hughes v Pump House Hotel Co [1902] 2 KB 190 153

IBL Ltd v Coussens [1991] 2 All ER 133 73
Illingworth v Houldsworth [1904] AC 355 189
Ind Coope & Co, Re [1911] 2 Ch 223 163
Indian Oil Corpn v Greenstone Shipping SA [1987] 3 All ER
    893 ....110, 111
Ingram v Little [1961] 1 QB 31 ....58, 116
Inland Revenue Commissioners v Rossminster [1980] AC 952 49
Inland Revenue Commissioners v Venderell [1966] Ch 261 112
International Factors Ltd v Rodriguez [1979] QB 351 ....63, 160
IRC v Muller and Co's Margarine Ltd [1901] AC 217 7
Irons v Smallpiece (1819) 2 B & Ald 551 94

Jag Shaki, The [1986] AC 337 46
James Morrison & Co v Shaw, Savill, and Albion Co [1916]
    2 KB 783 38

Jeffries v Great Western Railway Co (1856) 5 E & B 802 ....62, 65
Jerome v Bentley [1952] 2 All ER 114 ....119, 126
Jim Spicer Chev Olds Inc v Kinniburgh [1978] 1 WWR 253 123
Johnson v Credit Lyonnais (1877) 3 CPD 32 129
Johnson v Diprose [1893] 1 QB 512..193
Jones (F. C.) & Sons v Jones [1996] 3 WLR 703................................141
Jones v De Marchant (1916) 28 DLR 561 ....108, 109, 142
Jones v Lock (1865) 1 Ch App 25 101
Jones v Marshall (1889) 24 QBD 269..176
Joseph v Lyons (1884) 15 QBD 280..137

Kahler v Midland Bank [1950] AC 24 63
Keene v Carter (1994) 12 WAR 20 22
Keith v Burrows (1876) 1 CPD 722..179
Kemp v Falk (1882) 7 App Cas 573 44
Kirk v Gregory (1876) 1 Ex D 55..48, 50, 51
Kirkham v Attenborough [1897] 1 QB 201 85
Kronprinsessan Margareta, The [1921] 1 AC 486................................92
Kuwait Airways Corpn v Iraqi Airways Co [2002] UKHL 19 ....53, 57,
    72, 73, 74

Lackington v Atherton (1844) 7 Man & Gr 360....................................45
Ladenburg & Co v Goodwin, Ferreira & Co [1912] 3 KB 275...............92
Lamb v Attenborough (1862) 1 B & S 831..125
Lancashire Waggon Co v Fitzhugh (1861) 6 H & N 502 57
Lancashire and Yorkshire Railway Co v MacNicoll (1918) 88
    LJKB 601 ....53, 54, 55
Langen and Wind Ltd v Bell [1972] Ch 685 195
Langmead v Thyer Rubber Co [1947] SASR 29..........................133, 134
Langton v Higgins (1859) 4 H & N 402...90
Latec Investments Ltd v Hotel Terrigal Pty Ltd (1965) 113 CLR
    265, 290 114
Laurie and Morewood v Dudin and Sons [1926] 1 KB 223.....45, 88, 182
Law Debenture Trust Corpn v Ural Caspian Oil Corpn Ltd [1993]
    1 WLR 138; [1995] Ch 152 (CA)..33
Leake v Loveday (1842) 4 M & G 972..65
Lee v Butler [1893] 2 QB 318 ....41, 135
Legg v Evans (1840) 6 M & W 36 172
Letang v Cooper [1965] 1 QB 232...50
Lethbridge v Phillips (1819) 2 Stark 544 56
Lewis v Averay [1972] 1 QB 198 ....122, 123

Lickbarrow v Mason (1787) 2 Tr 63; (1790) 1 HB1 357................46, 121
Lilley v Doubleday (1881) 7 QBD 510 38
Linden Gardens Trust Ltd v Lenesta Sludge Disposals
    Ltd [1994] 1 AC 85 ....158, 160, 161, 162
Lipkin Gorman v Karpnale Ltd [1991] 2 AC 548.....................140, 141
Lloyds Bank v Bank of America National Trust [1938] 2 KB 146.......178
Lloyds and Scottish Finance v Williamson [1965] 1 All ER 641 128
Lock v Heath (1892) 8 TLR 295 95
London Country and Westminster Bank v Tompkins [1918]
    1 KB 515 ....185, 187
London Jewellers v Sutton (1934) 50 TLR 193 57
London Joint Stock Bank v Simmons [1892] AC 201.......................137
Lonrho plc v Fayed (No.2) [1992] 1 WLR 1 114
Lord Napier and Ettrick v Hunter [1993] AC 713...........................195
Lord Strathcona S.S. Co v Dominion Coal Co [1926] AC 108 33
Lord's Trustee v Great Eastern Railway Co [1908] 2 KB 54 171
Lotan v Cross (1810) 2 Camp 464 52
Lowther v Harris [1927] 1 KB 393 126
Lunn v Thornton (1845) 1 CB 379..180
Lyon & Co v London City and Midland Bank [1903] 2 KB 135.........105

McArdle, Re [1951] 1 Ch 669...150
McCombie v Davies (1805) 6 East 538 58
McEntire v Crossley Bros [1895] AC 457 ....41, 170, 192
McGrath v Wallis [1995] 2 FLR 114 101
Macleay, Re (1875) LR 20 Eq 186 99
Macmillan Inc v Bishopsgate Trust (No.3) [1995] 1 WLR 978...........129
McVicar v Herman (1958) 13 DLR (2d) 419 119
Madell v Thomas [1891] 1 QB 230..13
Manchester Trust v Furness [1895] 2 QB 39..............................129, 137
Manchester, Sheffield and Lincolnshire Railway v North Central
    Wagon Co (1888) 13 App Cas 554..................................192
Manton v Brocklebank [1923] 2 KB 212.......................................49
Marfani & Co v Midland Bank Ltd [1968] 1 WLR 956.....................75
Marlborough Hill, The [1921] 2 AC 444 46
Matthew v T. M. Sutton Ltd [1994] 4 All ER 793 176
MCC Proceeds Inc v Lehman Brothers International (Europe)
    [1998] 4 All ER 675 (CA) 63, 74, 137
Mears v London & South Western Railway Co (1862) 22
    CB(NS) 850...71

Mediana, The [1900] AC 113 49
Melluish v B.M.I. (No.3) Ltd [1996] AC 454, 473 106
Mendelssohn v Normand Ltd [1970] 1 QB 177 35
Mercantile Bank of India v Central Bank of India [1938] AC 287 ......120, 128
Mercantile Credit Ltd v Hamblin [1965] 2 QB 242 121
Mercer v Craven Grain Storage Ltd [1994] CLC 328 ....39, 40, 88
Merry v Green (1841) 7 M & W 623 21
M'Ewan v Smith (1849) 2 HLC 309 45
Michael Gerson (Leasing) Ltd v Wilkinson [2001] 1 All ER 148 (CA)..45, 131
Miller v Race (1758) 1 Burr 452 165
Milroy v Lord (1862) 4 De GF & J 264 101
Mirabita v Imperial Ottoman Bank (1878) 3 Ex D 164 92
Mitchell v Ealing London Borough Council [1979] 1 QB 1 38
Mitchell v Jones (1905) 24 NZLR 932 131
Moffatt v Kazana [1969] 2 QB 152 24
Monk v Whittenbury (1831) 2 B & Ad 484 125
Moorgate Mercantile Co Ltd v Twitchings [1977] AC 890 ....119, 121
Moorgate Mercantile Credit v Finch [1962] 1 QB 701 56
Morison v London County and Westminster Bank [1914] 3 KB 356 74
Morris v C. W. Martin & Sons Ltd [1966] 1 QB 716 ....34, 35
Morris v Pugh (1761) 3 Burr 1242 56
Morritt, Re (1886) 18 QBD 222 ....187, 193
Mulliner v Florence (1878) 3 QBD 484 ....172, 174
Munro v Willmott [1949] 1 KB 295 75

Nanka-Bruce v Commonwealth Trust [1926] AC 77 84
National Coal Board v Evans [1951] 2 KB 861 50
National Employers' Assurance v Jones [1988] 2 All ER 245 135
National Mercantile Bank v Rymill (1881) 144 LT 767 ....60, 61
National Provincial Bank v Ainsworth [1965] AC 1175 ....32, 138
National Provincial Bank v Charnley [1924] 1 KB 431 181
Newlove v Shrewsbury (1888) 21 QBD 41 ....192, 193
Newtons of Wembley Ltd v Williams [1965] 1 QB 560 ....123, 134
Nicholson v Harper [1895] 2 Ch 415 133
Nicolls v Bastard (1835) 2 Cr M & R 659 ....63, 64, 65
Nokes v Doncaster Amalgamated Collieries Ltd [1940] AC 1014..........7
Norglen Ltd v Reeds Rains Prudential Ltd [1996] 1 All ER 945 146

North Central Wagon & Finance Co v Graham [1950] 2 KB 7.......70, 71
North Western Bank Ltd v Poynter [1895] AC 56..............................178
Nyberg v Handelaar [1892] 2 QB 202..30

Oakley v Lyster [1931] 1 KB 148...53, 57
Oasis Merchandising Services Ltd, Re [1977] BCC 282 (CA)............146
Oatway, Re [1903] 2 Ch 356...109, 142
Official Assignee of Madras v Mercantile Bank of India Ltd
    [1935] AC 53..44, 46
On Demand Information plc v Michael Gerson (Finance) plc
    [2001] 1 WLR 155; [2002] UKHL 13 ....27, 28
Oppenheimer v Attenborough & Son [1908] 1 KB 221...............127, 134
Ord v Upton [2000] 1 All ER 193 (CA)...8
O'Sullivan v Williams [1992] 3 All ER 385..65
Owen, Re [1894] 3 Ch 220...186

Pacific Motor Auctions Ltd v Motor Credits Ltd [1965] AC 867 130
Palmer v Carey [1926] AC 703 182
Parker v British Airways Board [1982] QB 1004 (CA).........24, 25, 66, 67
Patrick v Colerick (1838) 3 M & W 483..78
Peachdart Ltd, Re [1984] Ch 131 ....91, 107, 109, 184
Penfolds Wines Pty Ltd v Elliott (1946) 74 CLR 204..........48, 49, 51, 55
Pennington v Reliance Motors Ltd [1923] 1 KB 127...........................172
Pennington v Waine [2002] EWCA Civ 227............................97, 98, 102
Percy Edwards Ltd v Vaughan (1910) 26 TLR 545 136
Perrin v Morgan [1943] AC 399..10
Pettitt v Pettitt [1970] AC 777 100
Pfeiffer (E.) Weinkellerei-Weineinkauf GmbH v Arbuthnot Factors
    [1988] 1 WLR 150...91, 164, 184
Phillips v Phillips (1862) 4 De GF & J 208 138
Photo Production Ltd v Securicor Transport Ltd [1980] AC 827 70
Pignataro v Gilroy [1919] 1 KB 459 90
Pilcher v Rawlins (1872) 7 Ch App 259...137
Pioneer Container, The [1994] 2 AC 324 34
Playa Larga, The [1983] 2 Lloyd's Rep 171 ....55, 73
Poole v Smith's Cars (Balham) Ltd [1962] 2 All ER 482 85
Port Line Ltd v Ben Line Steamers Ltd [1958] 2 QB 146....................32

R v Kelly [1998] 3 All ER 741...4
R v Preddy [1996] AC 815..38
Ramsay v Margret [1894] 2 QB 18 18

Rawlinson v Mort (1905) 93 LT 555 95

Rhodes v Allied Dunbar Pension Services Ltd [1989] 1 WLR 800 164

Rich v Aldred (1705) 6 Mod 216 27

Richards v Delbridge (1874) LR 18 Eq 11 101

Ridgway, Re (1885) 15 QBD 447 94

Robbie (N. W.) & Co v Witney Warehouse Co [1963] 3 All ER 613 156

Roberts v Wyatt (1810) 2 Taunt 268...73, 117

Robins & Co v Gray [1895] 2 QB 501 175

Rodick v Gandell (1852) 1 D M & G 763 182

Rogers Sons & Co v Lambert & Co [1892] 1 QB 318........................65

Rogers v Kennay (1846) 9 QB 592 ....63, 69

Rolls Royce v Jeffrey [1962] 1 All ER 801 6

Roscorla v Thomas (1842) 3 QB 234..150

Rosenthal v Alderton & Sons Ltd [1946] KB 374 72

Rose, Re [1952] Ch 499..97

Roxburghe v Cox (1881) 17 Ch D 520 155

Rugg v Minett (1809) 11 East 210..83, 84

St Albans City and District Council v International Computers Ltd
 [1996] 4 All ER 481 (CA)..8

Salford Van Hire (Contracts) Ltd v Bocholt Developments Ltd
 [1995] CLC 611 29

Sandeman (F. S.) & Sons v Tyzack and Branfoot Shipping Co
 [1913] AC 680 110

Sanders Bros v Maclean & Co (1883) 11 QBD 327 46

Santley v Wilde (1899) 2 Ch 474 179

Scaptrade, The [1983] 2 AC 694 28

Schebsmann, Re [1944] Ch 83...101

Sewell v Burdick (1884) 10 App Cas 74 ....93, 176, 177

Shaw v Commissioner of Police of the Metropolis [1987] 1 WLR
 1322 ....133, 136

Shepherd v Cartwright [1955] AC 432 ....98, 100

Shiloh Spinners Ltd v Harding [1973] AC 691 ....28, 138

Sifton v Sifton [1938] AC 656 100

Simmons v Lillystone (1853) 8 Ex 431 55

Singh v Ali [1960] AC 167 81

Smith (1995) 111 LQR 10 39

Smith v Bridgend Borough Council [2001] UKHL 58........................189

Smith v Lloyd's TSB Bank plc [2001] 1 All ER 424 (CA)....................74

Société Générale de Paris v Walker (1885) 11 App Cas 20 164

Somes v British Empire Shipping Co (1859) 28 LJQB 220 172
Sorrell v Paget [1950] 1 KB 252 55
South Australia Insurance Co v Randell (1869) LR 3 PC 101..............39
South Staffordshire Water Co v Sharman [1896] 2 QB 44....................25
Southcote's Case (1601) Cro Eliz 815 35
Spackman v Foster (1883) 11 QBD 99..58
Span Terza (No.2), The [1984] 1 WLR 27 42
Spence v Union Marine Insurance Co (1868) LR 3 CP 427........110, 111
Spencer v Clarke (1878) 9 Ch D 137 162
Sport Internationaal Bussum NV v Inter-Footwear Ltd 1984 1
    WLR 776..28
Staffs Motor Guarantee Ltd v British Wagon Co [1934] 2 KB
    305..131
Standing v Bowring (1885) 31 Ch D 282 ....98, 100, 148
Stapylton Fletcher Ltd, Re [1994] 1 WLR 1181 88
Stephens v Elwall (1815) 4 M & S 259 60
Stephens v Green [1895] 2 Ch 148 162
Stewart v Sculthorp (1894) 25 OR 544 40
Stoddart v Union Trust Ltd [1912] 1 KB 181................................156
Stoneham, Re [1919] 1 Ch 149..96
Strand Electric and Engineering Co v Brisford Entertainments
    [1952] 2 QB 246..49
Strong v Bird (1874) LR 18 Eq 315...96
Stucley, Re [1906] 1 Ch 67 194
Swift v Dairywise Farms Ltd [2000] 1 All ER 320; [2001] EWCA
    Civ 145..7
Swire v Leach (1865) 18 CB(NS) 479..63
Swiss Bank Corpn v Lloyds Bank Ltd [1982] AC 584 (CA).........32, 182,
    183, 185

Tailby v Official Receiver (1888) 13 App Cas 523 ....150, 181
Tancred v Allgood (1859) 4 H & N 38..71
Tancred v Delagoa Bay Railway Co (1889) 23 QBD 239 152
Tappenden v Artus [1964] 2 QB 185 ....170, 173, 174
Taylor v Russell [1892] AC 244 138
Tettenborn [1996] CLJ 36; [1998] LMCLQ 498 ....63, 161
Thames Guaranty v Campbell [1985] QB 210 183
Thames Iron Works Co v Patent Derrick Co (1860) 1 J & H 93 171,
    172, 173
Theakston v MGN Ltd [2002] EWHC 137..5

Thomas v Heelas 27 November 1986 (CAT No.1065).......................124
Thomas v Kelly (1888) 13 App Cas 506..............................193
Thomas v Times Book Co [1966] 2 All ER 241 96
Thompson v Dominy (1845) 14 M & W 403 168
Three Rivers District Council v Bank of England [1996] QB 292.......147
Tinsley v Milligan [1995] 1 AC 340..............................81, 101
Tolhurst v Associated Portland Cement Manufacturers (1900)
    Ltd (1902) 2 KB 660 158
Torkington v Magee [1902] 2 KB 427............................154, 164
Transag Haulage Ltd v Leyland DAF Finance [1994] 2 BCLC 88.......28
Transport and General Credit v Morgan [1939] 2 All ER 17..............194
Trendtex Trading Corporation v Credit Suisse [1982] AC 679 146
Tribe v Tribe [1996] Ch 107................................101
Trustees of the Property of Pehrsson v Von Greyerz
    (PC, unreported 16 June 1999)..............................97
Tubantia, The [1924] P 78 17
Turcan, Re (1880) 40 Ch D 5 160
Twinsectra Ltd v Yardley [2002] UKHL 12 112

Underwood Ltd v Burgh Castle Brick [1922] 1 KB 343..............84
United Dominion Trust Ltd v Parkway Motors [1955] 1 WLR
    719..159
United States of America v Dollfus Mieg et Cie SA [1952] AC
    582..16, 52

Vandepitte v Preferred Accident Assurance Corpn [1933] AC 70.......161
Vandervell v Inland Revenue Commissioners [1967] 2 AC 291..........112
Vandervell's Trusts (No.2), Re [1974] Ch 269.....................112
Varley v Whipp [1900] 2 QB 513.............................82
Vaudeville Electric Cinema Ltd v Muriset [1923] 2 Ch 74 105
Victoria Park Racing and Recreation Co v Taylor (1937) 58 CLR
    479 5
Vinogradoff, Re [1935] WN 68.............................100
Viscount Hill v Dowager Viscountess Hill [1897] 1 QB 483..................3

Wait and James v Midland Bank (1926) 31 Com Cas 172 87
Wait v Baker (1848) 2 Ex 1...............................44, 90, 92
Wait, Re [1927] 1 Ch 606 ....87, 88, 194
Wake v Hall (1883) 8 App Cas 195...........................105
Wallis & Simmonds (Builders) Ltd, Re [1974] 1 WLR 391 183
Ward (R. V.) Ltd v Bignall [1967] 2 QB 534 83

Ward v Duncombe [1893] AC 369...162, 163

Ward v Turner (1752) 1 Dick 170..102

Wardar's (Import and Export) Co v W. Norwood and Sons [1968]
2 QB 663 91

Watson, Laidlaw & Co v Pott, Cassels & Williamson (1914) 31
RPC 104 49

Waverley Borough Council v Fletcher [1996] QB 334 ....25, 28

Webb v Chief Constable of Merseyside [2000] QB 427 66

Weiner v Gill [1906] 2 KB 574...85

Wells, Re [1933] 1 Ch 29 23

Welsh Irish Ferries Ltd, Re [1986] Ch 471..183

Westdeutsche Landesbank Girozentrale v Islington
London Borough Council [1996] AC 669 (HL).............12, 111, 112, 113,
114, 142

Westover, Re [1919] 2 Ch 104 ....147, 154

Whitehorn Brothers v Davison [1911] 1 KB 463...............................124

Whiteley v Hilt [1918] 2 KB 808...28

Whitwham v Westminster Brymbo Coal and Coke Co [1896]
2 Ch 538 49

Wickham Holdings Ltd v Brooke House Motors Ltd [1967]
1 WLR 295 ....42, 74

Wilbraham v Snow (1669) 2 Wms Saund 47.....................................63

Williams v Atlantic Assurance Co [1933] 1 KB 81 153

Williams v Gesse (1837) 3 Bing NC 849...55

Willis (R. H.) & Son v British Car Auctions [1978] 1 WLR 438.....54, 60

Wilson v Lombank Ltd [1963] 1 WLR 1294 ....50, 51, 52

Winkfield, The [1902] P 42...63, 64, 68

Winter v Winter (1861) 4 LT 639..96

Woodard v Woodard [1995] 3 All ER 980 103

Worcester Works Finance v Cooden Engineering Co [1972]
1 QB 210...132

Wrightson v McArthur and Hutchinsons (1919) Ltd [1921]
2 KB 807 44

Wyatt, Re [1892] 1 Ch 188 162

Yorkshire Woolcombers Association Ltd, Re [1903] 2 Ch D
284, 295 189

Young v Hichens (1844) 6 QB 606...17

Young v Kitchin (1878) 3 Ex D 127...156

Table of Statutes

Administration of Estates Act 1925...2

Bank Charter Act 1844...10
Bankruptcy Act 1914, s 38(1)(c) 29
Bills of Exchange Act 1882 ....165, 167
   s 2..165
   s 3(1) 165, 166
   s 5(1)..165
   s 9(1)..166
   s 11 166
   s 17(2)...166
   s 23 166
   s 24 167
   s 29(1)...167
   s 31(2)–(3)...166
   s 34(1)...166
   s 35(1)...166
   s 59...9
   s 60..75
   s 64(1)..74
   s 73 166
   s 82..75
   s 83(1)...167
Bills of Lading Act 1855, s 1..168
Bills of Sale Act 1878 ....99, 192, 193
   s 4 ....192, 194
   s 10..193
Bills of Sale Act 1878 (Amendment) Act 1882...................186, 187, 192
   s 4 193
   s 7...187
   s 8–s 10 193
   s 13 187
   s 15..192
   s 17 193
   Sch 193

Bills of Sale Act 1890, s 1 194
Bills of Sale Acts 1878–1891 181

Carriage by Air Act 1961 37
Carriage of Goods by Sea Act 1971 37
Carriage of Goods by Sea Act 1992 ....46, 168
Carriers Act 1830 37
Cheques Act 1957 165
  s 4 75
Cheques Act 1992 165
Civil Aviation Act 1982, s 88 ....171, 173
Coinage Act 1971 10
Common Law Procedure Act 1854 76
  s 78 2
Companies Act 1985
  s 183 159
  s 360 164
  s 395 ....91, 179, 195
  s 396 ....91, 179
Consumer Credit Act 1974 136
  s 114–s 121 176
  s 120(1)(a) 177
  s 121 176
  s 121(3) 176
  s 123 165
  Sch.4 136
Copyright, Designs and Patents Act 1988
  s 1 7
  s 12 7
Currency Act 1983 10
Currency and Bank Notes Act 1954 10

Factors Act 1889 ....117, 125, 126, 129
  s 1(1) 125, 126
  s 1(2) 126, 130
  s 1(4) 128, 130
  s 2 ....124, 126, 127, 134
  s 2(1) 124
  s 2(2) 127, 134
  s 2(3) 128
  s 2(4) 127

s 5 131
s 8 ....124, 129, 130
s 9 ....124, 132, 135
s 9(2) 136

Hire Purchase Act 1964, Part III 136, 170
Hotel Proprietors Act 1956 175
s 2(2) 171

Increase of Rent and Mortgage Interest (War Restrictions)
    Act 1915 185
    s 1(4) 185
    s 2(4) 185, 186
Innkeepers Act 1878 172
Insolvency Act 1986 ....7, 8, 29, 192
    s 15(4) 139
    s 29(2) 188
    s 178 7
    s 238 99
    s 240 99
    s 283 13
    s 306 15
    s 315 7
    s 322 ....13, 15, 39
    s 339 99
    s 341 99
    s 386 190
    s 436 7
    Sch.1 188
    Sch.6 190

Law of Distress (Amendment) Act 1908, s 4(1) 29
Law of Property Act 1925
    s 1 3
    s 36(2) 31
    s 52 180
    s 53(1)(c) 102, 149, 154, 181
    s 85 ....179, 180, 182
    s 86 ....179, 182
    s 101 ....187, 188

s 109 188
s 136...145, 164
s 136(1) 151, 152, 154, 155
s 137(1) 163
s 137(3) 163
s 205(1)(xvi)...184, 188
Law of Property (Miscellaneous Provisions) Act 1989 96
　s 1(2)(a) 96
　s 1(3) 96
Law Reform (Enforcement of Contracts) Act 1954,
　s 1...81
Limitation Act 1980..79
　s 2 ....78, 79
　s 3 79
　s 3(1)–(2) 79
　s 4...79

Merchant Shipping Act 1995, s 8–s 10 29
Misrepresentation Act 1967, s 2(2) 123

Pawnbrokers Act 1872...176
Pawnbrokers Act 1960..176
Port of London Act 1968
　s 39 171
　s 146(4)..46

Sale of Goods Act 1893 ....80, 88
　s 4...81
　s 52...88
Sale of Goods Act 1979 ....8, 44, 82, 86, 117, 129
　s 1 129
　s 2(1) 30
　s 5(1) 82
　s 5(3) 86
　s 12 161
　s 16 ....86, 87
　s 17 ....82, 83, 91, 92, 93, 184
　s 18 170
　　r.1 83
　　r.2–r.3...83, 84
　　r.4..43, 84, 86

r.4(a)–(b) 84, 85
r.5 ....89, 91, 92
r.5(1)–(2) 89
r.5(3)–(4) 87
s 19 ....82, 91, 92
s 19(1)–(3) 92
s 20 81
s 20A–s 20B 89
s 21 117
s 22 117
s 22(1) 118
s 23 ....117, 118, 122, 124, 126, 133, 134
s 24 ....117, 124, 129, 130, 131, 132, 133, 135
s 25 ....117, 124, 132, 133, 134, 135, 136
s 25(1) 134
s 25(2) 136
s 26 117
s 29(2) 90
s 29(4) 44
s 32(1) 44, 90
s 39(1)(a) 173
s 39(2) 173
s 48 173
s 49 81
s 61(1) 30, 43, 80
s 61(5) 83
s 62(1) 81, 82
Sale of Goods (Amendment) Act 1995.....................86, 88, 91, 118, 140
Statute of Frauds 1677...3
  s 4 3
  s 17...3
Statute of Tenures 1660...2
Supply of Goods and Services Act 1982.................................8
Supreme Court Act 1981, s 37(1) 187
Supreme Court of Judicature Act 1873, s 25(6).........................145

Theft Act 1968 4
  s 1..21
Torts (Interference with Goods) Act 1977..................28, 47, 53, 64, 65,
                                                    68, 71, 73, 75, 76, 77

s 1...47
s 1(c)–(d)..71
s 2(1)..77
s 2(2)..56, 62
s 3..77
s 3(3)(b)..77
s 3(7)..75
s 4..77
s 5(1)...68, 72
s 5(4)..68
s 6(1)–(2)..75
s 7..67, 68
s 7(2)..67, 68
s 7(3)–(4)..68
s 8..67
s 8(1)..51
s 8(2)(c)..67
s 9..65
s 10..73
s 11(1)..76, 122
s 11(2)..58
s 11(3)..57
Sch.1, Part II..172
Treasure Act 1996...26
s 1(1)..26
s 1(1)(b)..26
s 1(2)..26
s 2..26
s 2(2)..26
s 3(3)..26
s 4(1)..26
s 10..26
s 10(3)(d)..26
s 10(6)..26

Unfair Contract Terms Act 1977.......................................37
Unsolicited Goods and Services Act 1971............................61

Wills Act 1540..2
Wills Act 1837..103

The meaning of personal property

In this introductory chapter, we shall consider how the subject matter of personal property is organized before turning our attention to a definition of property rights.

TYPES OF PROPERTY

PERSONAL PROPERTY AND LAND

It is a commonplace observation that personal property (or personalty) is all the property that is left once land, that is real property (or realty), has been subtracted. Personal property is therefore residual in character, an attribute that contributes to the somewhat formless nature of the subject. It is also capable of expansion, both in respect of the recognition of novel kinds of property and of its quantity. The American humorist, Will Rogers, advised the purchase of land because no more of it was being made (we may exclude the Netherlands). The same could not be said of shares in companies: as many companies exist as human ingenuity and enterprise can devise, and the number of shares issued by those companies will be dependent upon the national wealth generated and the investment outlook. Nor could the same be said of objects that we may heuristically refer to as widgets, manufactured from natural resources that for present purposes are assumed to be infinitely replenishable in response to a demand that is infinitely elastic.

The customary way to treat the definition of personal property is to break it down into its sub-categories once land has been eliminated. Before that is done, however, we should ask why land and personal property are distinguished. The answer, which is not surprising given the character of English law, is historical, which accounts for this deep division in property law that has produced a rift in the treatment of the subject, apparent in textbooks and university law courses.

The evolution of land law and personal property law differed in at least three respects. First of all, land after the Norman Conquest was subject to feudal tenure and thus held from or through the Crown. The major tenants in chief held land directly from the Crown in return for feudal dues and service. By a process of subinfeudation, lesser tenants held portions of the same land from the tenants in chief on similar terms and so on.[1] The system of tenure, expressed through the doctrine of estates, is very much in place today, though feudal dues as such no longer exist. No such structure of ownership ever applied to property other than land.

Secondly, interests in land were protected at law by the so-called real actions, which meant that the land itself could be recovered if the owner were wrongfully dispossessed.[2] This was not true of personal property, which after the demise of the appeal of felony could not thus be recovered *in rem* until the middle of the nineteenth century.[3] The owner's claim was a monetary one for damages. Nor was it true of all interests in land. The highest form of freehold estate, the fee simple, was a grant to an individual and his heirs and therefore open-ended in time. Leasehold interests, on the other hand, were finite with a defined beginning and a defined end. They were not recoverable in a real action, though a similar remedy was eventually developed through the medium of a personal action, the action of ejectment, which was an offshoot of the writ of trespass. Because of their remedial shortcomings, leasehold interests, as we shall note, have always been a category of personal property.

Thirdly, the rules relating to descent on death differed for land and personalty. Land went to the heir at law, usually the eldest son. By the Wills Act 1540 and the Statute of Tenures 1660, owners of land acquired the power to devise by will, but the old rule of descent persisted in the case of intestacy until 1926.[4] The order of descent on intestacy for the personal estate of the deceased followed the order laid down in the Statute of Distributions 1670; it went to the next of kin, including the widow, after first vesting in the personal representatives of the deceased. Since 1926, the rules for personalty and for realty have been the same: all property descends to the next of kin in a prescribed order.[5]

---

[1] Holdsworth, W., *A History of English Law*, vol II, 4th edn, 1956, pp 199–201, 250; Plucknett, T., *A Concise History of the Common Law*, 5th edn, London: Butterworth & Co., 1956, pp 506–520, 531–545; Pollock, F., and Maitland, F. W., *The History of English Law*, 2nd edn, Cambridge: Cambridge University Press, 1898 (rev. 1968 with an introduction by Milsom, S. F. C.), vol I, pp 210–218.

[2] Holdsworth, *op. cit.*, vol III, 5th edn, 1942, chapter 1; Pollock and Maitland, *op. cit.*, vol II, pp 570–572.

[3] Common Law Procedure Act 1854, s 78.

[4] Administration of Estates Act 1925.   [5] Administration of Estates Act 1925.

CHATTELS REAL AND PERSONAL

The analysis of personalty starts with chattels real. These consist principally of leasehold interests in land, the subject of personal rather than real actions. Since the 1925 property legislation, leaseholds have firmly been recognised as equivalent to other interests in land. Indeed, the term of years absolute is one of only two permitted legal estates in land, along with the fee simple.[6]

Chattels personal are those items of personalty that are not chattels real. They divide into two mutually exclusive types:[7] choses (or things) in possession and choses in action.

CHOSES IN POSSESSION

Choses in possession are tangible (or corporeal) movable things like a jacket, a book, or a bicycle. The size of a thing is no obstacle to its being a chose in possession: microdots and ships both fall into the category. When they form the subject matter of a sale or similar transaction, choses in possession are called goods, which, in an earlier generation of mercantile statutes, were more compendiously known as 'goods, wares, and merchandise'.[8] It is more convenient to refer to them generally as chattels, which will be the practice used throughout this book.

Certain objects that might appear sufficiently corporeal to qualify as chattels are in fact not so. Documents of title to land,[9] as well as the very narrow category of heirlooms,[10] are so closely affiliated to land as to be an appendage of it for practical purposes. Items may become chattels upon severance from the land; a large body of nineteenth century case law dealing with growing crops and natural produce distinguishes sale of land and sale of goods agreements for the purpose of the different contractual writing requirements for the two laid down in the Statute of Frauds 1677.[11] Conversely, items may become so attached to land as to constitute fixtures and therefore become part of it (see further chapter 4). This idea has even been extended to keys, because enjoyment of the land is so difficult without them,[12] though attachment in such a case can only be metaphysical. Certain items of valuable commercial paper, known as documentary intangibles, have a mobile and corporeal existence, but

---

[6] Law of Property Act 1925, s 1.   [7] *Colonial Bank v Whinney* (1885) 30 Ch D 261.
[8] Statute of Frauds 1677, s 17.   [9] *Harrington v Price* (1832) 3 B & Ad 170.
[10] *Viscount Hill v Dowager Viscountess Hill* [1897] 1 QB 483, *per* Chitty LJ.
[11] Sections 4 and 17.   [12] *Elliott v Bishop* (1855) 11 Ex 113.

because they are significant for what they represent rather than for what they are, they are not regarded simply as chattels.[13]

In the vast majority of cases, there is nothing controversial about the classification of tangible items as choses in possession. But advances in medical science have forced consideration of whether one can own body organs or even a human foetus. The Warnock Committee[14] recommended that there should be no ownership of the human foetus but muddied the waters by going on to recommend rights of disposal and sale, evidently rights of a proprietary character, in the foetus. In this same concessionary vein, it is hard to deny that recent developments in the law concerning corpses and body tissue support the view that they are capable of being the subject of some property rights.[15] Thus in *Dobson v North Tyneside Health Authority*,[16] the court held that those charged with the burial of a corpse have a legal right to its possession for the purposes of disposal and burial. Although there was no property as such in a corpse, it was 'properly arguable' that a corpse or a part of it could become property if subjected to a process such as embalming or stuffing. A medical student's skeleton ought on this account to be the subject of a conversion action[17] in appropriate circumstances. Similarly, the Court of Appeal has held that body parts used as anatomical specimens were capable of being property for the purpose of the Theft Act 1968, once they had taken on different attributes in consequence of human skill, for example, by dissection and preservation.[18] The likely future is one of increasing incremental acceptance, by statute or at common law, of the idea that corpses, body parts, and tissue are property: 'the common law does not stand still'.[19]

CHOSES IN ACTION

The other division of chattels personal is choses (or things) in action, which embraces diverse types of intangible (or incorporeal) property. These are what remain after the elimination of corporeal chattels and are the residual category of personal property. The expansion in modern times of forms of intangible property means that many commercial entities operating in post-manufacturing industries have intangible property rights greater in value than their tangible property. Examples of

[13] See below.

[14] *Report of the Committee of Inquiry into Human Fertilisation and Embryology* (Cmnd. 9314, 1984).

[15] See Magnusson, 'Proprietary Rights in Human Tissue', in Palmer, N., and McKendrick, E. (eds), *Interests in Goods*, 2nd edn, London and Hong Kong: LLP, 1998.

[16] [1997] 1 WLR 596.   [17] Chapter 3.   [18] *R v Kelly* [1998] 3 All ER 741.

[19] *Ibid*, p 750 (Rose LJ).

intangible property are: debts, goodwill, rights under an insurance policy, shares in a company, bills of exchange, and various forms of intellectual property. This last grouping, whose importance can barely be overestimated in modern commercial conditions, includes items such as patents, copyright, trade marks, registered industrial designs, trade secrets, and know-how.

As the name choses in action itself signifies, abstract personalty of this type could not physically be possessed. Entitlement to it had to be vindicated through legal action, not permitted by early common law courts (see chapter 6 for the reasons). It was left instead to equity and the law merchant to give recognition to property of this type. All personalty depends for its enjoyment upon the fact that the law imposes duties on one or more individuals not to interfere with the use or enjoyment of the personalty by its rightful owner or possessor. What use is a jacket to me if it is liable to be torn off my back in a lawless society that knows no means of supporting my ownership of it? Whereas, however, the jacket can be enjoyed in and of and for itself, providing the comfortable feeling of warmth as well as the comforting feeling that it is not liable to be taken away, the abstract thing that is a chose in action is purely a means by which others can be called upon to do or refrain from doing something in response to a duty imposed upon them.

Property, in the sense of things that can be owned, is not a static concept. It is in the case of choses in action above all that its dynamic properties and potential are best appreciated. A question that has not been satisfactorily resolved is whether information can constitute property.[20] If it can, a further question arises concerning how far the various rules of property law can properly apply to information. To put it another way, it may not be a stark choice between treating information as the subject of property rights or not. There may be an intermediate way that treats it as property only for certain purposes, thus avoiding some of the daunting problems of priority and remedies that would follow on from a proprietary analysis. And to the extent that an intermediate proprietary approach is adopted, it may not be materially different from existing approaches that use the law of trusts and tort to protect rights in respect of information in general and confidential information in particular.[21]

---

[20] See Kohler and Palmer, 'Information as Property', in Palmer, N., and McKendrick, E. (eds), *Interests in Goods*, 2nd edn, London and Hong Kong: LLP, 1998.

[21] *Douglas v Hello! Ltd* [2001] 2 All ER 289; *Theakston v MGN Ltd* [2002] EWHC 137 (QB). See also *Victoria Park Racing and Recreation Co v Taylor* (1937) 58 CLR 479 (denying tort protection).

In a tax case, Lord Radcliffe treated know-how as a form of property, intangible in the way that goodwill is,[22] just as half a century previously Lord Shaw had described trade secrets as property in a restraint of trade case.[23] Support for a property approach emerges from some of the speeches in *Boardman v Phipps*,[24] though Lord Upjohn in the same case was clear that information was not property, but yet the unlawful transmission of confidential information could be restrained.[25] In its report on *Breach of Confidence*,[26] the Law Commission preferred not to subject breach of confidence to treatment as a property matter since the law had evolved without property notions. An Australian judge has also declined to treat the transmission of information as a transfer of property, saying that having a richly stored mind does not make one a man of property.[27] This last case highlights one of the real problems of treating information as property: the transferor retains the information that was transmitted, which denies one of the features of a property right, namely its exclusivity. A diamond ring cannot support two wearers at the same time. To the extent that the transferor covenants not to make use of the information transmitted, or someone makes unlawful use of information, it seems therefore preferable to invoke the law of contract and tort rather than to deal with the matter by a heavy handed invocation of property law. If a property characterization of information adds nothing to the resolution of problems, then there is no need to go down a road full of pitfalls.

Choses in action break down into the two categories of pure intangibles and documentary intangibles.

Pure intangibles

Examples of pure intangibles include a debt, copyright and goodwill. A debt is a monetary obligation owed by one person to another which is an item of value because it can be transferred to a third party by way of sale or security for a loan (see further chapter 6). The debtor's duty to pay the creditor, which may or may not be recorded on a piece of paper, but which in principle can be purely informal, is a valuable piece of property because of its exchange value. If it could not be transferred in the above

---

[22] *Rolls Royce Ltd v Jeffrey* [1962] 1 All ER 801 at p 805.
[23] *Herbert Morris Ltd v Saxelby* [1916] 1 AC 688 at p 714. See also *Attorney-General v Guardian Newspapers Ltd* [1987] 1 WLR 1248 at p 1264 (Browne-Wilkinson VC).
[24] [1967] 2 AC 46 (Lords Hodson and Guest and Viscount Dilhorne).
[25] *Ibid*, pp 127–128.
[26] Report No. 110 (Cmnd 8388, 1981).
[27] *Federal Commissioner of Taxation v United Aircraft Corpn* (1944) 68 CLR 525 at p 535 (Latham CJ).

way, it would be no more than a contractual expectancy of the creditor's and not as such an item of property at all. Copyright is the exclusive entitlement of the creator of an intellectual work to copy, publish and distribute the work.[28] Goodwill is more than merely the factual expectation that the former clientele of a business will continue to patronize it notwithstanding the change of ownership. It is an item of property that may be used as security for a loan and disposed of apart from the underlying trade premises. Goodwill is 'whatever adds value to a business by reason of situation, name, and reputation, connection, introduction to old customers, and agreed absence from competition'.[29]

The law of insolvency is a testing ground for novel types of intangible property for various reasons, notably the duty resting on trustees-in-bankruptcy to gather in as much as possible so as to maximize returns to creditors. Another reason is the right given to trustees and liquidators to disclaim what is called 'onerous property',[30] which in broad terms is property (including contractual rights) that carries with it commitments or restrictions that on balance render it more of a liability than an asset. For example, a farmer's milk quota has been held to constitute property within the meaning of the Insolvency Act 1986, despite the limited and cumbersome way required for its transfer to another holder.[31] The statutory definition covered ' . . . every description of property whereever situated and also obligations and every description of interest, whether present or future or vested or contingent, arising out of, or incidental to, property . . . '[32] Whatever requirements the common law may impose in defining property—and statements to the effect that property takes its meaning from context[33] suggest these are few in number—they are liable to be overridden by expansive statutory draftsmanship. That same expansive definition led to the conclusion in another case that a waste management licence, the function of which was to render the holder immune from prosecution for performing certain acts, was property.[34] There was evidence of a market in such licences and the statutory machinery for their transfer required the active participation of both transferor and transferee. It is not necessary for something to have present value to

---

[28] Copyright, Designs and Patents Act 1988, ss 1, 12.
[29] *IRC v Muller and Co's Margarine Ltd* [1901] AC 217, *per* Lord Lindley.
[30] Insolvency Act 1986, ss 178, 315.
[31] *Swift v Dairywise Farms Ltd* [2000] 1 All ER 320, affirmed [2001] EWCA Civ 145.
[32] Section 436.
[33] For example, *Nokes v Doncaster Amalgamated Collieries Ltd* [1940] AC 1014 at p 1051.
[34] *Re Celtic Extraction Ltd* [1999] 4 All ER 684 (CA).

constitute property under the Insolvency Act. Hence, an expressly assignable preemption right over property that the owner might never decide to sell has been held to constitute property vesting in the grantee's trustee-in-bankruptcy.[35] There are nevertheless limits on the broad wording of the statutory definition. It does not include assets of a purely personal nature, even valuable ones, such as rights of action for damages for personal injury or injury to reputation[36] and the personal correspondence of a bankrupt.[37]

A difficult question of classification is presented by computer software which can be stored and downloaded by means of a portable disk. If the software as stored on these disks constitutes a chattel, then that chattel may amount to 'goods' for the purpose of a supplier's strict liability for the quality and fitness of goods under the Sale of Goods Act 1979 or the Supply of Goods and Services Act 1982. On the other hand, if the software represents intangible property stored for convenience on a disk, then strict liability under statute would not present itself and would exist in a given case only by virtue of a term implied in the contract pursuant to the parties' intention.[38] It cannot be said that the question of classification has been resolved but in logic it is hard to resist the conclusion that software is intangible property handled for convenience in a physical medium.

Documentary intangibles

Documentary intangibles are instruments or documents that are so much identified with the obligation embodied in them that the appropriate way to perform or transfer the obligation is through the medium of the document. The abstract intangible right acquires such a degree of concretized expression that it takes on some of the characteristics of a chattel. The document recording the right is itself a tangible thing and thus a chattel, and the right is thoroughly fused with the document.

For example, a bill of lading embraces the carrier's delivery obligation to surrender the cargo to the lawful holder at the journey's end. This holder might be a purchaser to whom the bill has been indorsed and delivered or even a bank that has provided an advance against the security of the bill. A carrier is bound to deliver the cargo to the lawful holder of

---

[35] *Dear v Reeves* [2001] EWCA Civ 277. [36] *Ord v Upton* [2000] 1 All ER 193 (CA).
[37] *Haig v Aitken* [2000] 3 All ER 80.
[38] See *St Albans City and District Council v International Computers Ltd* [1996] 4 All ER 481 (CA).

the bill of lading[39] and is liable for knowingly delivering to someone other than the lawful holder,[40] even the person consigning the goods for carriage in the first place. Again, the document might be a negotiable instrument such as a bill of exchange or promissory note. The promise to pay the stated sum of the acceptor of the bill, or the maker of the note, is to be performed in response to the demand of the holder of the bill or note, whoever that might be at the relevant time.[41] Where the bill of exchange has been made payable to bearer, that is to its unnamed holder from time to time, its easy portability and transferability display characteristics associated with chattels.

An insurance policy might be transferred, and the duty to the insurance company to indemnify in respect of the covered loss would be performed by paying the lawful holder of the policy.[42] Shares in a company would involve the payment of any dividend, for example, to the registered holder of the certificate at the time the dividend is declared.[43] The prospective development of paperless share transfer system promises faster transactions and therefore a greater volume of business turnover.

MONEY

This is an item of personalty that merits special mention. It is classically understood as both a medium of exchange and a store of value. As a medium of exchange, it ensures liquidity of transactions and the avoidance of cumbersome barters. The seller of wheat seeking to acquire tin does not have the burden of finding a rare trading partner whose desires are equal and opposite. In an inflationary economy, the attraction of money as a store of value diminishes. Placing money in an interest-bearing bank account involves exchanging it for an equivalent capital sum plus accruing interest; it does not involve merely storing it.[44] Before the deposit with interest is repaid, the bank comes under a personal obligation to repay the equivalent sum according to the terms of its contract with the depositor. In modern times, money has become a tradeable commodity in its own right, the subject of intense speculation on foreign exchange markets as pounds sterling are traded for dollars and so on.

---

[39] *Erichsen v Barkworth* (1858) 3 H & N 601.
[40] *Glyn, Mills & Co v East and West India Dock Co* (1882) 7 App Cas 591.
[41] Bills of Exchange Act 1882, s 59.
[42] Merkin, R., *Colinvaux's Law of Insurance*, 6th edn, London: Sweet & Maxwell, 1990, chapter 10.
[43] *Godfrey Phillips Ltd v Investment Trust Corpn Ltd* [1953] Ch 449.
[44] *Foley v Hill* (1848) 2 HLC 28.

Money as legal tender comprises coinage and banknotes. Coinage is issued by the Royal Mint exclusively, subject to Treasury permission.[45] Banknotes are issued exclusively in England and Wales by the Bank of England[46] in denominations and overall amounts approved by the Treasury.[47] The meaning of money may, however, become enlarged according to the context, a statute or a will[48] for example, in which the word is used.

The question whether money is a chattel or a chose in action is a purely analytical one, devoid of practical application. Although a banknote is literally cast in the form of a promissory note ('I promise to pay the bearer etc'), which is a documentary intangible, it is no longer redeemed by the maker of the note, the Bank of England, in gold or other precious metal. If taken into a clearing bank, the banknote may be used as a medium of exchange, if it is deposited in an account or used to acquire foreign exchange or surrendered for money in different denominations. The banknote has therefore become a chattel, and the same applies *a fortiori* to coins.

MOVABLE AND IMMOVABLE PROPERTY

A critical division in continental systems based upon Roman law is between movable and immovable property, which does not exactly correspond to its closest common law equivalent, that between personalty and land. English courts are faced from time to time with cases involving a foreign element. When the foreign element is duly established and proved, a body of choice of law rules dealing with such cases is brought into play. These rules may point to the application of a foreign law. In order to minimize the awkward effects of the transition from English law to a foreign law, English choice of law rules in the area of property are not based upon the division between personalty and land but upon the division between movables and immovables.[49] In brief, the category of immovable property includes certain examples of what we regard as personalty. Thus a mortgage debt secured on land is an immovable,[50] likewise a leasehold interest in land,[51] as well as land currently held under a trust for sale and expected to give rise at a future date to money proceeds.[52]

---

[45] Coinage Act 1971.   [46] Bank Charter Act 1844.
[47] Currency and Bank Notes Act 1954; Currency Act 1983.
[48] See *Perrin v Morgan* [1943] AC 399.
[49] *Re Hoyles* [1911] 1 Ch 179, *per* Farwell LJ.
[50] *Re Hoyles*.   [51] *Freke v Carbery* (1873) LR 16 Eq 461.
[52] *Re Berchtold* [1923] 1 Ch 192.

EQUITABLE DOCTRINE OF CONVERSION

In myriad instances, rules of equity modify the operation of common law rules. Equitable intervention is conventionally organized under the heading of a collection of maxims. One of these is that equity looks upon that as done which ought to be done. According to the doctrine of conversion, if an obligation exists to convert land into personalty, then equity will for various purposes deem that the conversion has already taken place and treat the obligee's interest in land as an interest in personalty instead.[53] Conversely, money held on trust terms for the purchase of land will be deemed to be land and not personalty. Greatly reduced in scope in the modern law, the doctrine of conversion is still important in the construction of wills and other instruments and in the interpretation of certain statutes.[54]

EQUITABLE INTERESTS

All interests in property recognized at common law may be the subject of divided ownership whereby one person has the bare legal ownership and the other the beneficial ownership, the latter having the substantial enjoyment of the thing.[55] Divided ownership most frequently occurs where items of property are held on trust. A trust is created where a settlor settles property on trust in favour of one or more beneficiaries, who may include the settlor himself. The settlor may himself be the trustee or he may transfer the property to a third party to hold as trustee. The trustee holds the legal interest and the beneficiary the beneficial interest. In certain cases, a trust may be imposed by operation of law. One example is the constructive trust which arises in numerous cases, for example where an agent makes a secret profit or accepts a bribe.[56] In some cases, a resulting trust[57] may arise by operation of law, as where a settlor transfers property to trustees without specifying the trusts on which the property is to be held. In other cases, a resulting trust may arise out of presumed intention, as where the legal interest in property is transferred to another in circumstances where no intention, actual or presumed, to transfer also the beneficial interest can be shown. Under a resulting trust, the transferee holds the property on trust for the transferor. A division of

---

[53] *Fletcher v Ashburner* (1779) 1 Bro CC 497.

[54] Bell, A. P., *Modern Law of Personal Property in England and Ireland*, London: Butterworth & Co, 1989, p 25.

[55] See further chapter 2.

[56] *Attorney-General of Hong Kong v Reid* [1994] 1 AC 324 (PC).

[57] See chapter 4.

ownership between legal and beneficial interest-holders is not peculiar to the trust; it can arise in other cases too.[58]

The only interests in personal property recognized at common law are rights of ownership and possession. Any other interest has to exist in equity and will thus suffer from a weakness affecting all equitable proprietary rights: it is overridden by a *bona fide* purchaser of the legal estate without notice of the equitable interest.

WHAT IS A PROPERTY RIGHT?

Having defined personal property, we must now consider rights in property. The question posed above is a fundamental one but surprisingly difficult to answer at the general level. We can start by saying that the question deals with the relationship between an individual and a thing, and the effect of that relationship on the world at large. Property rights come in various shapes and sizes. In the next chapter, we shall examine the common law rights of ownership and possession in some detail. There exists also a range of equitable rights over personalty. The touchstone of a property right is its universality: it can be asserted against the world at large and not, for example, only against another individual such as a contracting partner. If, under a contract of sale, I acquire the ownership of a chattel, my property right to that chattel may be asserted not just against the seller but against the whole world. This is not to say, however, that universal rights are invincible: common law property rights may in certain instances be overridden, and equitable rights, for example the interest of a trust beneficiary in the trust assets, are always vulnerable to the *bona fide* purchaser for value without notice of the legal estate.[59]

To say that a right is universal does not take us very far unless a further inquiry is launched into the remedial consequences of this universality. In chapter 3 we shall see that the dispossessed owner is not normally entitled to recover a chattel from someone who is wrongfully in possession of it. The wrongful possessor is answerable in the tort of conversion, the usual remedy for which is damages. In the case of a chose in action, such as a debt, physical recovery is obviously impossible. If the debt is paid to the wrong person in such a way that the debtor is not discharged, the debt still exists and its payment can be sought again by the creditor (see

---

[58] *Westdeutsche Landesbank Girozentrale v Islington London Borough Council* [1996] AC 669 (HL).

[59] See further chapter 5.

chapter 6). If its due payment is intercepted by a wrongdoer, the debt ceases to exist as such but the recipient of the proceeds of the debt will be amenable to a restitutionary action for the recovery of the money, which will in some instances at least be reinforced by an equitable tracing claim (see chapter 5). A number of special statutory and tort actions also exist to protect rights in intellectual property.

The infringement of a property right does not necessarily give rise to a proprietary (that is a real or *in rem*) remedy. How far the remedial consequences outlined above can be described as proprietary, and the practical consequences of their being so described, is best considered on the testing ground of insolvency. If, to take one example, an insolvent is wrongfully in possession of a chattel, the rightful claimant may maintain an action in conversion since the chattel is regarded as never forming part of the insolvent's estate. It therefore does not vest in the trustee in bankruptcy (individual insolvency) or the liquidator (corporate insolvency) as the case may be.[60] If the insolvent were subject only to a personal claim, as would be the case if the action were for breach of contract or for failing to pay a debt, then the claimant would have to lodge a proof for the claim in the insolvency,[61] which would yield very modest results from an estate inadequate to meet the various claims made upon it. If the conversion claim is made after the insolvent has already disposed of the chattel, the claim is necessarily only a personal one, as it would also be if the trustee in bankruptcy (or liquidator) had unlawfully disposed of a chattel not falling within the insolvent's estate.

Equitable proprietary rights and the remedies associated with them, such as tracing orders, are particularly significant in insolvency cases. Where the requirements for them are met,[62] a proprietary claim may be made against assets whose acquisition can be traced from the proceeds of the original unlawful disposition. If a tracing order is made and the defendant becomes insolvent, so many of the defendant's assets as are traceable to the wrongful disposition do not vest beneficially in the trustee in bankruptcy (or liquidator), for the trustee stands in the shoes of the insolvent.[63] A trustee who unlawfully interferes with a chattel will incur personal liability in conversion; one who fails to pay over a sum of money traced in the above way will become personally liable in a restitutionary action for money had and received.

---

[60] Insolvency Act 1986, s 283.   [61] Insolvency Act 1986, s 322.
[62] See chapter 5.   [63] *Madell v Thomas* [1891] 1 QB 230, *per* Kay LJ.

2

Interests in chattels

INTRODUCTION

In contrast with land, the law of personal property is conceptually under-developed. It was never subjected to the doctrine of estates which had, according to Maitland,[1] the following effect: 'Proprietary rights in land are, we may say, projected upon the plane of time. The category of quantity, of duration, is applied to them.' Land was permanent, ineradicable and unique; personalty, for the most part, was ephemeral and fungible. The tenure of land, an expression inappropriate to personalty, was an intimate feature of the feudal system, which did not extend to interests in personalty. This is not to say that personalty was incapable of being an important source of wealth. Maitland cites the likely surprise at such a statement of a thirteenth century Cistercian abbot with flocks of thousands of sheep.[2] After the demise in medieval times of the appeal of felony, there existed until the middle of the nineteenth century no means at common law for the recovery of goods of which the owner had been wrongfully dispossessed. The law of tort, as we shall see,[3] stepped in to protect property rights, more accurately to protect possession, by means of the award of damages. But the non-existence of proprietary remedies in the developing common law, such as the *vindicatio* of Roman law or its modern civilian equivalent of the revendication action in French law, makes it peculiarly difficult to define personal property law and thus to settle the contents of syllabuses and books on the subject.

Proprietary interests in chattels (tangible personal property) are defined[4] in terms of possession and ownership. Each is hard to explain. Moreover, ownership is largely expressed in terms of the vocabulary of possession since 'possession is in a normal state of things the outward

---

[1] Pollock, F., and Maitland, F. W., *The History of English Law*, vol II, 2nd edn, 1898, p 10.
[2] Pollock and Maitland, *op. cit.*, vol II, p 148.
[3] Chapter 3.
[4] More accurately described: Harris, D., 'The Concept of Possession in English Law', p 70, in Guest, A.G. (ed), *Oxford Essays in Jurisprudence*, Oxford: Oxford University Press, 1961.

sign of ownership'.[5] We may fairly say at this point that ownership amounts to the best available possessory right. Consequently, of the two, more space has to be devoted here to possession, which must be dealt with before we turn to ownership. The difficulty of understanding possession comes into focus with the circumstances of its acquisition and loss, since unsurprisingly these are the events that attract the primary concern of the law. The present chapter will concentrate on these aspects of possession. The corresponding aspects of ownership, more easily detached from an understanding of what ownership is, will be dealt with later.[6]

In the case of intangible personal property, possession is impossible. As we saw in chapter 1, rights in these choses in action have to be asserted through the medium of legal action. They can of course be owned; the acquisition of ownership is dealt with in chapter 6. Choses in action that amount to documentary intangibles can be possessed: statements about the possession of chattels can normally be extended to cover the case of documentary intangibles. In addition, documentary intangibles can be owned but the ownership of them is valued, and the possession of them deemed significant, according to what they represent since the paper embodying them has no intrinsic value. These matters will be dealt with in subsequent chapters.

Possession and ownership of a chattel are real rights rather than personal ones. An executory contract affecting a chattel does not normally create real rights over it. These only arise when possession is taken of the chattel or one party succeeds in conveying to the other his ownership rights in it, as the case may be.[7] The significance of real rights is that they bind others apart from the parties to the transaction. More particularly, they survive the insolvency of the person granting the right. They can be asserted against the trustee-in-bankruptcy (or company liquidator) charged with winding up the insolvent's estate,[8] the holder of such rights not being limited to proving in the insolvency[9] and receiving the pitifully small dividend that almost always results when the estate is finally wound up.

---

[5] Pollock, F., and Wright, R., *An Essay on Possession in the Common Law*, Oxford: Oxford University Press 1888, p 4.

[6] Chapters 4–5.

[7] Goode, R. M., *Commercial Law*, 2nd edn, Harmondsworth: Penguin Books, 1995, p 51.

[8] See Insolvency Act 1986, s 306.

[9] See Insolvency Act 1986, s 322.

POSSESSION

In this section, we shall consider the general features of how possession is acquired, before dealing with it at further length through a study of the cases on finding.

RELATIVITY OF POSSESSION

Earl Jowitt once confessed that English law had 'never worked out a completely logical and exhaustive definition of "possession"'.[10] The meaning of possession appears to vary according to context and indeed it sometimes appears in constructive and symbolic forms. Possession takes its meaning very much from the operative facts, so its application differs according to whether it applies to a signet ring or a supertanker.

THE HISTORY OF A CHATTEL

Chattels cannot be possessed before they come into existence or after they have perished. They do not, however, appear from nothing and they commonly disappear, sometimes leaving tangible remains. To the extent that processes are at work involving changes in the nature of chattels when they are worked, commingled, adapted and converted, these have consequences that affect ownership rights.[11] In routine cases, the minute history of a chattel will not be recorded; a seller, for example, will not be required to demonstrate a good root of title or the way in which the chattel came into his hands. Nevertheless, in so far as it is practicable to do so, the chain of lawful possession is traceable to the first lawful possessor. This individual may have spun polymer yarn from petrochemical ingredients, or have captured a wild animal, or have manufactured a compact disc from a variety of materials and processes, or have cut cloth to make a suit. The life of the ensuing chattel, as well as the number of transactions of which it is the subject matter, will obviously be variable. Polymer yarn may have a very brief existence before it is reworked into a wholly new product; a compact disc, on the other hand, has reached its mature form and is good only for scrap in the unlikely event of its destruction. Given the movable, commonly short-lived and protean character of chattels, it is hardly surprising that property rights in them should be defined in possessory rather than abstract terms.

---

[10] *United States of America v Dollfus Mieg et Cie SA* [1952] AC 582.
[11] See chapter 4.

LEGAL CHARACTER OF POSSESSION

Possession is largely a matter of fact, hence its relative nature. As a legal concept, it may be stated as consisting of two elements: first, the exercise of factual control over the chattel; and secondly, the concomitant intention to exclude others from the exercise of control. The presence of this second element, more than anything, serves to differentiate the legal meaning of possession from its looser, lay equivalent, which broadly approximates to the first element. The necessary degree of factual control is understood for present purposes to be established when the possessor has acquired such control as the nature of the case admits. This may be illustrated with the assistance of two decided cases. In *Young v Hichens*,[12] the claimant had almost encompassed a shoal of pilchards with a seine net when the defendant rowed his boat to the opening of the net, thereby preventing the claimant's placing of a stop net across the seven fathom gap to take the fish. The claimant's suit in trespass required him to show that he was in possession of the fish at the time of the disturbance.[13] Though the claimant contended that 'a strong probability of complete capture is enough to give a right of possession against a party preventing the capture', the court disagreed: it was not enough that it was 'almost certain' that the claimant would have had the fish without the defendant's interference.

A contrasting case is *The Tubantia*.[14] It involved interference by the defendants with the claimants' attempts to salve a sunken Dutch freighter, which lay in over a hundred feet of water. The behaviour of the defendants consisted in sending down their own divers and attempting to raise the claimants' grappling irons and anchor. By means of marker buoys and various lines in 'the nature of fixed plant on and around the *Tubantia*', the claimants were able to put in about twenty-five working days in the year in which they claimed possession of the wreck, the roughness of the seas and weather preventing any more than this. In the circumstances, they were held to have acquired possession of the wreck. They had the necessary possessory intention, had recovered some valuable items from the wreck and were exercising 'the use and occupation of which the subject matter was capable'. They were also in a position to prevent the defendants from asserting the same degree of control over the wreck as they (the claimants) themselves had already assumed. If the owner had done what the claimants had done, this would more clearly still have been enough to

---

[12] (1844) 6 QB 606.   [13] See chapter 3.   [14] [1924] P 78.

resume possession, given the 'presumption of law which aids the operative effect of the possessory acts of the owner'.[15]

This last point demonstrates also that the degree of control necessary
for the acquisition of possession in the first place may not be necessary for
possession to be maintained. Peace and social order, one of the goals of
the law in this area, would be at risk if too stringent a test were to be
applied to the retention of possession. The law is defined in such a way as
to avoid legitimizing a free-for-all over disputed chattels. There is no
need for the intention to exclude others to be constantly present to the
mind of the possessor[16] or for the possessor to have a very specific intention about the object of possession.[17] A person in possession may, with the
necessary intention, abandon it[18] so as to permit its occupancy by the first
person to assume control of it with the necessary possessory intention.
Even if a chattel has not been abandoned but has been seized by a wrongdoer, the latter may satisfy a court that it has thereby been reduced to his
possession; we shall see in chapter 3 that the wrongdoer is in principle
entitled to complain of a wrong done to his possession by someone other
than the true owner. The volume of evidence required to satisfy an
unsympathetic court, however, may be beyond the capabilities of some
wrongdoers.

Holmes[19] cites the example of someone who finds a purse of gold
which he leaves in his country house, 'lonely and slightly barred', while
he serves time in prison a hundred miles away. The only person within
twenty miles is 'a thoroughly equipped burglar' who is poised at the
window to take the purse. Holmes rightly concludes that, until the burglar succeeds in making off with the purse, the finder is still to be regarded
as being in possession, however precarious that possession may be. There
is a marked disinclination in the law, clear cases of abandonment apart, to
conclude that there has been a lapse in the possession of a chattel. The
same point comes out in an illustration given by Pollock and Wright.[20] It
concerns the careless banker who leaves the bank 'open and unguarded',
thus facilitating the theft of cash and securities. However reprehensible
that may be by the standards of careful bankers, the banker remains in
possession of those valuables until effectively dispossessed.

---

[15] See also *Ramsay v Margret* [1894] 2 QB 18 for the resolution of evidentiary doubt in
favour of the owner.
[16] Markby, Sir W., *Elements of Law*, 6th edn, Oxford: Clarendon Press, 1905, p 190.
[17] See the finding cases, below.
[18] *Brown v Mallett* (1848) 5 CB 599 *per* Maule J.
[19] *The Common Law*, 1881, p 237.   [20] *Op. cit.*, p 15.

INDIVISIBILITY OF POSSESSION

Possession, it is sometimes said, may not be shared,[21] given that it is based upon the exclusion of others.[22] This statement should be read carefully. It seems clear that adverse claimants will not share possession; the law will rule that one of them has succeeded in excluding the other. Nevertheless, it seems perfectly possible for there to be a consensually shared possession, as would commonly be the case with co-owners, 'each . . . in possession of the whole and of the half'.[23] Moreover, the proposition has been accepted, for the purpose of suit in trespass[24] that both bailor and bailee at will are in possession of the chattel bailed. The recognition that a bailee, able to call for the return of the chattel at any time, has possession is clearly a pragmatic, instrumental extension of the idea that underlines the relativity of possession.

The same pragmatism appears to be evident in certain cases dealing with liens.[25] A good illustration is the House of Lords decision in *Great Eastern Railway Co v Lord's Trustee*.[26] A railway company let to a merchant for the storage of coal certain allotments in one of its yards, which coal it also carried on behalf of the merchant. Under a 'ledger agreement', the railway was to have a continual lien on the contents of those allotments, which varied with the addition and withdrawal of coal from time to time, for all charges due to it from the merchant. This meant that, if payment was not duly made by the merchant, the railway had the right to sell the coal and pay itself out of the proceeds. The railway had the keys of the yard gates, the merchant not having a set, and the yard was kept closed outside business hours. Upon default by Lord, the railway closed the yard gates and detained the coal. Its action was challenged by Lord's trustee in bankruptcy, acting on behalf of his other creditors, on the ground that it had taken place under an unregistered, and therefore unlawful, bill of sale. Briefly, the legislation governing bills of sale[27] requires certain onerous formalities to be observed where a licence or equitable right is given to take possession of chattels in certain instances. The outcome of the case depended upon whether the railway company was already in possession of the coal stored in the allotments at all

---

[21] Fitzgerald, P.J., *Salmond on Jurisprudence*, 12th edn, London: Sweet & Maxwell, 1966, p 287; Markby, *op. cit.*, p 203.
[22] Holmes, *op. cit.*, p 220.   [23] Markby, *op. cit.*, p 204.
[24] See chapter 3; *Ancona v Rogers* (1876) 1 Ex D 285.
[25] Discussed further in chapter 7.
[26] [1909] AC 109.   [27] See further chapter 7.

material times, because if this were so, there was no need to comply with the legislation.

By a bare majority, the House of Lords concluded that the legislation did not apply, since the railway was in possession of the coal and so could not be said to have taken it when it refused to allow Lord to carry it off. It did not matter that Lord could be said to be in occupation of the allotments containing the coal, nor, evidently, that Lord could normally, during business hours, remove the coal without let or hindrance before the axe fell. The courts of this period were concerned not to apply too readily bills of sale legislation, with its ponderous requirements difficult to satisfy, especially where this would lead to the frustration of normal business transactions not falling in Lord Macnaghten's words 'within the mischief at which the Act was aimed'. Possession was therefore given an expansive reading of the kind that a more dispassionate review of the facts would not have afforded. Apart from Lord Macnaghten's observation that Lord had possession of the coal 'in a sense', the result of the case was not justified in terms of a joint possession. It is hard to see how Lord's control over the coal on a daily basis, coupled with his intention to exercise ownership rights over it, fell short of possession.

CONTROL FALLING SHORT OF POSSESSION

The result in the above case prompts a reference to those cases where occupation of a chattel falls short of the legal sense of possession. The most obvious example is that of the employee, who is recognized as against the employer as not possessing the employer's chattels but rather as having only custody of them. As an employee of University College London, I therefore have custody over the word processor on which the manuscript for this book is being typed, whilst possession is enjoyed by my employer, even though other employees, never mind anyone representing the directing mind and will of the corporate entity that is the university, rarely ever come near the word processor. Such a legal conclusion cannot be said to follow from a neutral evaluation of fact.

The above rule (for that is what it comes to) was formulated at a time when the offence of larceny required amongst other things an asportation (or removal) of the chattel from the possession of the owner. If the employee were already in possession of the chattel before forming a dishonest intention, the offence of larceny could not be committed. Treating the employer as still being in possession meant that the law of larceny could work within the employment relationship to protect the employer's property rights. The offence of larceny has now been superseded by theft,[28] which no longer demands an asportation but rather any act of sufficient interference with the owner's property rights. Thus the custody rule, not affected by this development, has been separated from the criminal law's function as the protector of property rights.

The conclusion that an employee, even with extensive control, has only custody of the employer's chattels can always be excluded by the clear assertion of an intention by the employee to possess exclusively. Such an intention wrongfully to dispossess the employer would on the evidence involve the commission by the employee of a tort[29] or of a breach of the employment contract.

The same approach to custody can also be found in other circumstances where close physical control is exercised over a chattel. A hotel guest does not possess movable items in the hotel room, with the likely exception of disposable bathroom products when these, in response to the hotel's mute invitation, are packed away in the guest's suitcase. A diner does not possess the condiments on a restaurant table, though it would be regarded as a gross breach of etiquette, if not a trespass, for a neighbouring diner to remove these without permission.

Physical control falling short of possession and causing problems under the old law of larceny emerges in another context. In *Cartwright v Green*[30] a bureau was entrusted to a carpenter for repair, neither party at the time being aware that a very large sum of money had been placed in a secret drawer. The carpenter found the money and appropriated it, and the question arose whether this was a felonious taking and therefore a larceny. If the carpenter had been entrusted with possession of the bureau together with its contents, then he could not be said to have taken the money for the purpose of committing larceny. But he was entrusted only with the bureau for a limited purpose, so, by analogy with the case of a common carrier who breaks open a parcel entrusted to him for carriage and appropriates its contents, he committed a trespassory (and therefore a larcenous) taking when he opened the secret drawer and removed the money.

The circumstances were different in *Merry v Green*,[31] where a bureau, sold at auction, was found by the purchaser to contain a substantial sum of coin and valuables in a secret drawer. On the question of felonious taking, the case supports the view that no such taking could have

---

[28] Theft Act 1968, s 1.   [29] See chapter 3.
[30] (1803) 8 Ves Jun 405.   [31] (1841) 7 M & W 623.

occurred if the auctioneer's intention had been to sell the bureau together with its contents (not difficult to infer in such a case), for this would have involved a surrender of total possession to the purchaser. It is more likely there will be a limited intention where an owner entrusts something for repair than where a seller disposes outright of his interest in the chattel containing the hidden contents.

ACQUISITION OF POSSESSION BY FINDING

Chattels may be lost or abandoned. In both cases, subsequent finders may acquire property rights in the chattel. The finder of a lost chattel acquires a possessory title to it that is usually effective against all but the true owner; the rights of the finder of an abandoned chattel are more difficult to state. First of all, abandonment may go to either or both of possession and ownership. The abandonment of possession means the voluntary surrender of that possession; the abandonment of ownership means that the owner is voluntarily abdicating ownership. To the extent that only possession is being abandoned by an owner, the owner is entitled to resume possession at a later date. The finder, meanwhile, will still acquire a possessory title to the chattel, but one that, if the chattel is more easily traceable, is likely to be more precarious than the possessory title of the finder of a lost chattel.

As for ownership, the law on abandonment is obscure and difficult to relate to modern conditions.[32] Early law was resistant to the idea that ownership could be abandoned, even to the point of holding in one case that burial shrouds had not been abandoned by their former owners and present wearers.[33] Blackstone, however, states that 'the right to take or resume possession' of a sunken ship can be lost by abandonment.[34] The abandonment of ownership gains further support from the House of Lords in *The Crystal*,[35] where a statutory claim was made by harbour commissioners against the owner of a sunken ship for expenses incurred in disposing of the wreck. Since the owners had given notice of abandonment prior to the incurring of expenses, they could not be regarded as the 'owner' under the Act. The outcome is consistent with the view that a

---

[32] For a fuller statement, see Hudson, A., 'Abandonment', in Palmer, N., and McKendrick, E., *Interests in Goods*, 2nd edn, London and Hong Kong: LLP, 1998.

[33] *Haynes's Case* (1614) 12 Co Rep 113. See also C. St. Germain, *Doctor and Student* (1551), 91 Selden Society at pp 290–292.

[34] *Commentaries on the Laws of England* (1765), Book I, chapter 8 'Of the King's Revenue', at p 285.

[35] *Arrow Shipping Co Ltd v Tyne Improvement Commissioners (The Crystal)* [1894] AC 508. See also *Keene v Carter* (1994) 12 WAR 20.

statutory liability with no common law counterpart will not receive an expansive interpretation, but *The Crystal* does contain broad statements of support for the abandonment of ownership of vessels on the high seas.[36] Lord Macnaghten echoes Blackstone's language[37] but then leaves open the possibility that the property remains in the original owners despite the abandonment.

Lord Macnaghten also indicates that, if ownership has indeed been abandoned, then the ownership of the wreck vests in the Crown as *bona vacantia* (that is, as goods otherwise without an owner).[38] If this view is correct, it has restrictive implications for the rights of finders since they would necessarily take subject to the rights of the Crown, though it has to be said that the distinction between lost and abandoned chattels is illusory if there is no one on hand to explain the circumstances of abandonment or loss. Nevertheless, Romer LJ once confined the rights of finders to keep chattels to those cases where chattels had been lost rather than abandoned.[39] It is however questionable that all ownerless property belongs to the Crown. Furthermore, Blackstone asserts that chattels can exist without an owner when he writes that 'absolutely abandoned' chattels have been 'returned . . . into the common stock'. Since they are thus 'in a state of nature', they will belong to 'the first occupant or finder'.[40] In authorities dealing with intangible property, there seems to be a greater reluctance to infer abandonment, possibly in view of the prospect of the property in question reverting to the Crown as *bona vacantia*, with a consequent inference of a resulting trust in favour of the supposed abandoner.[41]

Assuming then that the ownership of a chattel can be abandoned effectively by the true owner and that the Crown has no *bona vacantia* claim, the finder first to take possession would succeed to the position of the true owner. If a chattel has been lost, or if only the possession of it has been abandoned, then the finder who takes possession acquires a proprietary right that is good against all the world with the exception of the true owner. This is subject to the law on treasure trove.[42] To legitimize such behaviour in assuming control of the chattel in this way, the law deems

---

[36] *Ibid*, pp 519 (Lord Herschell) and 521 (Lord Watson).

[37] *Ibid*, p 532 (abandonment of the 'right to retake or resume possession').

[38] See Bell, 'Bona Vacantia', in Palmer, N., and McKendrick, E., *Interests in Goods*, 2nd edn, London and Hong Kong: LLP, 1998.

[39] *Re Wells* [1933] 1 Ch 29 at p 56.

[40] *Commentaries on the Laws of England* (1765), Book I, chapter 8 'Of the King's Revenue', at p 285.

[41] See chapter 4.   [42] See below.

the finder to hold it under the terms of a fictitious bailment.[43] This fiction also submits the finder to the obligations of a bailee.[44] So, if the finder's subsequent behaviour is so serious a denial of the true owner's title that it would be a conversion[45] if committed by a bailee, it will be similarly wrongful on the part of the finder.[46] The finder acquiring a possessory title in this way seems also under a duty to seek out the true owner. In *Parker v British Airways Board*,[47] Donaldson LJ stated that a finder 'has an obligation to take such measures as in all the circumstances are reasonable to acquaint the true owner of the finding and present whereabouts of the chattel . . . ' If this is correct, it would seem not to be a condition of the finder acquiring and retaining a lawful possessory title. Rather, the inactive finder would lose the immunity from liability in conversion that arises within the protective walls of the fictitious bailment. This is borne out by Donaldson LJ going on to refer to the finder's duty to take care of the chattel. Any finder who uses or abuses the chattel to an extent not allowed a bailee will be liable in conversion, though the true owner's claim against the finder may become statute-barred.[48] The scope of such liability is, however, unclear since different types of bailment permit use and consumption in varying degrees.

In one category of case, acute difficulties have been caused in determining who acquires the possession of lost goods, namely where one person discovers a chattel on land occupied by another. In *Parker v British Airways Board*, a passenger at Heathrow Airport found a gold bracelet in the executive lounge. He handed it in to the airport authority, requiring it to be returned to him if the true owner were not found. The authority, however, sold the bracelet and appropriated the proceeds of sale when the search for the owner proved unavailing. The ensuing contest between authority and passenger was adjudicated in favour of the passenger, with the following principles emerging from the judgments. First, the issue depended on whether the authority had already acquired a possessory title to the bracelet before the passenger discovered it. If not, the law would protect the finder's claim against subsequent claimants.[49] Secondly, whether the authority already had possession at the moment of finding depended upon whether it had shown a sufficiently strong

---

[43] *Gilchrist Watt & Sanderson Pty Ltd v York Products Pty Ltd* [1970] 3 All ER 825; Palmer, N.E., *Bailment*, 2nd edn, London: Sweet & Maxwell, 1991, pp 32–34.

[44] See below.   [45] See chapter 3.

[46] *Moffatt v Kazana* [1969] 2 QB 152.   [47] [1982] QB 1004 (CA).

[48] See chapter 3.

[49] See also *Armory v Delamirie* (1722) 1 Stra 505.

intention to control both the premises on which the bracelet was found as well as 'the things which may be on or in it'. No such intention had been shown by the authority, so it followed that the passenger had established a prior and therefore superior possessory claim.[50] Thirdly, in the case of chattels becoming attached to or embedded in the land, the decision will go in favour of the occupier of the land, because possession of land also carries with it possession of things attached to or under the land.[51] In such a case, it might have been better to say that the occupier of land will find it easier to establish the necessary possessory intention to establish a claim that is prior to that of the finder. Legal possession being a function of both physical control and an intention to exclude others, the greater the physical control possessed by the occupier the less forcefully an excluding intention would have to be asserted. But it seems clear that a rule of law favours the occupier of land. This is borne out by *Waverley Borough Council v Fletcher*,[52] where a local authority was held to be entitled to a medieval brooch which was discovered underground by a finder with a metal detector, notwithstanding that the authority held the land under the terms of a covenant empowering it to allow access to the land for recreational purposes. The fourth principle in *Parker v British Airways Board* is that, as a matter of public policy, the law will rule in favour of the occupier when the finder is trespassing upon the land at the time of the finding.

Another point emerging from *Parker v British Airways Board* is that, as between an employer and an employee, when the latter finds something in the course of employment it must be accounted for to the employer.[53] This complements the rule that the employee does not possess, but merely has custody of, the employer's chattels.

TREASURE TROVE

Whatever may be the relative outcome of a dispute between the occupier of land and the finder, the prerogative claim of the Crown will be paramount (provided the true owner does not appear) if the chattel found is treasure trove. At common law, treasure trove is 'money or coin, gold, silver, plate, or bullion' that has been hidden.[54] The significance of the hiding is that it negatives an intention by the owner to abandon the

---

[50] See also *Bridges v Hawksworth* (1851) 21 LJQB 75; *Hannah v Peel* [1945] KB 509.
[51] *South Staffordshire Water Co v Sharman* [1896] 2 QB 44; Goodhart (1929) 3 CLJ 195.
[52] [1996] QB 334.
[53] See also *City of London Corpn v Appleyard* [1963] 2 All ER 843.
[54] Blackstone, *op. cit.*, Book I, chapter 8, p 285.

valuables. Where such objects are found buried or in a place of conceal-
ment, the Crown benefits from a presumption that they have been hidden.[55] This presumption is not displaced by 'fanciful suggestions more
suited to the poem of a Celtic bard than the prose of an English law
reporter'[56] that valuables have been given up (and not hidden) as votive
offerings to the gods.

The Treasure Act 1996 recasts and expands the range of the common
law of treasure trove, and thus has important ramifications for the rights
of finder and occupier over certain objects found in or upon land. For the
purpose of the Act, 'treasure' means, in addition to objects within the
common law definition of treasure trove, a range of objects that are at
least 300 years old; this includes coins (defined in terms of age, com-
position, and number) together with other metallic objects having a gold
or silver content of at least ten *per cent*.[57] In addition—and this departs
from the narrow common law definition—the Secretary of State is
empowered to designate as treasure objects that are at least 200 years old
and have 'outstanding historical, archaeological or cultural importance'.[58]
Conversely, the Secretary of State also has power to exclude objects from
the definition of treasure that otherwise would be considered treasure.[59]
Treasure, when found, vests in the Crown, except where there is a fran-
chisee (the Duke of Cornwall, for example) with a prior entitlement.[60]
The previous system of discretionary payments to finders has now been
put on a statutory footing[61] but remains a discretionary system.[62] It would
seem that the Secretary of State could divide any reward between the
finder and the owner of the land on or in which the treasure is found.[63]
Finally, the common law requirement that the treasure be hidden,
together with the concomitant presumption that treasure trove was
hidden, has been dispensed with under the new law.

POSSESSION AS A PROTECTED PROPERTY INTEREST

Proprietary rights, as stated above, bind those who are not parties to the
transactions that create them. To that extent they differ from contractual
rights, which, in accordance with the doctrine of privity of contract, do
not impose burdens on third parties. The distinction between property
rights and contractual rights is not free from difficulty and is tested by an

---

[55] *Attorney-General v Trustees of the British Museum* [1903] 2 Ch 598.
[56] *Ibid.*   [57] Sections 1(1), 3(3).
[58] Sections 1(1)(b), 2.   [59] Sections 1(2), 2(2)
[60] Section 4(1).   [61] Section 10.
[62] Section 10(6).   [63] Section 10(3)(d).

examination of the rights acquired by a hirer under a lease of chattels, which is a type of bailment. It has been argued that the hirer of a chattel does not have a proprietary right that can be opposed against someone purchasing it from the lessor.[64] If this argument is correct, it means that the possessory right of a hirer is a precarious one, whose vulnerability to a purchaser would defeat conventional commercial expectations. This argument, if successfully advanced, would also draw an invidious line between the rights of a hirer and the rights of a pledgee of a chattel,[65] since the latter certainly acquires a valuable security right that would not be overreached on a sale of the pledged chattel. A lease of chattels and a pledge equally confer on the party in possession rights of a proprietary and not merely of a contractual kind.[66] There is moreover the considerable authority of Lord Holt that the purchaser takes subject to a bailee's possessory right.[67] Possessory rights, furthermore, can be asserted against the owner's insolvency representatives,[68] insolvency being a well-defined, indeed the best, touchstone for determining whether rights are proprietary and not merely contractual. Sometimes, proprietary rights are contrasted with 'rights of possession and use',[69] but in a way that assimilates 'proprietary' to ownership without relegating all possessory rights to the status of mere contractual rights.

The proprietary character of the hirer's rights is confirmed by recent authorities on relief against forfeiture. Briefly, if a contracting party commits a discharging breach of contract and the other party exercises termination rights, equity will not step in to relieve the former party from the rough features of the contract.[70] Nevertheless, the Court of Appeal in *On Demand Information plc v Michael Gerson (Finance) plc*[71] held that the possessory right of a hirer of chattels under finance leases could be protected from forfeiture consequent upon the termination of the leases as a result of the hirer's stated default, which was entry into receivership. This relief was available provided that the forfeiture provision was

---

[64] Swadling, 'The Proprietary Effect of a Hire of Goods', in Palmer, N., and McKendrick, E., *Interests in Goods*, 2nd edn, London and Hong Kong: LLP, 1998.

[65] See chapter 7.

[66] *Franklin v Neate* (1844) 13 M & W 481.

[67] *Rich v Aldred* (1705) 6 Mod 216; see Calnan, 'Property, Security and Possession in Insolvency Law: *Re Cosslett (Contractors) Ltd*' (1997) 11 JIBFL 530 at pp 535–536.

[68] *Re Cosslett (Contractors) Ltd* [1998] Ch 495.

[69] *Ibid*, p 508 (Millett LJ).

[70] See in general the attitude of Lord Radcliffe in *Bridge v Campbell Discount Co Ltd* [1962] AC 600, 626.

[71] [2001] 1 WLR 155, affirmed on this point by the House of Lords at [2002] UKHL 13, but reversed in the result on another ground.

inserted in the lease primarily to attain a result that could be attained by other means when the matter came to court.[72] Those other means would almost always be the payment of moneys outstanding under the lease agreement. In the normal case, the lease would continue in the event of the owner's financial interest being protected in this way.

Forfeiture relief, however, is not tantamount to reviving a contract that has been lawfully terminated because of a party's discharging breach. Hence, it was held not to be available where a contracting party's rights were merely contractual, which was why it could not be given to time charterers, who do not take possession of the vessel, upon its withdrawal from hire because of late payment by the charterer.[73] Similarly, no relief is available to the licensee of trade marks or other intellectual property rights.[74] The decision in *On Demand* goes a step beyond the hire purchase cases, where forfeiture relief has been granted,[75] in that the hirer in such cases has an option to purchase which in the past has itself been treated as proprietary in character.[76] *On Demand* establishes beyond any doubt that a hirer's right to possession is proprietary and not merely contractual.

OWNERSHIP

RELATIVITY OF OWNERSHIP

It is common to speak of ownership as though it were an absolute thing. The literature is full of references to the true owner, the proprietary equivalent of the true cross or the philosopher's stone. Yet proprietary disputes are solved in bilateral litigation where the court has traditionally been called upon only to adjudicate in favour of one or the other of two claimants, an exercise in the relative rather than the absolute. It has rightly been said that 'the English law of ownership and possession, unlike that of Roman law, is not a system of identifying absolute entitlement, but of priority of entitlement'.[77] Changes introduced in 1977[78] have created the procedural possibility of all potential claimants being made party to litigation involving a disputed chattel. Because more than two parties may be involved, this creates a search for the best instead of the

---

[72] *Shiloh Spinners Ltd v Harding* [1973] AC 691.
[73] *The Scaptrade* [1983] 2 AC 694.
[74] *Sport Internationaal Bussum NV v Inter-Footwear Ltd* [1984] 1 WLR 776.
[75] For example, *Transag Haulage Ltd v Leyland DAF Finance* [1994] 2 BCLC 88.
[76] *Whiteley v Hilt* [1918] 2 KB 808. For a description of hire purchase, see below.
[77] *Waverley Borough Council v Fletcher* [1996] QB 334, *per* Auld LJ at p 345.
[78] Torts (Interference with Goods) Act 1977: see chapter 3.

better possessory right. It does not, however, quite equate to the discovery of the absolute owner. Registers of chattel ownership do not, except in unusual cases,[79] exist and, as we have seen, the history of ownership of a chattel, as well as the history of a chattel as a thing with an identity of its own, are not explored when transactions are concluded. Consequently, it may not be possible in proceedings to track down all parties with an interest in a disputed chattel. Commerce, furthermore, would become paralysed if the care and deliberation taken when investigating title to land were also taken when chattels are bought and sold.

This is why the owner of a chattel may be described as the person with the best possessory interest in it. The affinity between possession and ownership has long been recognized by the law. Under the old bankruptcy law, goods in the 'possession, order or disposition' of a bankrupt were liable to be distributed amongst his creditors where the bankrupt 'appeared the reputed owner thereof'.[80] The link between possession and ownership is not so obvious in a credit economy where suppliers notoriously reserve ownership until they are paid (see for example the discussion of hire purchase, below) and where non-possessory security is taken by creditors,[81] so the doctrine of reputed ownership is absent from modern legislation on the subject.[82] It survives, however, in legislation governing a landlord's right to distrain property found on the rented premises for rent unpaid by the tenant.[83] Even here, the modern trend is to restrict the operation of reputed ownership.[84]

The grant by the owner of extensive rights of possession may almost eviscerate ownership. When we examine the law of bailment, we shall see that the owner may have granted possessory rights for such a lengthy term that the reversionary value of a wasting chattel is slight. This grant may be subject to conditions that, if not observed, result in a premature reversion of the chattel to the owner before the term has expired. Thus the owner's otherwise negligible reversionary rights are endowed with a little more substance.

A distinction ought to be drawn between the above definition of the owner and a definition of ownership. Ownership may be regarded as the

---

[79] For example, British ships: Merchant Shipping Act 1995, ss 8–10.
[80] Bankruptcy Act 1914, s. 38(1)(c).
[81] See below.
[82] Insolvency Act 1986.
[83] See Law of Distress (Amendment) Act 1908, s 4(1).
[84] See *Salford Van Hire (Contracts) Ltd v Bocholt Developments Ltd* [1995] CLC 611.

'*greatest possible interest in a thing which a mature system of law recognizes*' (original emphasis), consisting of a bundle of rights and incidents in respect of the thing.[85] For our purposes, the most important rights may be abbreviated as: the perpetual right to possess and enjoy the thing; the perpetual right to the fruits and profits generated by it; and the right to alienate, bequeath or destroy it. Ownership may also attract certain incidents such as the legal obligation to purchase a licence, the amenability of the thing to execution pursuant to a judgment and the obligation not to use it so as to breach a duty imposed by law (for example, allowing a car to be driven on the road in an unroadworthy state; not abandoning a chattel in such a way as to cause a public nuisance or offend against litter legislation). The above rights may be surrendered in part without surrendering ownership of the thing itself. For example, I may lend you my book for an agreed period of one month. Until you actually obtain possession of the book pursuant to our antecedent agreement, you have a personal, contractual right to the book which becomes the proprietary right of possession once I deliver it to you.[86] In a very real sense, the owner is the person who has residual rights in the thing whatever lesser interests may have been granted in respect of it.[87]

GENERAL AND SPECIAL PROPERTY

In sale of goods transactions, the ownership of the seller, the transfer of which for a money consideration is the hallmark of a sale, is called the general property[88] and is defined as being other than the special property.[89] The latter expression is certainly used to signify the possessory entitlement of a pledgee[90] but is also used in a looser way to describe the possessory right of a bailee, who may hold as against the owner but whose right falls short of ownership.[91] Possession and ownership[92] together exhausting the category of legal property rights in a chattel, it follows that the general property is the ownership, in view of the identification of the special property with possession. Apart from defining a sale of goods

---

[85] See Honore, A., 'Ownership', in Guest, A. G. (ed), *Oxford Essays in Jurisprudence*, Oxford: Oxford University Press, 1961.

[86] See Goode, *op. cit.*, p 51.   [87] Honore, *op. cit.*, pp 126–128.

[88] Sale of Goods Act 1979, s 2(1).   [89] *Ibid*, s 61(1).

[90] See chapter 7.

[91] Holmes, *op. cit.*, p 242; *Nyberg v Handelaar* [1892] 2 QB 202; *Donald v Suckling* (1866) LR 1 QB 585, where special property is used to differentiate pledge and lien as opposed to pledge and other forms of bailment.

[92] Plus the immediate right thereto: see chapter 3.

agreement, the distinction between special and general property seems largely to be of terminological significance only.

INDIVISIBILITY AND CO-OWNERSHIP

It was stated earlier that personal property was never subjected to the doctrine of estates by which ownership can be divided on the temporal plane.[93] The quality of ownership can, however, be affected by the possession enjoyed by someone else. But the transfer by the owner of possession is not in law the grant of ownership rights. That legal principle can be pressed hard by practical reality is evident in the case of bailment, which is capable of definition in terms of the life span of the person receiving possession of the chattel, namely the bailee, or of the useful life of the chattel itself. The bailee, nevertheless, acquires only a possessory interest and not ownership since the chattel, however devalued and however lax the terms on which it is bailed, will revert to the bailor at the end of the bailment. As small as the bailor's residue might be, its existence prevents the transaction from effecting a transfer of ownership.

Chattels may be the subject of co-ownership, taking the form of either a joint tenancy or a tenancy in common, the latter being a form of co-ownership that is no longer possible in the case of land.[94] The difference between the two forms is that the ownership rights of a joint tenant descend on death to the other joint tenant(s). By contrast, each tenant in common, while sharing possession of the whole, owns only his share of the whole, which therefore goes to his next-of-kin on death. The notion of tenancy in common may have a useful part to play where chattels are commingled to form an undifferentiated mass.[95]

EQUITABLE INTERESTS IN PERSONALTY

The principle that the law does not recognize the divisibility of ownership of personalty is subject to a most important exception. The ownership of personalty, just as much as land, can be divided between the legal owner (the trustee) and the beneficial owner (the beneficiary or *cestui que trust*). The effect of this is that the trustee has the bare legal ownership while the fruits of beneficial ownership go to the beneficiaries whose interest may be of either a vested or contingent kind. Through the structure of the trust, the ownership of personalty may therefore be divided in myriad

---

[93] See also Goode, *op. cit.*, pp 37–39.   [94] Law of Property Act 1925, s 36(2).
[95] See chapter 4.

ways and the common law's limitation of proprietary interests to owner-ship and possession is exploded.

Trusts may arise in various circumstances. They may be created expressly where A, the owner, settles property on B on trust for C, or where A declares himself trustee in favour of B. Trusts are commonly set up in testamentary instruments and sometimes imposed by statute. They are sometimes used to establish security rights favouring creditors. Constructive trusts, very much at the forefront in modern commercial law developments as well as in other areas of law, are imposed in an instrumental way to render effective certain equitable obligations affecting the conscience of the constructive trustee. Since the beneficiary obtains a proprietary interest in the subject matter of the trust, this property right is shielded from the creditors of the trustee. The subject of trusts is much too large to deal with here except in the broadest outline. The vulnerability of beneficial interests to those acquiring a legal interest in the subject matter of the trust will be dealt with in chapter 5.

Besides those equitable proprietary interests arising under a trust, there exists also a category of mere equities,[96] largely of significance in the case of land, which in some instances have proprietary consequences.[97]

CONTRACTUAL RIGHTS IN RESPECT OF CHATTELS

In the case of land, covenants of a negative nature (that the land shall not be used in a certain way) or sometimes of a positive nature (that something shall be done on the land) may run with the land so as to bind successors in title who were not privy to the giving of the covenant. Suppose that A covenants in favour of B and subsequently disposes of the land to C. Since its beneficiary (B) obtains a proprietary right, the covenant diminishes the proprietary entitlement of the disponee of the land (C). The attempt in *De Mattos v Gibson*[98] to extend to chattels the doctrine of covenants in land law has not generally found favour.[99] A straightforward application of the doctrine of indivisible ownership of personalty would have it that covenants do not have a proprietary effect outside land. Nevertheless, there may be exceptional cases where a contractual coven-

---

[96] See *National Provincial Bank v Ainsworth* [1965] AC 1175.
[97] See further the standard trust and land law texts.
[98] (1858) 4 D & J 276, *per* Knight Bruce LJ.
[99] See *Port Line Ltd v Ben Line Steamers Ltd* [1958] 2 QB 146; *Swiss Bank Corpn v Lloyds Bank Ltd* [1982] AC 584 (CA); Treitel, G. H., *The Law of Contract*, 10th edn, London: Sweet & Maxwell, 1999, pp 570–575.

ant will bind a third party acquiring the chattel[100] with notice of the covenant.[101] It would also seem that the third party acquirer in such cases can only be restrained in negative terms from acting in disregard of the covenant, and may not be enjoined in positive terms to perform the contractual covenants of his predecessor in title.[102] It is clear that the doctrine in *De Mattos v Gibson* will remain exceptional in its scope so as not to 'provide a panacea for outflanking the doctrine of privity of contract'.[103] Someone acquiring a chattel may, however, do so with the knowledge that its acquisition gives rise to a breach of contract by the transferor. The acquirer may thereby incur liability in tort for interfering with the contractual relations of covenantor and covenantee.[104] The need for knowledge is what separates a duty in tort not to interfere with the contractual rights of others from a universal obligation in property law to respect restrictions, originating in contract, on the use and enjoyment of a chattel.

BAILMENT

DEFINITION OF BAILMENT

We have already made a number of references in this chapter to bailment. Bailment is a possessory relationship by which a bailor transfers possession of a chattel to a bailee. The bailment may be at will, in which case the bailor has the right to call for the return of the goods at any time, or it may be for a fixed or determinable period, in which case the bailee has the right to resist a demand for the early return of the chattel. At the end of the bailment, the bailee must place the goods at the disposal of the bailor, either to be delivered to the bailor or dealt with according to the bailor's instructions. Whether it is the bailee's duty actively to return the chattel or simply to make it available for the bailor to collect will depend upon the construction of the relationship, in particular, upon the terms of any contract governing the bailment. The bailment may serve one or more of a wide variety of economic and social purposes. If executed pursuant to a contract, the contractual incidents will be added to those that flow out of the proprietary relationship of bailor and bailee. If no contract exists, the

---

[100] *Lord Strathcona S.S. Co v Dominion Coal Co* [1926] AC 108.

[101] *Law Debenture Trust Corpn v Ural Caspian Oil Corpn Ltd* [1993] 1 WLR 138, at p 143, treating the covenant as giving rise to only an equitable right in the covenantee.

[102] *Ibid*, at p 146.

[103] *Ibid*, at p 144.

[104] *Law Debenture Trust Corpn v Ural Caspian Oil Corpn Ltd* [1995] Ch 152 (CA).

rights and duties of the bailor and bailee *inter se* may be defined according to law of torts.[105] There is no such thing as a form of action, or latterly a cause of action, in bailment.[106] Tort principles, however, have to be specially adapted at times in their application to bailment relationships.

SUB-BAILMENT

Where the bailor consents, the bailee may sub-bail the chattel to another, who now stands as a sub-bailee in relation to the bailor.[107] The relationship between bailor and sub-bailee remains unclear; it has been brought into play, for instrumental reasons, to circumvent the doctrine of privity of contract in circumstances where the application of the doctrine would be commercially inconvenient. Consequently, a furrier, to whom a mink stole had been sub-bailed for specialist cleaning by the bailee dry-cleaner, was held in *Morris v C. W. Martin & Sons Ltd*[108] to owe the bailor a duty to take reasonable care of the stole and a duty not to convert it. If the language of the exclusion clause in the contract between bailee and sub-bailee had been apt to give the latter protection from the consequences of its employee's theft of the stole, Lord Denning MR would have been prepared to modify the relationship of bailor and sub-bailee in accordance with the clause, because the terms of the bailor's consent to the receipt of the stole by the sub-bailee were usual in the trade. Otherwise, the imposition of restrictions on the rights of the bailor against the bailee could hardly be justified if it depended upon subjecting the bailor to burdens arising under a contract between bailee and sub-bailee to which he was not privy.

The doctrine of sub-bailment on terms was applied also by the Privy Council in *The Pioneer Container*,[109] where the owners of cargo were held to have consented to an exclusive jurisdiction clause in a contract concluded between the carrier and a sub-bailee carrier brought in for the last leg of the journey. The decision of the Privy Council reveals a curious doctrine. A bailment relationship is consummated directly between the bailor and the sub-bailee without, it seems, displacing the other bailment

---

[105] *Morris v C. W. Martin & Sons Ltd* [1966] 1 QB 716; but see Palmer, *op. cit.*, pp 44–63.

[106] But *cf. The Pioneer Container* [1994] 2 AC 324, *per* Lord Goff of Chieveley.

[107] Pollock and Wright, *op. cit.*, p 169.

[108] [1966] 1 QB 716. See also *Gilchrist Watt & Sanderson Pty Ltd v York Products Pty Ltd* [1970] 3 All ER 825 (PC); Bell, 'Sub-Bailment on Terms', in Palmer, N., and McKendrick, E. (eds), *Interests in Goods*, 2nd edn, London and Hong Kong: LLP, 1998.

[109] [1994] 2 AC 324.

relationships (bailor/bailee, bailee/sub-bailee). As against the bailor, the sub-bailee is a bailee for reward, even though the sub-bailee is paid by the bailee and not by the bailor. Furthermore, this bailment relationship between bailor and sub-bailee exists even though the latter has not yet 'attorned'[110] to the former. This last conclusion is difficult to reconcile with basic principles of bailment law. A more natural characterization of the relationship would have been one of implied contract, but this expedient was rejected by the Privy Council for unstated reasons.[111] This route could not be used in *Morris v C. W. Martin & Sons Ltd* since the trial judge found a contract to be lacking and this finding was not challenged on appeal.

BAILMENT AND POSSESSION

If the possession of a chattel is not transferred, there can be no bailment. This is illustrated by the well-known case of *Ashby v Tolhurst*,[112] where the owner of a car left it in a private car park. He paid his parking fee and received a ticket. A thief later appeared and was permitted by the attendant to take away the car, though he had neither the ticket nor the key. Because of a clause on the ticket exempting the car park from liability, the outcome of the case turned upon whether there had been a misdelivery of the car by the car park as bailee. Reversing the trial judge, the Court of Appeal held that the owner of the car had merely availed himself of a permission (or licence) to park his car on the other's land. Possession of the car had not passed to the car park (which had been paid in advance). Whether transactions of this kind can amount to a bailment involves construing the relationship, in deciding which the handing over of keys to an attendant will argue strongly in favour of the transfer of possession of the car.[113]

TYPES OF BAILMENT

The nature of the bailee's liability depends to some extent upon the type of bailment relationship created. Before Lord Holt's masterly summary of bailment law, drawing upon Roman law principles and categories, in *Coggs v Bernard*,[114] the view was that a bailee was absolutely liable for the loss or destruction of the chattel.[115] This position complemented the bailee's entitlement to sue third party wrongdoers and recover the value

---

[110] See below.

[111] *Ibid*, at p 339.

[112] [1937] 2 KB 242.

[113] See *Mendelssohn v Normand Ltd* [1970] 1 QB 177.

[114] (1703) 2 Ld Raym 909.

[115] *Southcote's Case* (1601) Cro Eliz 815.

of the chattel in full.[116] It is unclear whether the bailee was absolutely liable because of this extensive entitlement to sue[117] or whether each rule was predicated upon the other.[118]

In *Coggs v Bernard* itself, the defendant promised to take up the claimant's brandy from one cellar and lay it down carefully in another. One of the casks was staved and a great quantity was spilled. Seeking to prevent judgment being given in the claimant's favour, the defendant made the pleading point that, since he could only be liable if he had been paid to perform the task (which would have been implied if he had been engaged as a common carrier), the claimant ought to have expressly mentioned payment (or the common carrier status of the defendant) in the declaration setting out his grievance. The defendant's attempt to arrest judgment was unsuccessful, the court ruling that the claimant could succeed on the promise without necessarily paying for the service.

The significance of the case lies principally in Lord Holt's attempt to classify various types of bailment and lay down the principles governing the bailee's liability when handling the subject matter of the bailment. He said there were six types of bailment: first, a deposit of the chattel with the bailee for the bailor's purpose (for example, luggage left for safeguarding); secondly, a gratuitous loan for the bailee's purpose (for example, a book); thirdly, the hire of a chattel to be paid for by the bailee (for example, a carriage); fourthly, a pledge of valuables as security for a loan made by the bailee;[119] fifthly, delivery of a chattel to permit the bailee to perform a service for which the bailor pays (for example, goods to be transported); and sixthly, delivery of a chattel for the purpose of a gratuitous service (as the transaction in *Coggs v Bernard* was for procedural reasons assumed to be).

THE BAILEE'S LIABILITY

The liability of bailors for goods supplied, a matter of contract law, may be left to the texts that deal with sale of goods and similar agreements. Similarly, there is no need to analyse in great detail the various degrees of duty that, in Lord Holt's view, the different bailees owed to their bailors, though it is useful to look at the matter for the light it throws on the

---

[116] See chapter 3.

[117] Holmes, *op. cit.*, p 167: '[A]s all the remedies were in the bailee's hands, . . . he was bound to hold his bailor harmless.'

[118] Pollock and Maitland, *op. cit.*, p 172: 'The bailee had the action because he was liable and was liable because he had the action.'

[119] See chapter 7.

relationship of bailment. Whatever duty is laid down, it may be excluded or varied by any contract between the parties, subject to controls abridging freedom of contract contained in the Unfair Contract Terms Act 1977.[120] The levels of duty as classically articulated respond to the following standards of liability: first, liability for slight negligence; secondly, liability for ordinary negligence; thirdly, liability for gross negligence; and fourthly, strict liability (subject to the defence of act of God or the King's enemies).

Liability for slight negligence was seen by Lord Holt as appropriate where the bailee benefited from the bailment (the second and third of his categories of bailment). Liability for ordinary negligence was appropriate for pledge (the fourth category) and liability for gross negligence applied where the bailment benefited the bailor (the first and sixth categories). In the case of *Coggs v Bernard* itself, the bailee's promise to answer to a higher standard of care superseded the lower imposed standard. Strict liability governed in the case of Lord Holt's fifth category (common carriers); it was needed to maintain the honesty of carriers. Furthermore, the public nature of the carrier's employment made his conduct a matter of importance to the whole community.[121]

Although the circumstances of bailment are different from the driving of a car, Lord Holt's attempt to calibrate in refined degrees the obligation to take care has largely fallen foul of the twentieth-century trend to standardize the duty of care in the tort of negligence as one of reasonable care. Consequently, the notions of slight and gross negligence have fallen by the wayside.[122] Strict liability has remained, but may be displaced by a contractual exemption clause or by the assumption by a common carrier of the status of private carrier. Furthermore, various statutes exist permitting or prescribing the means by which liability may be excluded or limited in monetary or other terms, some of them pursuant to international conventions.[123]

The negligence liability of a bailee, however, differs from that of other defendants in the law of tort in at least one major respect. The burden of proof lies upon the bailee to show that any loss or damage occurred despite the fact that reasonable care was taken.[124] This is a pragmatic

---

[120] For which see the standard contract texts.

[121] *Clarke v West Ham Corporation* [1909] 2 KB 858.

[122] *Houghland v R. R. Low (Luxury Coaches) Ltd* [1962] 1 QB 694.

[123] For example, the Carriers Act 1830, Carriage of Goods by Sea Act 1971, Carriage by Air Act 1961: see generally Palmer, *op. cit.*

[124] *Houghland v R. R. Low (Luxury Coaches) Ltd.*

response to the fact that the bailee, having controlled the chattel, knows its bailment history better than the bailor. Even if the bailee establishes, for example, that the chattel was stolen despite the taking of reasonable care, the bailee will be liable in the event of a failure to take steps to secure its recovery, if unable to show that such steps would have been unavailing in any event.[125] Similarly, a bailee who deviates in the conduct of a bailment, whether by storing a chattel in other than the agreed place,[126] or by entrusting it without authority to another,[127] or by carrying it other than by the prescribed route, will be liable for its loss or destruction unless able to prove that this would have occurred even without the deviation. Thus, in *James Morrison & Co v Shaw, Savill, and Albion Co*,[128] a ship carrying a consignment of New Zealand wool was sunk while deviating to Le Havre. The carrier, unable to shift the above burden, was left with the liability of an insurer for the loss that occurred. Furthermore, the carrier lost the protection of a clause in the contract giving protection for loss caused by the actions of the King's enemies.

While the bailee must in general exercise reasonable care, the standard becomes very much stricter if the bailee refuses, or inexcusably fails, to surrender the chattel at the end of the bailment in response to a demand made at that time by the bailor.[129] The bailee's liability now becomes that of an insurer and so the bailee will be liable if the goods are stolen, even if no amount of care would have prevented the theft.

LOANS FOR CONSUMPTION

If you place money in a bank, whether in a current, savings or deposit account, the relationship between you and the bank is that of creditor and debtor.[130] It is not a case of bailment at all. The bank is under no obligation to deliver to you the original coinage or bank notes left with it. Rather, it owes you a personal obligation to repay the debt in accordance with the terms of its contract with you. Consequently, if you authorize your bank to debit your account and credit someone else's account in another bank, no money is transferred between the two banks.[131] The first bank's indebtedness to the payer is reduced by the amount transferred, and the second bank's indebtedness to the payee commensurately increased.

---

[125] *Coldman v Hill* [1919] 1 KB 443.   [126] *Lilley v Doubleday* (1881) 7 QBD 510.
[127] *Edwards v Newland & Co* [1950] 2 KB 534.
[128] [1916] 2 KB 783.
[129] *Mitchell v Ealing London Borough Council* [1979] 1 QB 1.
[130] *Foley v Hill* (1848) 2 HLC 28.   [131] *R v Preddy* [1996] AC 815.

Certain agreements involve the storage of fungible chattels, such as wheat or other types of grain, and permit the chattels to be mixed with the indistinguishable chattels of others in a common stock. It may be that the depositor ends up selling the chattels in question to the storage company or it may be that it is contemplated that the same quantity as that deposited will later be returned. In the latter of these eventualities, it is important for various reasons to know whether the transaction amounts to a loan of fungible goods, like the agreement with the bank in the sense that the original chattels deposited need not be returned, or whether it is a genuine bailment. If it is merely a loan to be repaid by the delivery of equivalent chattels, the insolvency of the storage company, for example, would leave the depositor in the position of an unsecured creditor having to prove for the amount owed when the insolvent's estate is wound up.[132] If the transaction is one of bailment, however, the depositor has a real, proprietary right which can be maintained in full against the liquidator of the storage company (providing the grain or whatever it is has not altogether disappeared). Until the decision of the House of Lords in *Mercer v Craven Grain Storage Ltd*,[133] it could have been said that the above transaction was not a bailment, the reason being that bailment requires the return of the original chattel as opposed to an equivalent quantity of an otherwise identical chattel.[134] In *Mercer*, however, the House of Lords by a bare majority on a summary judgment appeal found a bailment in the deposit of grain on terms calling, not for the return of the very same grain, but of an equivalent quantity. The various depositors were tenants in common of all of the grain so deposited and mixed. No mention was made of any of the relevant authorities and the issue of principle was not discussed. It may not be safe to rely upon this decision, but it is consonant with the recent resurgence of the notion of tenancy in common.[135] Furthermore, the decision of the court on this point, though casually reached, was trenchantly expressed.

In *Crawford v Kingston*,[136] a Canadian court refused to recognize as a bailment the delivery of cattle on terms calling for the return of the survivors together with their young at the end of a stated period. As the

---

[132] Insolvency Act 1986, s 322.

[133] [1994] CLC 328; Smith (1995) 111 LQR 10.

[134] *South Australia Insurance Co v Randell* (1869) LR 3 PC 101; *Chapman Bros v Verco Bros & Co* (1933) 49 CLR 306.

[135] See chapter 4 below.

[136] [1952] OR 714 (Ontario); cf. *Harding v Commissioner of Inland Revenue* [1977] 1 NZLR 337.

law stood before *Mercer*, the arguments were quite delicately poised. On the one hand, it may be that none of the original cattle will survive and it cannot be known in advance which ones will survive. On the other hand, it is perfectly possible for there to be a bailment if, during its course, the chattel perishes for whatever reason. In the light of *Mercer*, this would be more clearly seen as a bailment.

A bailment may exist even if it is contemplated that changes will be made to the chattel during the bailment, such as the repair or modification of a car. One Canadian case appears to take this point too far in holding that the delivery of seed to a farmer, with an obligation on him to return the mature produce represented by the seed, was a bailment.[137] Where some of the necessary materials were provided by the Crown to an arms manufacturer in order to permit the latter to make them up, with additional materials, into rifles, which were then to be supplied to the Crown at an agreed price, the House of Lords held that the manufacturer had sold the rifles to the Crown.[138] It could not be said that the Crown had bailed the materials that it provided to the manufacturer. Bailment ought not to be the conclusion where the parties contemplate a change in the basic nature of the chattel supplied.

HIRE PURCHASE AND RELATED BAILMENTS

On the face of it, it seems odd to classify as a bailment a transaction contemplating that the bailee will never return the chattel to the bailor and will indeed enjoy it beneficially for the rest of its useful life. This is precisely the case with the contract of hire purchase which is regarded as a bailment until the hirer exercises a future and contingent option to purchase the subject matter of the contract.

A common type of hire purchase takes the form of a bailment of a chattel (a car, for example) by a finance company to a hirer after the finance company has purchased the car from a car dealer. Preliminary discussions will take place between the hirer and the car dealer, the latter forwarding the hirer's request for finance to the finance company, which will accept or reject it according to the degree of risk involved. The hirer will pay a deposit, taking the form of cash or a trade-in vehicle, which will be retained by the dealer and deducted from the purchase price of the car to be received by the dealer from the finance company. The finance company is unlikely to see the car before the hirer takes possession and

---

[137] *Stewart v Sculthorp* (1894) 25 OR 544.
[138] *Dixon v London Small Arms Co* (1876) 1 App Cas 632.

fervently hopes that it will not physically have to deal with the car in the untoward event of a serious default by the hirer. If the hirer duly makes payment of the monthly instalments for, say, the agreed term of twenty-four months, the hirer may exercise an option to purchase the car for (invariably) a nominal consideration. Consequently, once consummated, the dealings between hirer and finance company consist of a bailment for the agreed period followed by a sale.

Thus stated, hire purchase is a legal fiction sanctioned as such by the highest courts and the legislature. The economic purpose of the transaction is to permit the acquisition of a chattel for consumption by a buyer who cannot yet (or does not want to) pay the price. The finance company's purpose in structuring its relations through the medium of bailment is two-fold. First, it wishes to avoid the conclusion that it is taking a non-possessory security interest in the chattel by way of a mortgage,[139] for this would involve compliance with intricate and tiresome bills of sale legislation.[140] If successful, it would also succeed in demonstrating that it was not in the business of lending money. The House of Lords in *McEntire v Crossley Bros*[141] gave the finance company its full backing on this issue. Secondly, the finance company, at the time hire purchase in its modern form was devised, wished to avoid the conclusion that the hirer was really someone who had agreed to buy the goods, for otherwise (as the law then stood) the finance company's retained ownership rights would be at risk if the hirer disposed of the chattel to a *bona fide* purchaser for value without notice.[142] This conclusion could be avoided by treating the hirer as someone who at no time ever promised to buy the chattel. The hirer in a hire purchase agreement never agrees to buy, but rather agrees to hire and unilaterally decides to buy at the end of the hire purchase term when it makes overwhelming economic sense to exercise the purchase option. The House of Lords gave the finance company its full backing on this issue too in *Helby v Matthews*.[143]

For reasons connected with the relative power of hirers and owners to transfer to purchasers a title that overrides the owner's property rights,[144] it may be in the interest of owners to draft a contract that is in the form of a hire purchase agreement but nevertheless maximizes the instalment payment obligations of the 'hirer' in a way that is consistent with conditional sale. This occurred in *Forthright Finance Ltd v Carlyle Finance*

[139] See chapter 7.   [140] Chapter 7.   [141] [1895] AC 457.
[142] See chapter 5.   [143] [1895] AC 471; see also *Lee v Butler* [1893] 2 QB 318.
[144] See chapter 5.

Ltd,[145] where the agreement required the 'hirer' to pay all of the instalments making up the price of a car, whereupon it would be deemed to have exercised the hirer's purchase option 'unless the hirer has told the owner before that time that such is not the case'. This was dismissed as a 'specious' attempt to dress up conditional sale as hire purchase.

In other respects, however, the courts have not assiduously respected the form of hire purchase contracts as bailments. One example concerns the liability in tort of a third party who converts the chattel[146] where the courts are prepared to look through the transaction and recognize that the finance company's only real interest in the chattel is measured by the (diminishing) amount of the unpaid instalments.[147] Although in this, and in certain other respects, finance companies have not succeeded in persuading courts to accept fully the bailment characterization of their dealings, hire purchase has successfully withstood the test of time in furthering their interests. An offshoot of it, which may have tax advantages for the hirer, is the simple financial lease by which, without obtaining an option to purchase, the hirer simply agrees to hire the chattel over a lengthy period, commonly the economic life of the chattel. The finance company's interest in, for example, a worn out office computer system or photocopier at the end of the lease is too inconsiderable to engage our attention.

Another example of what might be termed a wasting bailment, where it is contemplated that the chattel will never be returned to the bailor, more particularly that there will not be a chattel at the end of the bailment term, is afforded by the House of Lords decision in *The Span Terza (No. 2)*.[148] The time charterers of a ship, the possession of which at all material times remained with the shipowners, had the usual right to direct the ship to various ports for the purpose of loading and unloading cargoes. Under the charterparty agreement, it was the charterers' obligation to supply the bunker fuels needed to operate the ship. When the ship was arrested and thus immobilized by one of the shipowners' creditors, the charterers put an end to the time charterparty. They then sought a declaration that they were the owners of valuable bunker fuels still on board and were successful. The possession of the bunker fuels had been transferred by the charterers to the shipowners who, as bailees, had a contractual duty to see to it that the fuels were used by the ship's master

---

[145] [1997] 4 All ER 90 (CA).   [146] See chapter 3.
[147] *Wickham Holdings Ltd v Brooke House Motors Ltd* [1967] 1 WLR 295.
[148] [1984] 1 WLR 27.

in responding to the voyage directions given by the charterers from time to time. It was not a case where the ownership of the fuels had been transferred outright to the shipowners.

Bailment akin to sale emerges in another way too. A chattel may be sent on approval (for personal consumption) or on sale or return (for resale purposes) to a potential buyer who need not yet buy but, in the meantime, holds the chattel as a bailee. Needless to say, the potential buyer pays no hire during the course of the bailment. The Sale of Goods Act 1979[149] contains rules that assist in determining when the bailment has been superseded by a sale between the two parties.

TRANSFERRING POSSESSION

DELIVERY

The transfer of possession by manual means is effected by delivery. Whilst delivery is not confined to the performance of sale of goods agreements, it achieves there its most characteristic and comprehensive definition. Sale can therefore serve as the medium through which we explore delivery, though the consequences of delivery within the contract of sale need not detain us. The transfer of possession by constructive means will also be discussed in this section.

According to s 61(1) of the Sale of Goods Act 1979, ' "delivery" means voluntary transfer of possession from one person to another'. The seller will therefore deliver to the buyer when effective control over the chattel is surrendered in favour of the buyer, who simultaneously demonstrates an intention to assume effective control. Delivery is therefore a bilateral matter; it would not occur if the seller tendered the chattel to the buyer who refused to assume control over it. In certain cases, it will be a question of some difficulty to determine whether the seller has permitted the buyer such liberties with a chattel as to surrender possession thereto.[150] Notwithstanding the above, delivery will be deemed to have occurred if the seller and buyer agree as from a certain time that the seller shall thereafter retain the chattel in the capacity of bailee.[151] In such a case, possession and delivery go their separate ways since the seller's possession is unbroken.

---

[149] Section 18 *Rule 4*; see chapter 4.

[150] *Cooper v Bill* (1865) 3 H & C 722: possession lost because buyer allowed to treat, measure and stamp timber.

[151] *Dublin City Distillery v Doherty* [1914] AC 823.

CONSTRUCTIVE DELIVERY

Delivery may occur where the effective means of securing the chattel is transferred rather than the chattel itself. In *Wrightson v McArthur and Hutchinsons (1919) Ltd*,[152] the keys to various rooms in the defendants' premises were transferred to the claimant, who was not given a key to the outer door, which was kept locked outside business hours. A true delivery was held to have occurred since the claimant, by means of an irrevocable licence to enter the premises, had effective control of the contents of the locked rooms. The court was at pains to say that the delivery was not merely 'symbolic'[153] and could not adequately be described as 'constructive'. A more accurate example of symbolic delivery would occur if the seller handed over a portion of the contract goods with the accompanying intention, shared by the buyer, that this would be representative of the whole.[154]

A clear case of constructive delivery occurs where chattels are transferred to an agent of the buyer who holds them on account of the buyer. If the agent were an employee, it would be more accurate to call this a true delivery since the employee only has custody of the employer's chattels. The agent, however, might be an independent operator such as a carrier who, under the Sale of Goods Act 1979, is *prima facie* the agent for the buyer.[155] Delivery to the carrier is therefore delivery to the buyer, even though the carrier holds the chattel under the terms of a carriage bailment.

Another type of constructive delivery occurs where, at the time of the contract of sale, the goods are held by a third party, such as a wharfinger or warehouseman, under the terms of a bailment with the seller. It may be that the buyer will collect the chattel, in which case a delivery occurs at that time. But it may be that the buyer is content to allow the third party to retain possession but to hold the chattel thereafter on the buyer's account. In the latter case, it will be necessary for a new bailment between the buyer and the third party to be substituted for the old one between the seller and the third party. This is accomplished not merely by the seller instructing the third party to hold the chattel for the buyer; the third party must 'acknowledge to the buyer that he holds the goods on his behalf'.[156] This process is known as an attornment. A warehouseman who

---

[152] [1921] 2 KB 807.
[153] But see *Official Assignee of Madras v Mercantile Bank of India Ltd* [1935] AC 53.
[154] *Kemp v Falk* (1882) 7 App Cas 573 *per* Lord Blackburn.
[155] See s 32(1); *Wait v Baker* (1848) 2 Ex 1.   [156] Sale of Goods Act 1979, s 29(4).

merely entered details of the sale in his books without more ado could not therefore be said to have attorned to the buyer so as to incur the responsibilities as bailee to the buyer.[157]

Attornment and constructive delivery present themselves in another common commercial case where an owner of goods sells them to a financier and then takes a leaseback of the goods which in the meantime never leave his possession. The seller's acknowledgment that he holds the goods on account of the buyer amounts to a delivery, so that thereafter he retains the goods as bailee.[158]

DELIVERY DOCUMENTS

Suppose that the seller delivers to the buyer a document, concerning a chattel held by a third party, whose purpose is to effectuate a later physical delivery of the chattel to the buyer. May this document be described as a documentary intangible so that its delivery to the buyer is tantamount to delivery of the chattel itself?

The short answer is that it depends upon whether the document is a document of title as that expression is understood at common law. To discover what this means, it is convenient to begin by defining the types of document. For our purposes (though note that the terminology in the cases is not always consistent), we may distinguish between a delivery order and a delivery warrant. A delivery order is a command issued by the seller to the warehouseman that the chattel be given up to the buyer. A warehouseman failing to respond to that order may well be in breach of an obligation owed to the seller under the warehousing contract, but he owes no duty to the buyer unless and until an attornment to the buyer occurs. It follows that a seller has not delivered under the contract of sale before the warehouseman attorns, whether the delivery order is given to the buyer[159] or to the warehouseman.[160]

A delivery warrant, on the other hand, is a document generated by the warehouseman (or other bailee) and not by the seller. It records an undertaking[161] by the warehouseman to deliver to the seller 'or order'. By virtue of the latter words, the seller may indorse and deliver (that is, negotiate) the warrant to the buyer, who may do likewise for a sub-buyer and so on. Though it might have made perfect sense to regard the warehouseman's undertaking

---

[157] *Laurie and Morewood v Dudin and Sons* [1926] 1 KB 223.
[158] *Michael Gerson (Leasing) Ltd v Wilkinson* [2001] 1 All ER 148 (CA).
[159] *Lackington v Atherton* (1844) 7 Man & Gr 360.
[160] *M'Ewan v Smith* (1849) 2 HLC 309.
[161] *Gunn v Bolckow, Vaughan & Co* (1875) LR 10 Ch App 451.

in the warrant to deliver to order as an advance attornment, the position is well established that a constructive delivery does not occur when the warrant is negotiated to the buyer.[162] An attornment remains necessary.

Certain documents containing a bailee's undertaking, however, may work a constructive delivery upon their negotiation. By virtue of the law merchant, bills of lading have long been accepted as negotiable documents of title in that the carrier's delivery obligation is transferred to the holder of the bill when it is duly negotiated.[163] Left to its own devices, the common law would have been content to treat bills of lading in the same way as it treats delivery warrants in general, namely as 'mere tokens of an authority to receive possession'.[164] A carrier who delivers to someone other than the holder of the bill of lading commits the tort of conversion.[165] Nevertheless, delays in the transmission by post of bills of lading mean that carriers often surrender the cargo to a consignee buyer, not yet in receipt of the bill of lading, against the posting of a suitable indemnity against such liability by the buyer. The Carriage of Goods by Sea Act 1992 has extended the range of claimants entitled to bring suit against a carrier for breach of the contract of carriage, but it has not effected changes to the nature of a document of title as discussed above.

There is some controversy about what constitutes a bill of lading for present purposes, but the better view is that it is a document issued by a carrier attesting to the fact that the cargo has actually been shipped on board and not merely received for shipment.[166] Only where it is confidently known that the cargo is on board, locked in the 'floating warehouse',[167] may transactions be effected through the documentary intangible ('the key') that represents the cargo.

Certain special statutes extend to particular documents the above attributes of a negotiable bill of lading.[168] In addition, documents that fall short of being negotiable may yet constitute 'tokens of an authority to receive possession' so that dealings in them in favour of *bona fide* purchasers, even if not authorized by the owners of the chattels they represent, have proprietary consequences in favour of those purchasers.[169]

---

[162] *Farina v Home* (1846) 16 M & W 119; *The Future Express* [1992] 2 Lloyd's Rep 79.

[163] *Lickbarrow v Mason* (1787) 2 TR 63, (1790) 1 H Bl 357.

[164] *Official Assignee of Madras v Mercantile Bank of India Ltd* [1935] AC 53.

[165] *The Jag Shakti* [1986] AC 337.

[166] *Diamond Alkali Export Corpn v Fl Bourgeois* [1923] 3 KB 443; *cf. The Marlborough Hill* [1921] 2 AC 444.

[167] *Sanders Bros v Maclean & Co* (1883) 11 QBD 327.

[168] For example, the Port of London Act 1968, s 146(4) (dock warrants).

[169] See chapter 5.

3

The protection of property interests

INTRODUCTION

This chapter deals with the protection of property interests in chattels. The common law's treatment of this subject differs from that of civil law systems in at least two respects. First,[1] the common law has no notion of ownership in the sense of absolute title. As we shall see, however, certain statutory changes go some way towards defining such an absolute title.[2] Secondly, in consequence of this, the primary remedy at common law for the protection of property interests is not the compulsory return of the property to the claimant but rather damages. Hence the protection of property interests is a category of the law of torts (the so-called property torts) rather than of the law of property. The regrettable tendency in recent years is to drop the property torts from tort syllabuses, as much for their failure to fit in comfortably there as for the tendency of an expanding tort of negligence to crowd them out.

Historically, the most important torts were trespass *de bonis asportatis*, detinue and conversion. But for the accidents of history and the ingenuity of generations of pleaders, each tort might have occupied its separate share of the field, with trespass concerning itself with unlawful taking, detinue with unlawful detention and conversion with unlawful disposal. However, trespass grants protection in cases going beyond taking (or asportation) and conversion has also swallowed up unlawful taking. Moreover, conversion, easily the most important of these torts, had already assimilated certain instances of unlawful detention before the Torts (Interference with Goods) Act 1977 (hereinafter the 1977 Act) abolished detinue. It is unclear how much of detinue was added to conversion at this time. That Act, besides abolishing detinue, was concerned largely with rationalizing the various remedies associated with the property torts. It did not amount to a codification of the law and did not, despite its title and s 1, which defines a 'wrongful interference with goods', create a new tort of that name.

[1] See chapter 2.   [2] See below.

Trespass is the fountainhead of the law of tort so our treatment of the subject will begin with it, though it is dwarfed by conversion in terms of practical significance.

TRESPASS TO CHATTELS

TYPES OF BEHAVIOUR

Like other forms of trespass, trespass to chattels requires there to be a direct link between the behaviour of the defendant and the chattel: the name of its related tort against the person, trespass *vi et armis*, illustrates graphically the forceful and direct character of the tort. The distinction between direct and indirect is commonly brought out by standard examples of the kind that distinguish between laying down poisoned meat for the claimant's dog to find (indirect) and feeding the meat to the claimant's dog (direct). It would be a trespass if I immobilized your car by removing the rotor arm from the engine but not if I surrounded your car with other items to make it impossible for you to drive it away.

As the name trespass *de bonis asportatis* indicates, the tort was originally concerned with interference that involved carrying off the chattel. It was therefore committed when the sister-in-law of the deceased removed jewellery without authority from one room to another;[3] and when tyres were removed from a car in *G W K Ltd v Dunlop Rubber Co*;[4] it would be committed if a horse were to be led from one field to another.[5] Trespass subsequently expanded to catch other forms of interference like the infliction of damage, for example, the scratching of a coach panel,[6] and the shooting of the claimant's pigeons.[7] As Latham CJ put it in *Penfolds Wines Pty Ltd v Elliott*:[8]

> Unauthorized use of goods is a trespass; unauthorized acts of riding a horse, driving a motor car, using a bottle, are all equally trespasses, even though the horse may be returned unharmed or the motor car unwrecked or the bottle unbroken. The normal use of a bottle is as a container, and the use of it for this purpose is a trespass if . . . it is not authorized . . .

Despite some authority to the contrary,[9] the better view is that trespass

---

[3] *Kirk v Gregory* (1876) 1 Ex D 55.   [4] (1926) 42 TLR 593.
[5] *Fouldes v Willoughby* (1841) 8 M & W 540, *per* Rolfe B.
[6] *Fouldes v Willoughby*, *per* Alderson B.
[7] *Hamps v Darby* [1948] 2 KB 311.
[8] (1946) 74 CLR 204.   [9] See *Everitt v Martin* [1953] NZLR 29.

is actionable *per se* and without proof of special damage.[10] In the absence of a proprietary remedy that serves a declaratory function in the settling of disputes between competing claimants, this function can only be performed by the tort of trespass. Consequently, there is a practical need for trespass to lie, even in the absence of estimable damage. No good reason exists for treating trespass to chattels differently from trespass to land, which is actionable *per se* and thus able to perform this function of resolving title.[11] Similarly, trespass would be a useful expedient for dealing with irritating antisocial behaviour like the touching of museum exhibits. Actionability *per se* would assist trespass to perform a role in the protection of civil liberties. If the mere handling of another's papers is trespass,[12] then public officials will more readily be called upon to discharge the burden of establishing any available statutory defence of reasonable cause.

Moreover, to return to the example quoted earlier of the horse returned unharmed, such chattels possess earning power for the owner. A borrower would normally be expected to pay hire, so the actionability of trespass *per se* would make it easier to justify the award of damages calculated on this basis.[13] A long line of cases justifies the award of damages against a trespassing defendant measured according to the benefit accruing to the defendant rather than any loss incurred by the plaintiff.[14] Lord Halsbury pointed out in *The Mediana*[15] that it did not avail a wrongdoer depriving the plaintiff of the use of a chair that the plaintiff did not usually sit on it or that there were other chairs in the room.

THE MENTAL ELEMENT

Trespass requires there to be at least a wilful act on the part of the defendant; an involuntary act will not suffice. For that reason, a trespass is not committed by the owner of a mare when it bites the claimant's horse, though the result would probably be otherwise if the defendant trained his dog to remove golf balls.[16] Nor is trespass committed if the defendant is pushed against the claimant's chattel.

---

[10] See *Penfolds Wines Pty Ltd v Elliott*, *per* Latham CJ: no need to show 'material damage' for asportation.

[11] *Entick v Carrington* (1765) 2 Wils KB 275.

[12] See Lord Diplock in *Inland Revenue Commissioners v Rossminster* [1980] AC 952.

[13] See the example of the unauthorized borrowing of the livery horse in *Watson, Laidlaw & Co v Pott, Cassels & Williamson* (1914) 31 RPC 104, *per* Lord Shaw of Dunfermline.

[14] For example, *Whitwham v Westminster Brymbo Coal and Coke Co* [1896] 2 Ch 538; *Strand Electric and Engineering Co v Brisford Enterainments* [1952] 2 QB 246.

[15] [1900] AC 113, at p 117.

[16] *Manton v Brocklebank* [1923] 2 KB 212, *per* Atkin LJ.

Apart from the need for a wilful act, does the defendant have to intend to make contact with the claimant's chattel? Or is it sufficient if the defendant is negligent? Or is a wilful act sufficient without proof of either intention or negligence? Let us take first the question whether liability is so strict that the tort can be committed even in the absence of an intention to make contact or of negligent contact. In *National Coal Board v Evans*,[17] the defendants were not liable in trespass for damaging the claimant's power cable. When digging a trench on land belonging to a third party, they had no idea at all that there was a buried cable. Though the act of digging was a voluntary one, they could not be said to have made intentional contact with the cable. Furthermore, they were not negligent, for the claimant had trespassed upon the land and buried the cable without the knowledge and consent of the third party occupier. The case demonstrates that the defendant may escape liability by establishing the defence of inevitable accident. Later developments in the area of trespass to the person,[18] if brought over as they should be into the law relating to chattels, would go further and put the burden on the claimant to show that the defendant intended to make contact with the chattel. The tort of negligence, actionable only upon proof of damage, would be the appropriate form of recourse for damage inflicted unintentionally. The burden of proof of establishing negligence would of course fall upon the claimant. Trespass, given also its actionability *per se*, would be well defined to play a title protection role.

Once an intentional act has been shown, it is no defence, to amplify earlier examples, for the defendant in *Kirk v Gregory* to show that she moved the jewellery to what she thought was a safe place because of the revelry taking place in the house of the deceased, or for the man leading the animal (Rolfe B's example in *Fouldes v Willoughby*) to explain his mistaken belief that the animal had strayed. Motive and mistake do not assist the defendant. Again, where a finance company repossesses a car in the mistaken belief that the car belongs to it, and then returns it to another finance company which it discovers to be the true owner, it will have no defence to a trespass action brought by the person from whom the car was seized.[19] It would have been different if the defendant had seized the car in the capacity of agent for the true owner, for then the act of the defendant would have been the act of the owner.

---

[17] [1951] 2 KB 861.
[18] See *Fowler v Lanning* [1959] 1 QB 426; *Letang v Cooper* [1965] 1 QB 232.
[19] *Wilson v Lombank Ltd* [1963] 1 WLR 1294.

The quality of the defendant's behaviour, if not relevant to the issue of liability, might yet be taken into account in the assessment of damages at the discretionary margins of the tort. A tort that is actionable *per se* will always yield at least nominal damages. The well-meaning defendant in *Kirk v Gregory* was thus required to pay only nominal damages: it is anyway hard to see that her behaviour caused the later loss or theft of the jewellery. But, possibly because of its arbitrary action, the defendant in *Wilson v Lombank* was required to pay for the full value of the car, notwithstanding that the claimant's possessory interest in it was worth very little once the true owner was informed of its whereabouts. This comes close to an award of punitive damages. It is likely that s 8(1) of the Torts (Interference with Goods) Act 1977 would now operate so as to allow the defendant finance company to raise against the claimant the superior title of the true owner. This should serve to reduce the damages recoverable, without as such acquitting the defendant of liability.

WHO MAY SUE IN TRESPASS?

The rule is well established that only claimants in possession of the chattel at the time of the interference may sue, but possession is defined in such a way as to blur the line between possession and the right to immediate possession.

In *Penfolds Wines Pty Ltd v Elliott*,[20] the Australian High Court[21] in an extensive review of the law concluded forcefully that actual possession, not a right to immediate possession, was needed for a trespass action. Otherwise, there would have been no need for a separate action in conversion. Trespass is a tort of forcible and direct interference and it is not easy to see how it can be committed to someone's right to immediate possession as opposed to someone's actual possession.

On the other hand, in *Wilson v Lombank*, a car had been left with a garage for repair when it was repossessed by the defendant finance company. The defendant contended that the claimant had neither possession nor a right to immediate possession at the time of the repossession, since the garage would have been able to exercise a repairer's lien for its charges. The claimant accepted the defendant's apparent concession that a right to immediate possession was sufficient to qualify for an action in trespass and went on to argue, successfully, that it existed here because

---

[20] (1946) 74 CLR 204.
[21] Relying on Pollock F. and Wright R., *An Essay on Possession in the Common Law, op. cit.*, 1888.

the garage's lien had been given up in return for a monthly settlement of accounts between the claimant and the garage.

Much of the difficulty in this area stems from the tendency to assume that the right to immediate possession is tantamount to possession itself and indeed a constructive form thereof.[22] If English courts continue to take that fictitious view, which it is submitted they should not, then a right to immediate possession masquerading as possession will support a trespass action. But it is hard to see that a bailor at will is in possession when the bailee and the goods might be many miles away. It is also not easy to see how a bailor and bailee at will can both possess a chattel for the purpose of suit, as apparently they can.[23]

There are others apart from bailees at will whose constructive possession is recognized for the purpose of suit, for example, executors and administrators of estates for torts committed before letters of probate are granted, trustees where the beneficiary holds goods under the terms of the trust,[24] and the owners of franchises in wrecks.[25]

LIABILITY IN CONVERSION

DEVELOPMENT

The tort of conversion was developed from the writ of trover, itself a late fifteenth century offshoot of the writ of trespass on the case. As initially formulated, trover contained the following four averments by the claimant; first, that the claimant was possessed of a chattel; secondly, that the claimant casually (*casualiter et per infortunatem*) lost it; thirdly, that the defendant found it (hence trover); and fourthly, that the defendant converted the chattel to his own use. The second and third requirements were fictitious and non-traversable by the defendant; eventually they were dropped. Over time, the right to sue was extended beyond those who were in actual possession at the time of the conversion. It came to include those with a right to immediate possession, a category including bailors at will and unlawfully dispossessed owners following chattels down a chain of transactions involving their transfer. Conversion expanded to embrace certain examples (not all) of unlawful asportation as well as certain

---

[22] See *United States of America v Dollfus Mieg et Cie SA* [1952] AC 582, *per* Lord Porter; *Wilson v Lombank Ltd*; *Lotan v Cross* (1810) 2 Camp 464.

[23] See below.

[24] *Barker v Furlong* [1891] 2 Ch 172.

[25] *Bailiffs of Dunwich v Sterry* (1831) 1 B & Ad 831.

examples (again not all) of unlawful detention. The 1977 Act enacted some of the recommendations of the Law Reform Committee,[26] but not the recommendation that trespass, detinue and conversion all be super-seded by a new tort of unlawful interference with goods (or chattels). Instead, the 1977 Act retained conversion, adding to it elements of the abolished tort of detinue and making a number of changes, mainly of a remedial nature.

DEFINITION AND INTENTION

Perhaps the best definition of conversion is given by Atkin J in *Lancashire and Yorkshire Railway Co v MacNicoll*:[27]

> It appears to me plain that dealing with goods in a manner inconsistent with the right of the true owner amounts to a conversion, provided that it is also established that there is also an intention on the part of the defendant in so doing to deny the owner's right or to assert a right which is inconsistent with the owner's right.

Baron Bramwell once conceded that no true definition of the tort was possible.[28] Lord Nicholls, asserting that 'a precise definition of universal application is well nigh impossible', has laid emphasis upon conduct that has the three properties of being deliberate, inconsistent with the rights of the true owner, and 'so extensive an encroachment on the rights of the owner as to exclude him from use and possession of goods'.[29] Neverthe-less, Prosser has remarked[30] that, as difficult as it is to define the tort, judicial decisions on the subject have attained a high degree of consist-ency. Consequently, the best way to understand the tort is to follow in the steps of the numerous textbook writers and consider various examples of the way in which it can be committed. There is, of course, no definitive list of examples.

The tort is actionable *per se* but it should be understood that not every interference with chattels will ground an action in conversion. The inter-ference must be so serious as to amount to a denial of the claimant's title. Obstructive behaviour by a defendant making it difficult for an owner to recover goods, for example the owner of land who refuses to allow access for the recovery of the claimant's goods, may not involve a sufficiently

---

[26] 18th Report on Conversion and Detinue 1971, Cmnd. 4774, hereinafter LRC 18th Report.
[27] (1918) 88 LJKB 601, approved by Scrutton LJ in *Oakley v Lyster* [1931] 1 KB 148.
[28] *Burroughes v Bayne* (1860) 5 H & N 296.
[29] *Kuwait Airways Corpn v Iraqi Airways Co* [2002] UKHL 19 at [39].
[30] (1957) 42 Cornell LQ 168.

direct denial of the claimant's title to engender liability.[31] Conversion is a tort of strict liability and yet the element of intention is commonly stressed, as in Atkin J's definition in *Lancashire and Yorkshire Railway Co v MacNicoll*. The key to this apparent inconsistency is to understand that the defendant can be liable without at all being aware of the existence, or the superior entitlement, of the claimant. The element of intention goes only to the nature of the claimant's act: as we shall see in the various examples, the defendant must intend to assert an entitlement of his own or of someone else, which in fact is seriously inconsistent with the claimant's superior entitlement. Cleasby B in *Fowler v Hollins*[32] spoke of the 'salutary rule for the protection of property' by which 'persons deal with the property in chattels or exercise acts of ownership over them at their peril'. Yet the strictness of the tort causes judicial heartache from time to time,[33] though it has appositely been observed that those exercising professional callings are able to insure against this type of liability.[34]

Conversion has been defined as a tort that protects ownership,[35] unlike trespass which protects possession. When we come to look at the range of those entitled to sue, we shall see that this statement cannot be taken quite at face value.

ASPORTATION AS CONVERSION

Whilst a wrongful asportation may suffice for liability in trespass, something more is usually required for conversion. The leading case is *Fouldes v Willoughby*.[36] The defendant, who managed the ferry between Birkenhead and Liverpool, came on board and received complaints about the claimant's behaviour. He put the claimant's two horses ashore, after unsuccessfully asking the claimant to leave the ferry, but this action did not have the intended effect of persuading the claimant to follow them. Because the defendant had no intention of exercising any personal entitlement or dominion over the horses, his action was held not to be a conversion. All he did was to assert his control over the ferry and what he was prepared to carry on it, doing the minimum necessary to remove the horses from the ferry. As in other areas of conversion, liability turns on questions of degree. If, for example, in order to induce the claimant to leave the boat, the defendant had refused to allow the claimant's agent ashore to take the horses in charge, this might well have constituted a

---

[31] *England v Cowley* (1873) LR 8 Ex 126.   [32] (1872) LR 7 QB 616.
[33] See Blackburn J in *Hollins v Fowler* (1875) LR 7 HL 757.
[34] See Lord Denning in *R. H. Willis & Son v British Car Auctions* [1978] 1 WLR 438.
[35] See LRC 18th Report.   [36] (1841) 8 M & W 540.

conversion. A temporary deprivation of possession may in special circumstances constitute a conversion.[37] Leading the claimant's straying heifer from a railway line to a place of safety has however been held not to be a wrongful act, still less a conversion.[38]

DAMAGE, DESTRUCTION AND LOSS

We saw that scratching the panel of a coach would be a trespass. The conventional view is that minor acts of damage[39] do not amount to conversion. Cutting a log in two has been said not to be a conversion.[40] It would surely be different if the defendant did this with the intention of demonstrating in as vivid a way as possible an entitlement inconsistent with the claimant's. Altering the nature of the goods, however, is a conversion, as where a miller grinds corn into flour, or oats are made into oatmeal,[41] or water is poured into wine, or the seals cut from a deed.[42] Similarly, to participate in a string of paper transactions, the effect of which is to strip from the claimant's lorries valuable heavy goods licences, will give rise to liability.[43] Using goods in such a way as to make it impossible to return them to their earlier state may be a conversion, as where the defendant poured a quantity of carbolic acid into his tank in the mistaken belief that it was the creosote that he had ordered.[44] To destroy goods intentionally is a clear act of conversion: we have already seen that it is no defence for the defendant to be unaware of the claimant's interest in them. Suppose, however, that the defendant performs this act at the behest of someone who claims to be the true owner. The defendant is in the same position as the innocent miller (in Blackburn J's example) and is therefore strictly liable in conversion. Liability in conversion exists where the defendant asserts a title inconsistent with the true owner's, whether it be his own title or that of someone else.

It is well settled that, at common law, liability in conversion does not lie for negligent loss or destruction.[45] So a theatrical producer was not liable for the loss of a playwright's script that he had not requested,[46] and a

---

[37] *The Playa Larga* [1983] 2 Lloyd's Rep 171.
[38] *Sorrell v Paget* [1950] 1 KB 252; see also Blackburn J in *Hollins v Fowler* (1875) LR 7 HL 757.
[39] Or use: *Penfolds Wines Pty Ltd v Elliott* (1946) 74 CLR 204.
[40] *Simmons v Lillystone* (1853) 8 Ex 431, *per* Parke B.
[41] *Hollins v Fowler*, *per* Blackburn J.
[42] *Penfolds Wines Pty Ltd v Elliott*, *per* Dixon J.
[43] *Douglas Valley Finance Co v S Hughes (Hirers) Ltd* [1969] 1 QB 738.
[44] *Lancashire and Yorkshire Railway Co v MacNicoll* (1918) 88 LJKB 601.
[45] *Williams v Gesse* (1837) 3 Bing NC 849.
[46] *Howard v Harris* (1884) Cab & El 253.

person given charge of a valuable miniature painting was not liable for carelessly leaving it too near the stove.[47] The position was different in the tort of detinue where it was well settled that a negligent bailee could be liable in detinue.[48] With the abolition of detinue in 1977, conversion was explicitly extended by statute to cover this case.[49] In one case at common law, a defendant bailee had already been held liable for the unintentional loss of goods. In *Moorgate Mercantile Credit v Finch*,[50] a hire purchase car had been sub-bailed to one of the defendants (Read) who used it to smuggle watches into the country. When Read was caught, the car was forfeited under statute. Read was held to have converted the car since, at the time he obtained it, he was minded to use it for the commission of an illegal act. This act posed a grave risk to the claimant's interest in the car and Read was taken to have intended the natural and probable consequences of his action.

DETENTION

It is not a conversion to be in possession of someone else's chattel without authority.[51] Suppose, however, that the defendant in possession is faced with a demand by the true owner (or anyone with a superior title). A refusal to deliver in these circumstances would have been treated as an unlawful detention for the purpose of liability in detinue.[52] It is also evidence of a conversion though not necessarily conversion *per se*.[53] To that extent, the abolition of detinue may have created a small hole in the liability network,[54] easily filled nevertheless by an insistent demand and an adamant refusal to surrender the chattel that can be treated as conversion on the facts. In *Howard Perry & Co v British Railways Board*[55] the defendants refused to allow the claimant company to take delivery of its steel because they feared retaliatory action from their own employees who were supporting certain industrial action taken by steelworkers. This was a serious and unjustified interference with the claimant's right, not excused by the fact that the defendants were not asserting any personal claim to the steel. They were held liable even though it could not at the time of the refusal to surrender the steel be predicted how long the industrial disturbance would last.

---

[47] *Lethbridge v Phillips* (1819) 2 Stark 544.   [48] *The Arpad* [1934] P 189.
[49] 1977 Act, s 2(2).   [50] [1962] 1 QB 701.
[51] *Caxton Publishing Co v Sutherland Publishing Co* [1939] AC 178.
[52] *Alicia Hosiery Ltd v Brown Shipley Ltd* [1970] 1 QB 195.
[53] *Morris v Pugh* (1761) 3 Burr 1242.
[54] See Palmer, N.E., *Bailment*, 2nd edn, London: Sweet & Maxwell, 1991, p 247.
[55] [1980] 1 WLR 1375.

More recently, Lord Nicholls has confirmed that detention alone can amount to conversion provided that it is adverse to the owner as where the party in possession intends to keep the chattel. Such an intention may be inferred from a demand and a refusal to deliver up the chattel,[56] which shows the liability hole produced by the abolition of detinue to be more apparent than real.

The defendant is not liable in conversion merely because he delays in order to make inquiries when faced with the demand.[57] Furthermore, the defendant responds adequately to a lawful demand if the goods are made available for the claimant to collect; the defendant does not have to go to the further trouble, in the absence of a contractual duty to do so, of actively returning the chattel to the claimant.[58]

Liability can arise on the basis of a detention without a demand and refusal;[59] the wilful detention of a chattel, coupled with the intention of denying the true owner, may therefore entail liability.[60]

DISPOSITIONS OF CHATTELS

We shall examine in chapter 5 how the disposition of chattels may occur in circumstances where the disponee acquires a good title by way of exception to the rule of *nemo dat quod non habet*. Where this occurs, the disponee's act in accepting the goods will be a lawful one and, by virtue of acquiring a title superior to that of the earlier owner, the disponee will not be liable in conversion. The action of the disponor remains wrongful, however, and thus attracts liability.

It is well settled that the delivery of a chattel under a contract of sale is a conversion of it. It would be difficult to imagine a clearer assertion of title. The sale alone without the delivery will not suffice[61] apart from those cases where a *nemo dat* exception arises even before delivery occurs.[62] Section 11(3) of the 1977 Act accords with this approach in that it reversed earlier law,[63] whose supposed effect was to impose liability where the defendant simply denied the claimant's title without a physical intermeddling or other behaviour with injurious effects. The receipt of goods by a buyer who is not protected by a *nemo dat* exception will be a

---

[56] *Kuwait Airways Corpn v Iraqi Airways Co* [2002] UKHL 19 at [42].
[57] *Clayton v Le Roy* [1911] 2 KB 1031; *Alexander v Southey* (1821) 5 B & Ald 247.
[58] *Capital Finance Co v Bray* [1964] 1 WLR 323.
[59] *London Jewellers v Sutton* (1934) 50 TLR 193.
[60] *Clayton v Le Roy* [1911] 2 KB 1031.
[61] *Lancashire Waggon Co v Fitzhugh* (1861) 6 H & N 502.
[62] *Ibid*; LRC 18th Report.   [63] *Oakely v Lyster* [1931] 1 KB 148.

conversion.[64] According to Lord Ellenborough in *McCombie v Davies*:[65] 'Certainly a man is guilty who takes my property by assignment from another who has no authority to dispose of it; for what is that but assisting that other in carrying his wrongful act into effect.' Where goods are unlawfully pledged, the taking of them by the pledgee is now to be regarded as a conversion,[66] which reversed earlier law.[67] Not all unauthorized pledges by a bailee, however, will amount to a conversion by the bailee,[68] in which case the action of the pledgee in taking delivery of the goods also ought not to be conversion.

AGENTS AND INTERMEDIARIES

Perhaps the most difficult question in the area of conversion lies in determining the liability of those who assist others in denying the claimant's title. Does this act of assistance by agents and intermediaries mean they commit conversion too? Whilst it is sufficient for conversion that the defendant asserts a personal title so as to deny the claimant's title, this is not a necessary requirement. The defendant may be liable for asserting the title of a third party. Before we turn our attention to individual categories of agent, it is worth noting at the outset that brokers and auctioneers run a considerable liability risk whilst carriers and freight forwarding agents do not. The distinction is brought out in the judgment of Romer J in *Barker v Furlong*[69] and justified on the ground that an agent who is a broker or auctioneer, in some cases at least, 'takes part in transferring the property in a chattel', whereas carriers and packing agents 'merely purport to change the position of the goods, and not the property in them'. Liability in this tort of strict liability may therefore depend, in some cases at least, upon the defendant's knowledge of what is happening.[70]

The leading case on the liability of brokers is *Hollins v Fowler*. A rogue, falsely claiming to be the purchasing agent for a reputable trader, obtained possession of thirteen bales of the claimant's cotton. He offered it for sale to the defendant broker who, having found a buyer, sent a delivery order to the rogue requesting delivery to a third party. The cotton was received by the third party and spun into yarn at its factory. The defendant paid the sale price to the rogue and was reimbursed this

---

[64] *Ingram v Little* [1961] 1 QB 31; *Farrant v Thompson* (1822) 5 B & Ald 826.
[65] (1805) 6 East 538.   [66] 1977 Act, s 11(2).
[67] *Spackman v Foster* (1883) 11 QBD 99.
[68] *Donald v Suckling* (1866) LR 1 QB 585.
[69] [1891] 2 Ch 172.   [70] Blackburn J in *Hollins v Fowler* (1875) LR 7 HL 757.

amount, together with a brokerage commission, by the third party. Though the defendant was found to have acted as agent for the third party principal, he was held liable in conversion.

The following words of Blackburn J, called in to advise the House of Lords on the liability of intermediaries, summarize the principle governing liability:

> [O]ne who deals with goods at the request of the person who has the actual custody of them, in the *bona fide* belief that the custodier is the true owner, or has the authority of the true owner, should be excused for what he does, if his act is of such a nature as would be excused if done by the authority of the person in possession [,] if he was a finder of the goods, or entrusted with their custody.

Calling the person with actual custody A and the intermediary who deals with the goods B, the test may be rephrased as follows. Deeming A to be a bailee, B will not be liable in conversion for handling the goods if B's action is consistent with A's duty to return the goods to, or hold them at the disposition of, the true owner (who is the deemed bailor). So if B participates in the sale of the goods to C, B will be liable because this sale is inconsistent with A's duty as bailee to return the goods or hold them pending instructions from the bailor. On the other hand, to use Blackburn J's own illustration, a warehouse-man is not liable in conversion for returning the goods to the person who deposited them with him because this action is in no way inconsistent with the terms of the deemed bailment by which the depositor acquires the goods.

With rather more difficulty, we can say that a carrier (B) is not liable in conversion merely for accepting goods from a consignor (A) and delivering them to or to the order of a consignee (C). The carrier knows nothing of the relations between consignor and consignee and performs an act that may be quite consistent with the terms of a loan between consignor and consignee, which in turn may be perfectly consistent with the deemed bailment between the consignor/bailee and the owner/bailor. The knowledge of the intermediary (B) is therefore relevant, but only to the extent that it goes to an awareness that ownership of the chattel is being purportedly transferred under the transaction in which the intermediary gets involved. To return to Blackburn J, speaking of a railway company carrying goods from Liverpool to Stockport:

> [M]erely to transfer the custody of goods from a warehouse at Liverpool to one at Stockport, is *prima facie* an act justifiable in any one who has the lawful custody of the goods as a finder, or bailee, and the railway company . . . would be in complete ignorance that more was done. But if the railway company . . .

could have been fixed with knowledge that more was done than merely changing the custody, and knew that [its] servants were transferring the property
from one who had it in fact to another who was going to use it up, the question
would very nearly be the same as in the present case. It would, however, be very
difficult, if not impossible, to fix a railway company with such knowledge . . .

A case commonly considered to be a hard one is *Stephens v Elwall*.[71]
The defendant clerk, employed by a London trading house and 'act[ing]
under unavoidable ignorance and for his master's benefit', was held liable
in conversion merely for the physical act of consigning goods to his
master in America. Given the defendant's ignorance of the ownership
dimension of what he was doing, the case is impossible to justify in the
light of *Hollins v Fowler*, unless the view is taken that the realities of early
nineteenth-century shipping meant that the clerk must have known that
the goods could not have been returned from America to the true owner
as the deemed bailor.

The liability of auctioneers has been considered on a number of occasions. It was held in *Consolidated Co v Curtis*[72] that auctioneers who sold
goods on behalf of their principal and delivered them to the buyer were
liable to the owner in conversion. Yet the Court of Appeal in *National
Mercantile Bank v Rymill*[73] had earlier found in favour of an auctioneer
where certain horses, present in the auctioneers' repository and entered
in their sale catalogue, were sold by private treaty in their yard before the
auction took place. The purchase money was paid to the auctioneers who
took their commission and delivered the horses to the buyer. By Blackburn J's test in *Hollins v Fowler*, this should have been a clear case of
liability, even though the auctioneers played no part in initiating and
negotiating the sale. Lord Denning, in *R. H. Willis & Son v British Car
Auctions*,[74] saw no reason for distinguishing between sales under the
hammer and sales following a provisional bid since, in the latter instance,
the intervention of the auctioneer 'was an efficient cause of the sale and
he got his commission for what he did'. He observed that a well-
developed system of insurance served to protect private property and
spread the loss of dishonesty throughout the auction-going public.[75] In
the *British Car Auctions* case itself, the sale occurred by private treaty in
the office of the auctioneer, who accepted a lower commission on a sale to
the earlier highest bidder at the auction, whose bid had fallen below the
reserve. The Court of Appeal, in finding the auctioneer liable, left no

---

[71] (1815) 4 M & S 259.   [72] [1892] 1 QB 495.   [73] (1881) 144 LT 767.
[74] [1978] 1 WLR 438.   [75] See also LRC 18th Report.

room for a principled argument that the *Rymill* case was distinguishable on its facts. If the law is to be consistent in this area, the *Rymill* case ought not to be followed.

INVOLUNTARY BAILEES

Suppose that someone receives unsolicited goods. Where the Unsolicited Goods and Services Act 1971 applies, the recipient may, as between the sender and himself, 'use, deal with or dispose of [unsolicited goods] as if they were an unconditional gift to him, and any right of the sender to the goods shall be extinguished', provided certain conditions are met. These are that the goods were sent to the recipient with a view to his acquiring them; and that the recipient has no reasonable ground for believing that the goods were sent with a view to their being acquired for a trade or business. The statutory remedy is therefore, broadly, one made available to consumers. Further conditions are that the sender did not resume possession of the goods within six months of their receipt or did not respond to a written warning within thirty days (expiring within the six month period) that the recipient's statutory right of acquisition would be exercised. In the doubtless unusual case of title under the statute being acquired by the recipient, the previous owner is in no position to complain about acts that would otherwise be a conversion.

The involuntary receipt of unrequested goods is not a conversion[76] and the law has displayed a degree of tenderness to the victims of an ingenious but simple fraud that takes the following form. A rogue orders goods in the name of the recipient and the owner dispatches goods in response. Before the goods arrive, the rogue contacts the recipient to say that a mistake has been made and that unordered goods will be arriving. The rogue (or a confederate) is on hand to take the goods off the recipient's hands and the recipient obliges, believing naturally that only someone acting for the owner could have been so well informed about the movement of the goods. When this happened in *Elvin and Powell Ltd v Plummer Roddis Ltd*,[77] the court found the bailee's behaviour to be reasonable and declined to hold it liable in conversion in view of the jury's finding that negligence was absent. A different result was reached in *Hiort v Bott*,[78] where the defendant received an invoice and delivery order for a quantity of barley dispatched by rail. The delivery order was made out to consignor or consignee, so the consignee need not have done anything to

---

[76] See Burnett (1960) 76 LQR 364.   [77] (1933) 50 TLR 158.
[78] (1874) LR 9 Ex 86.

permit the consignor, or his agent, to recover the goods from the railway company. Despite this, the consignee innocently indorsed the delivery order in the name given by the rogue and the rogue was able to obtain the goods and decamp with them. Since this was an unnecessary act of intermeddling, 'assuming a control over the disposition of these goods' (Bramwell B), the defendant consignee was made liable in conversion. His action went beyond the implied authority given by the mistaken consignor (Bramwell B), which the consignor was estopped from denying (Cleasby B), to take reasonable steps with regard to the goods.

MISDELIVERY

We saw earlier that a carrier unable to deliver because of negligence is liable in conversion since the enactment of s 2(2) of the 1977 Act. The delivery by a carrier or other bailee to the wrong person will also entail liability, even if the misdelivery is unintentional,[79] though it is hard to see why the matter should not be disposed of under the contract giving rise to the bailment or in the tort of negligence, where appropriate.

ENTITLEMENT TO SUE IN CONVERSION

POSSESSION

We have seen that the common law failed to develop a sophisticated concept of ownership of personalty. The place of ownership was occupied by possession, which had the consequence that the protection of property interests was left to the law of tort. According to Pollock and Wright:[80]

> The Common Law never had any adequate process in the case of land, or any process at all in the case of goods, for the vindication of ownership pure and simple. So feeble and precarious was property without possession, or rather without possessory remedies, in the eyes of medieval lawyers, that Possession largely usurped not only the substance but the name of Property . . .

Lord Campbell once said that 'the person who has possession has the property'.[81] Conversion, a tort concerned with the protection of ownership, lay therefore at the behest of those in possession of the chattel at the time of the wrongful act and was later extended, because of the limitations of possession, to those with a right to immediate possession.

---

[79] *Devereux v Barclay* (1819) 2 B & Ald 702.
[80] *An Essay on Possession in the Common Law*, 1888, p 5.
[81] *Jeffries v Great Western Railway Co* (1856) 5 E & B 802.

Despite assertions sometimes made to the contrary,[82] it does not as such lie in favour of those with an equitable interest in chattels. Such persons still need to point in addition to possession or a right to immediate possession in order to sue in conversion, for otherwise they would need to join the legal owner as a party to the action.[83] Even where the equitable claimant could sue independently, the claimant would fail against a defendant acquiring a legal interest in the chattel without notice of the claimant's equitable interest,[84] just as any claimant with a legal interest is in narrower circumstances vulnerable to categories of purchasers able to override his legal interest.[85]

An owner out of possession and without the right to immediate possession will not be able to sue in conversion,[86] though the owner may be joined in proceedings brought by someone else with an entitlement to sue.[87] Such will be the position of an owner who has bailed a chattel under a term bailment. If, however, there is a bailment at will, the bailor will be able to maintain a conversion action, since the bailor's right to call for the return of the goods without delay means that the bailor has the right to immediate possession.[88] The bailee at will also has the right to sue.[89] Since the right to sue depends upon possession, it follows that a pledgee,[90] a sheriff,[91] and a lienee[92] may sue in conversion.

The bailee's right to sue was considered at length in the leading case of *The Winkfield*,[93] where the action lay in negligence (the rule here is the same as for conversion) against a ship that collided with another carrying mails from Cape Town to Southampton. The Postmaster-General, as bailee of the letters and parcels in transit, brought an action based upon the claims made against him by the bailors of the mails, though at all stages in the case it was assumed that he was under no liability at all to the various bailors. He was allowed to recover in full, the court taking the view that the matter of his liability to the bailors for the loss was not germane to the claim made against the defendant. It was accepted, however, that the right of the bailee to recover in this way was historically

---

[82] *International Factors Ltd v Rodriguez* [1979] QB 351 at p 359 (CA).
[83] *MCC Proceeds Inc v Lehman Brothers International (Europe)* [1998] 4 All ER 675 (CA). See Tettenborn [1996] CLJ 36.
[84] *Ibid.*　　　　　　　　　　　　　　[85] See chapter 5.
[86] *Gordon v Harper* (1796) 7 TR 9.　　　[87] See below.
[88] *Kahler v Midland Bank* [1950] AC 24, *per* Lord Radcliffe.
[89] *Nicolls v Bastard* (1835) 2 CrM & R 659.　　[90] *Swire v Leach* (1865) 18 CB (NS) 479.
[91] *Wilbraham v Snow* (1669) 2 Wms Saund 47.
[92] *Rogers v Kennay* (1846) 9 QB 592—at least in those cases, not all, where the lienee can be said to be in possession of the chattel.
[93] [1902] P 42.

linked to the bailee's former strict liability to the bailor.[94] Furthermore, the Postmaster-General was under a personal obligation to account to the bailors for moneys recovered in excess of his own (surely negligible) loss.

BAILMENT AND LIABILITY

Bailment at will throws up an example with more than one potential plaintiff. So does a term bailment to the extent that, though only the bailee has standing to sue in conversion, the bailor out of possession has an action for damages for any injury done to his reversionary interest.[95] There are other instances outside bailment, for example, finder and true owner, and other possibilities involving parties in a lengthy disposition chain. The existence of more than one claimant, in those cases of separate proceedings that give rise to liability measured by the value of the chattel rather than the claimant's interest in it,[96] creates the risk of unfair prejudice to the defendant. Double liability exceeding the value of the chattel would also concomitantly give rise to unjustified enrichment of those successful claimants retaining damages in excess of the value of their limited interest in the chattel.

Various common law mechanisms exist to avoid double liability and unjust enrichment. They are in evidence in proceedings brought by bailor and bailee. Outside bailment, the Torts (Interference with Goods) Act 1977 contains elaborate mechanisms to avoid the twin evils of double liability and unjustified enrichment.

The Winkfield states that a successful bailee has a duty to account to the bailor for that portion of the recovered damages exceeding his, the bailee's, interest, which 'serves to soothe a mind disconcerted by the notion that a person who is not himself the complete owner should be entitled to receive back the full value of the chattel converted or destroyed'.[97] Furthermore, once the bailee recovers damages from the defendant, the latter has a defence to any action brought by the bailor.[98] Since a term bailor cannot sue a wrongdoer in conversion (except in the case of a bailment terminated by the bailee's wrongdoing[99]), the action barred here is the action for damage done to the bailor's reversionary interest as well as the conversion action of the bailor at will.

It may be that a bailor's action against the wrongdoer is launched before proceedings are brought by the bailee. If so, the same principles

---

[94] See Pollock, F. and Maitland, F., *The History of English Law*, vol II, p 170.
[95] See below.　　　　[96] See below.　　　　[97] [1902] P 42, at p 600.
[98] *Nicolls v Bastard*; *The Winkfield*.　　　　[99] See below.

apply.[100] A successful action by the bailor will serve to bar recovery by the bailee. The bailor incurs a personal obligation to account to the bailee (to the extent of the bailee's interest) out of the damages award.[101] If the bailment is a gratuitous one, then there will be no duty to account.[102] If the bailor sues only for damage done to his reversionary interest, then in principle the bailee ought to be allowed to sue subsequently in respect of his residual interest. The rules in the 1977 Act[103] could be invoked to prevent excessive recovery by the bailee in such a case.

Where separate proceedings brought by bailor and bailee are running simultaneously against the wrongdoer, it is sensible to have these proceedings joined in order to effectuate the settlement of liabilities stated above. The 1977 Act[104] contains provisions for facilitating joinder when these separate proceedings are brought at different court levels.

POSSESSION AND THE *IUS TERTII*

Before the 1977 Act, the emphasis laid upon possession, as the property entitlement grounding a claimant's right to sue, was so strong that it was in general no defence for the wrongdoer to plead that someone else (the *tertius*) had, in relative terms, a better possessory right than the claimant. In the words of Pollock and Wright:

> A possessor may be a mere wrongdoer against the true owner, and a wrongdoer for the very reason that he has got possession; while yet his possession is not only legal but, as against all third persons not claiming under the true owner, fully protected by the law.

Where the defendant invaded the claimant's possession, the defence of *ius tertii* never lay: it was, said Lord Campbell, in society's interests that peaceable possession be protected against wrongdoers.[105] If, however, the claimant was relying upon a right to immediate possession, the above rationalization did not apply. The general rule in this case was that the *ius tertii* could be pleaded.[106] To this second rule, there was nevertheless an exception. A bailee was estopped, when sued by the bailor, from pleading the superior entitlement of a third party,[107] though the bailee had a good defence if actually evicted by title paramount by the true owner.[108] Faced with competing claims, the best course for the bailee would be to

---

[100] *Nicolls v Bastard* (1835), *per* Parke B (*arguendo*).
[101] *O'Sullivan v Williams* [1992] 3 All ER 385.
[102] *Ibid.*   [103] See below.   [104] In s 9.
[105] *Jeffries v Great Western Railway Co* (1856) 5 E & B 802.
[106] *Leake v Loveday* (1842) 4 M & G 972.   [107] *Biddle v Bond* (1865) 6 B & S 225.
[108] *Rogers Sons & Co v Lambert & Co* [1892] 1 QB 318.

interplead, that is, pay the chattel into court to permit the bailor and the other claimant to fight it out between them. A bailee defending the bailor's action in the name of the true owner, or *vice versa*, would take the risk of backing the losing side, thus incurring personal liability for resisting the claim.

The logical consequence of the identification of possession with property was that the defendant could not object that the claimant's possession was acquired wrongfully in the first place. Thus a jeweller was liable in conversion for refusing to return to a chimney sweep's boy a jewel that the boy handed over for valuation, despite the inference that the boy must have found the jewel in someone else's chimney.[109] Similarly, the finder of a can of money under a poolroom was able to recover from the local municipality when the latter insisted on retaining the money until the true owner appeared.[110] In the latter case, it was said that it did not matter 'whether the taking [by the finder] was with felonious intent or not'.[111]

The matter of unlawful possession was considered at length in *Costello v Chief Constable of Derbyshire*,[112] where the claimant had been found in possession of a stolen car which he was aware had been stolen. Now, the police have statutory powers of confiscation,[113] but have no residual common law power to retain property unlawfully obtained.[114] So far as the police alternatively have the power of temporary detention, the possessory rights of the previous possessor revive once the period of detention expires.[115] In *Costello*, the defendant argued that possession unlawfully obtained did not give the claimant title to sue in conversion. It had previously been asserted by Donaldson LJ that public policy demanded a ruling in favour of the occupier of land if the competing claim of a finder was based upon a trespass on the land.[116] It would not have taken any great extension of public policy to deny a claim manifestly based upon an unlawful taking, but the Court of Appeal refused to take this extra step, thereby undermining the logic of Donaldson LJ's earlier dictum. Donaldson LJ himself had conceded that the thief had a 'frail' title, but the

---

[109] *Armory v Delamirie* (1722) 1 Stra 505.
[110] *Bird v Town of Fort Frances* [1949] 2 DLR 791 (Ontario).
[111] See also *Buckley v Gross* (1863) 3 B & S 566.
[112] [2001] 3 All ER 150 (CA).
[113] See the Proceeds of Crime Bill 2001 for, *inter alia*, a consolidation of existing powers and the creation of new powers.
[114] *Webb v Chief Constable of Merseyside* [2000] QB 427.
[115] *Ibid.*   [116] *Parker v British Airways Board* [1982] QB 1004.

court in *Costello* went further in holding that possession, whether lawfully or unlawfully obtained, attracted the same degree of protection in law. The party in possession, further to the relativity of title principle, had a title good against the whole world with the exception of someone who could show a better title. This exception would clearly include the person from whom the chattel was stolen, as well as anyone else with a superior title to the person in possession at the time of the theft.

The meaning of a thief's 'frail' title is uncertain. It seems true to say that is it more difficult to establish on the facts that a possessory title has been acquired where the circumstances surrounding the claimant's claim are suspect: 'hostile or ambiguous occupation must make itself good at every step'.[117] Where the finder's claim is contested by the occupier of the land on which the chattel was found, public policy will dictate a ruling in favour of the occupier where the finder was trespassing on the land at the time.[118]

The subject of competing rights to chattels is dealt with in s 8 of the 1977 Act. It provides that any rule of law preventing the defendant from pleading the *ius tertii* is abolished. Rules of court require the claimant in a wrongful interference action to indorse his writ or originating summons with particulars of his title 'identifying any other person who, to his knowledge, has or claims any interest in the goods'. At any time after giving notice of his intention to defend and before judgment, the defendant may apply for directions as to whether any person so named shall be joined[119] 'with a view to establishing whether he has a better right than the claimant, or has a claim as a result of which the defendant might be doubly liable'.[120] This formula probably excludes the great majority of bailor/bailee claims. The common law already prevents double liability in such cases, and the term bailor's right to sue for damage done to his reversionary interest is not so much 'better' than the bailee's right to sue in conversion as different (and *vice versa*).

Statutory provision for the avoidance of double liability is to be found in s 7. This is achieved in two ways. Let us assume that there are only two claimants, appearing in chronological order as A and B, and no claim for special damages to complicate the issue. First of all, if both A and B are before the court, damages will be awarded (and presumably apportioned between them) in such a way as to avoid the defendant's double liability.[121]

---

[117] Pollock, F. and Wright, R., *An Essay on Possession in the Common Law*, p 14.
[118] *Parker v British Airways Board* [1982] QB 1004.   [119] In the language of s 8(2)(c).
[120] Within s 7 of the 1977 Act.   [121] Section 7(2).

Presumptively, the damages that are thus apportioned will not exceed the market value of the converted chattel.

Secondly, if only A is before the court and successful in the action, there will be recovery in full of the value of the chattel, as under the antecedent law. To the extent that the damages recovered exceed the value of A's interest, A has a duty to account to B (as under *The Wink-field*[122] the bailee has to account to the bailor) who has not yet appeared, since A has been overcompensated by the defendant to the extent of B's interest in the chattel.[123] If subsequently B appears with a valuable claim, though one that is inferior to A's, the defendant will have a partial defence,[124] having bought out A's interest on satisfaction of the judgment debt.[125] The defence will be complete if A has already accounted to B[126] for the overcompensation. The defence will again be complete if, in view of the strength of A's claim, B's claim is valueless. If B's claim is so superior to A's that the latter's claim is valueless, recovery in full will in principle take place again, unless A has already accounted to B.[127] The defendant will then have the right to recover all moneys previously paid to A, since A has been unjustly enriched at the defendant's expense.[128] The 1977 Act[130] contemplates A paying B who then pays the defendant, but the principle expressed in s 7(4) should permit a direct action by the defendant against A to recover the damages (but presumably not the costs) previously paid. If A has a valuable but inferior interest, the damages liability of the defendant to B in the second action will be reduced to that extent in order to avoid unjust enrichment.[130] Furthermore, the defendant will then have a right to recover from A the amount by which the damages previously awarded to A exceeded the value of A's interest.[131] Justice tends to complicate matters; absolute justice complicates matters absolutely.

The 1977 Act does not deal with separate claimants suing separate defendants, which is improbable but not impossible in the case of a complex disposition chain. The common law,[132] coupled with s 5(1) of the Act, will however cope with the abuse of a single claimant attempting to recover double damages by suing different defendants.

---

[122] [1902] P 42.   [123] Section 7(3).
[124] Section 7(2) (*semble*), to avoid invoking the cumbersome machinery in the rest of s 7.
[125] *Brinsmead v Harrison* (1872) LR 7 CP 547; s 5(1) of the 1977 Act.
[126] Section 5(4) of the 1977 Act.   [127] Section 5(4) of the 1977 Act.
[128] Section 7(4) of the 1977 Act.   [129] See the example in s 7(4).
[130] See s 7(4) of the 1977 Act.   [131] *Ibid.*
[132] *Brinsmead v Harrison.*

THE RIGHT TO IMMEDIATE POSSESSION

As stated above, the right to immediate possession will support a conversion action. The emergence of this head of entitlement to sue is a little obscure. The right to immediate possession should not be confused with references in some of the older cases to 'an immediate right of possession'. The latter expression was used in *Rogers v Kennay*[133] to underline the legitimacy of a lienee's actual possession when resisting an attempt by a sheriff to levy execution on the goods. A right to immediate possession may be understood for practical purposes as embracing two types of claimant: first, the bailor at will, who in the case of trespass has been treated fictitiously as being in actual possession; and secondly, the true owner (a category that may include a bailor at will) who pursues down a disposition chain successive wrongdoers whose tort was committed at a time when the true owner (or his bailee at will) had already been dispossessed. An example of a disposition chain should clarify the second category of claimant, who has no entitlement to sue in trespass. Suppose that the goods of A are bailed at will to B who is dispossessed by C before C is in turn dispossessed by D. Considering now only A's entitlement, A may sue C in either conversion or trespass but may sue D only in conversion. D interfered with C's possession, not with A's, but D's action amounted to a denial of A's title and A had the right to immediate possession at the time of D's wrongful act.

It ought to be possible for there to be more than one person with a right to immediate possession, and not just the true owner. Suppose A loses goods that are found by B. C wrongfully dispossesses B and is wrongfully dispossessed in turn by D. A certainly has the right of immediate possession as against D, but so, surely, has B. Otherwise B, the finder, would have no tortious remedy against D. It may be that B's damages will be insubstantial, where A can be identified, but circumstances might arise in which B is admittedly a finder but it is impossible to locate A.

To return to the first of the above examples, if the bailment between A and B had been for a term, then A would not have had the right to initiate suit against either C or D, subject to the following exception. At the very moment a term bailee commits a wrongful act that amounts to a repudiation of the bailment, for example a wrongful sale or the wilful destruction of the goods, then the bailor acquires the right to immediate possession and, besides claiming against the bailee, may pursue the buyer as well as anyone else asserting an inconsistent title. It would be quite

[133] (1846) 9 QB 592.

impracticable to leave litigation in the hands of a bailee whose actions have been unlawful and who would certainly be met with an estoppel or similar plea by the buyer. In *Fenn v Bittleston*,[134] Malpas as security for a loan gave a bill of sale over certain goods to Rhoades. Malpas was to retain possession of the goods unless and until he failed to repay principal and interest within fourteen days after a demand by Rhoades. Subsequently, Malpas's assignee in bankruptcy sold the goods (and not merely Malpas's reversionary interest in them) without at any material time Malpas defaulting on the loan. Although Malpas's holding of the goods was not as a bailee at will, Rhoades was entitled to bring trover against the assignee in bankruptcy. The act of selling the goods, 'entirely inconsistent with the terms of the bailment', destroyed the bailment so that the possessory title reverted to Rhoades.

Another example, this time drawn from the field of hire purchase, is *North Central Wagon & Finance Co v Graham*,[135] where the hirer of a car under a hire purchase agreement placed it with an auctioneer for the purpose of sale in clear breach of the terms of the agreement. The finance company was able to maintain a conversion action against the auctioneer whether because of the *Fenn* v *Bittleston* principle (Cohen LJ) or because the terms of the agreement gave it the right to terminate the agreement for breach of any of the hirer's duties without giving prior notice of an intention to that effect (Asquith and Cohen LJJ).

As convenient as it may be for the property torts to permit the bailor to sue in the above circumstances, it is difficult to reconcile the bailor's entitlement to sue with recent developments in the area of contract law. It has now been firmly established at the highest judicial level that repudiatory breaches do not of themselves terminate a contract. Instead, they give the injured party an election to affirm the contract or to terminate it.[136] The rule in *Fenn v Bittleston*, stated above, has the consequence of making the buyer immediately liable to the bailor at the moment the goods are purchased from the bailee, even before any agreement enshrining the bailment is terminated by the bailor. One response is that the *Fenn v Bittleston* rule is a matter of bailment law rather than contract. This response, however, does not fully meet the contractual arm of the decision in *North Central Wagon & Finance Co v Graham* where the bailor's right to terminate the bailment can be expanded by the terms of the

---

[134] (1851) 7 Ex 152.   [135] [1950] 2 KB 7.
[136] *Photo Production Ltd v Securicor Transport Ltd* [1980] AC 827.

agreement, beyond acts destructive of the bailment, so as to embrace any breach of the hirer's duties (though on the facts of *North Central Wagon* the hirer's act did indeed destroy the bailment). The solution to these difficulties is to assert that the bailor has the right to immediate possession if, whether at common law or under the terms of an agreement, the bailor has the immediate right to terminate a bailment. One can surely have a right to immediate possession without being aware that the right exists or without yet having decided to avail oneself of the right.

REVERSIONARY INTERESTS

Though the owner out of possession and without the right to immediate possession may not sue in conversion, it has long been settled that such an individual may bring a special action on the case for any damage done to his reversionary interest in the goods.[137] In so far as the action denies full recovery of the value of the chattel to the claimant owner, it is consistent with changes introduced by the 1977 Act to the level of damages awards in conversion cases where the claimant has only a limited interest in the goods.[138] This head of liability, which is brought within the definition of wrongful interference for the purposes of the 1977 Act (s 1(d)), is therefore close to being swallowed up whole by conversion. Yet not all acts of conversion will necessarily damage the owner's reversionary interest.[139] Furthermore, the reversionary action, besides applying as a matter of strict liability,[140] also embraces negligent conduct damaging the reversionary interest. Although the 1977 Act lists as separate heads of wrongful interference 'negligence' and 'any other tort so far as it results in damage to goods or to an interest in goods', a separate mention of negligence is needed for those cases where the claimant is in possession of the goods at the time of the negligent act.[141] It is a pity that the recommendation of the Law Reform Committee,[142] that this relic of forms of action thinking be absorbed in the larger category of wrongful interference liability, was not implemented in the 1977 Act.

---

[137] *Mears v London & South Western Railway Co* (1862) 22 CB(NS) 850.
[138] See above.
[139] LRC 18th Report.
[140] *Tancred v Allgood* (1859) 4 H & N 38.
[141] Section 1(c), (d).
[142] 18th Report.

REMEDIES ISSUES

MEASURE OF DAMAGES

Liability in conversion entails 'the forced judicial sale of the chattel to the defendant'.[143] It is therefore not any injurious behaviour of the defendant to the chattel that defines the damages award but rather the value of the chattel itself, which is the price the defendant has to pay to buy out the claimant's interest. The transfer of the claimant's interest to the defendant takes place, not upon entry of judgment in the claimant's favour, but upon satisfaction of it.[144] The damages awarded generally represent the value of the chattel at the date of the conversion,[145] though the logic of a forced judicial sale would make the date of judgment more appropriate, as it used to be in the case of detinue.[146] A reference will be made to the market, if one exists, to calculate the value of the chattel, but, if through the wrongdoing of the defendant the value cannot be determined, any doubt will be resolved in the claimant's favour.[147] This will be accomplished, in cases of uncertainty, for example where the chattel has disappeared, by ascribing to it the highest value that it could possess, provided the other evidence in the case is consistent with this approach.[148] In one unusual case, the claimant recovered damages where a quantity of shares in a company were unlawfully sold, only to be replaced later by the same quantity of shares in the same company. Damages were assessed as the difference between the value of the shares at the conversion date less the value of the repurchased shares on a falling market.[149]

Unless they are too remote or might have been mitigated by the claimant, consequential damages may also, if suffered, be recovered by the claimant. As for the appropriate remoteness test to apply in conversion, the House of Lords in *Kuwait Airways Corpn v Iraqi Airways Co* has drawn a distinction between cases where the defendant has acted in good faith and cases where the defendant has acted dishonestly. In the former case, the less stringent test of 'foreseeability' should be applied to the defendant, while in the latter case the defendant should be visited with the

---

[143] Prosser (1957) 42 Cornell LQ 168.
[144] *Brinsmead v Harrison* (1872) LR 7 CP 547; s 5(1) of the 1977 Act.
[145] *General & Finance Facilities v Cooks Cars (Romford) Ltd* [1963] 1 WLR 644, *per* Diplock LJ.
[146] *Rosenthal v Alderton & Sons Ltd* [1946] KB 374.
[147] *Armory v Delamirie* (1722) 1 Stra 505.
[148] *Colbeck v Diamanta Ltd* [2002] EWHC 616 (QB).
[149] *BBMB Finance (Hong Kong) Ltd v Eda Holdings Ltd* [1991] 2 All ER 129.

harsher consequences of a test that looks to the direct and natural consequences of the defendant's act.[150] Consequential damages might include the loss of the post-conversion appreciation in value of the converted chattel,[151] so that in substance the claimant would recover damages representing the value of the chattel at the judgment date. The 1977 Act gives no express assistance on the date of assessment of damages and, in particular, does not clarify the position regarding the date of assessment in those cases where formerly the claimant might have maintained an action in detinue. In such a case, nevertheless, it has been held that there is no firm rule that damages should be assessed at either the date of the conversion or the date of judgment. Instead, damages ought fairly to compensate the claimant's loss and so might take account of matters such as whether the claimant might have sold or retained the chattel had no conversion occurred, or whether a loss has arisen because of the claimant's inability to use the chattel.[152]

We saw above that the 1977 Act allows for a reduction in the measure of damages in certain cases where the claimant has only a limited title to the chattel.[153] Other common law examples of limited recovery exist. If the claimant consents to the return of the chattel before judgment, then nominal damages should be an appropriate measure.[154] Nominal damages may also be appropriate where the chattel would, even without the defendant's conversion, have been lost in any event.[155] Principles of causation apply when settling damages in the tort of conversion as they do elsewhere, though the forced judicial sale aspect of conversion, where it occurs, tends to cloud one's understanding of this point. Where the defendant has a property interest in the goods, the claimant's damages will be commensurately reduced.[156] This will be the position, for example, where one co-owner sues the other in those cases where a conversion action will lie.[157] Furthermore, though the law cannot be said to be wholly consistent in its recognition of the underlying commercial logic of hire purchase when this conflicts with the legal form of the transaction, it is well settled that a finance company suing in conversion will be

---

[150] [2002] UKHL 19 at [95]–[104].

[151] *The Playa Larga* [1983] 2 Lloyd's Rep 171.

[152] *IBL Ltd v Coussens* [1991] 2 All ER 133.

[153] See above.

[154] *Roberts v Wyatt* (1810) 2 Taunt 268.

[155] *Kuwait Airways Corpn v Iraqi Airways Co* [2002] UKHL 19 at [63], explaining *Hiort v London and North Western Railway Co* (1879) 4 Ex D 188.

[156] *Belsize Motor Supply Co v Cox* [1914] 1 KB 244.

[157] See s 10 of the 1977 Act: destruction and disposal of the goods.

permitted to recover damages based only upon the sum of unpaid instalments, and not upon the value of the chattel itself.[158] This is so even though the transaction itself purports to deny the hirer any proprietary interest in the chattel until the instalments have been paid in full and the option to purchase has been exercised.

In *Kuwait Airways Corpn v Iraqi Airways Co*, Lord Nicholls has also pointed to the possibility of a defendant in the tort of conversion incurring a restitutionary liability, subject to the usual defences such as change of position, in respect of benefits gained from the chattel.[159] Nevertheless, in the conventional case where damages represent a forced judicial sale and are assessed at the date of the conversion, damages representing the capital value of the chattel should also include its income earning power. The power of a chattel to generate benefits is a function of its capital value, with the result that it would be a mistake to make an additional restitutionary award for benefits received by the defendant in such cases.

DOCUMENTARY INTANGIBLES

The tort of conversion developed to protect interests in tangible personalty, namely chattels. Nevertheless, it has also assumed a role in connection with documentary intangibles, where damages are based not upon the intrinsic value of the paper but upon the value of the obligation locked up in it.[160] The documentary intangibles in question include cheques, bills of lading, and share certificates.[161] In the case of a validly drawn cheque, this will be the face value of the cheque unless the cheque has previously been subject to a material alteration. The material alteration of a cheque often renders it a worthless piece of paper. This is because a materially altered cheque is avoided against all parties liable on the cheque with the exception of a party to it who has made the alteration.[162] In *Smith v Lloyds TSB Bank plc*,[163] the alteration—a change in the name of the payee—had been carried out by a thief who was not a party to the cheque. The defendant in this case was the collecting bank, which had presented the cheque for payment. In cases where the cheque has not been materially altered, the business of banks, constantly involved in the collection of cheques for their customers, and in the payment of

---

[158] *Wickham Holdings Ltd v Brooke House Motors Ltd* [1967] 1 WLR 295.
[159] *Kuwait Airways Corpn v Iraqi Airways Co* [2002] UKHL 19 at [79].
[160] *Morison v London County and Westminster Bank* [1914] 3 KB 356.
[161] *MCC Proceeds Inc v Lehman Brothers International (Europe)* [1998] 4 All ER 675 (CA).
[162] Bills of Exchange Act 1882, s 64(1).
[163] [2001] 1 All ER 424 (CA).

cheques presented by collecting banks, would be fraught with the risk of strict liability in conversion were it not for certain statutory defences against liability[164] where they have not been guilty of negligence.[165]

IMPROVEMENTS TO CHATTELS

In chapter 4, we shall examine the principles dealing with the expansion of property rights in chattels transformed by accession, commingling and similar processes. Let us take the example of a chattel which, after its initial conversion, is increased in value by an accession or other improvement, such as servicing or repair. A straightforward application of property principles to a conversion action, based upon a later denial of title by the defendant, would lead to the unjust enrichment of the claimant if damages were based upon the improved value of the chattel. Although the claimant is the owner of the improved chattel, damages in a conversion action against the defendant improver will be reduced to give the latter credit for the improved value.[166] The claimant will not be allowed any practical benefit from making a tactical choice between acts of conversion occurring before and after the improvement. If, as a result of interpleader proceedings launched by a third party, the chattel is given up to the true owner, then the improver (the unsuccessful party in the interpleader proceedings) will have to be given credit for the improvements made.[167] It has been stressed that the improvements must have been made in the honest belief that the improver is entitled to the chattel.[168]

The 1977 Act also addresses the question of improvements made after the claimant has been dispossessed and before the chattel comes into the hands of the defendant. Even though the defendant has not personally incurred expense in improving the chattel, it is a reasonable inference that the price paid by the defendant to acquire the chattel reflects improvements made to it by an intermediate party. Consequently, s 6(2) of the Act provides for a reduction of damages, on the same principle as that set out above (provided the defendant has acted in good faith), and s 3(7) permits corresponding terms to be imposed by a court when requiring the defendant to surrender the chattel[169] to the claimant.

The 1977 Act has nothing to say about the claim of an improver who is

---

[164] Bills of Exchange Act 1882, ss 60 and 82; Cheques Act 1957, s 4.
[165] See *Marfani & Co v Midland Bank Ltd* [1968] 1 WLR 956.
[166] Section 6(1) of the Torts (Interference with Goods) Act 1977 (the 1977 Act); and see *Munro v Willmott* [1949] 1 KB 295, which gave credit for the expense incurred by the defendant.
[167] *Greenwood v Bennett* [1973] QB 195; s 3(7) of the 1977 Act.
[168] *Ibid.*   [169] See below.

no longer in possession of the chattel, as might occur where the owner has exercised the right of recaption. In *Greenwood v Bennett*, contrasting views were expressed about whether a claim could be maintained in such circumstances by a repairer (*pro* Denning MR; *contra* Cairns LJ). The existence of such a claim by the improver (and what about someone who has paid a previous improver in the chain?), a debatable matter, should be determined methodically in accordance with restitutionary principles.[170]

CONTRIBUTORY NEGLIGENCE

Although some support was given in the antecedent case law for a reduction of damages in conversion for the claimant's contributory negligence, the 1977 Act has now established beyond doubt that there is no such defence to conversion and trespass actions.[171] It is in any case not easy to see upon what principle a division of loss could be effected as between the claimant's negligence and the defendant's strict liability. Despite the laconism of s 11(1), it is most unlikely that, at common law, contributory negligence would be a partial defence to an action for intentional interference with a bailor's reversionary interest.

RECOVERY OF THE CHATTEL

Given the nature of conversion as a forced judicial sale, it is unsurprising that the remedy exclusively took the form of damages. What is remarkable is that no remedy existed in the old tort of detinue by way of specific delivery (or restitution) of the chattel until the Common Law Procedure Act 1854. More than anything, this historical feature highlights the anomaly of the protection of property rights being entrusted to the law of tort.

Before the 1977 Act, a detinue judgment might have taken one of three forms. The defendant might have been required to pay damages or to surrender the chattel or to elect between paying damages or surrendering the chattel.[172] It was rare for a judgment to compel the defendant to surrender the chattel since courts proceeded upon the same basis as that governing the award of specific performance in contract actions. Specific relief did not issue if damages adequately compensated the claimant, which they did in the case of ordinary articles of commerce.[173] The

---

[170] See McKendrick, E., 'Restitution and the Misuse of Chattels—The Need for a Principled Approach', in Palmer, N., and McKendrick, E. (eds), *Interests in Goods*, 2nd edn, London and Hong Kong: LLP, 1998.

[171] Section 11(1).

[172] *General & Finance Facilities v Cooks Cars (Romford) Ltd* [1963] 1 WLR 644.

[173] *Cohen v Roche* [1927] 1 KB 169, where even Hepplewhite chairs were articles of commerce in the hands of an antiques dealer.

statutory outcome of the abolition of detinue[174] was that the three forms of judgment outlined above also became available for conversion in its expanded form.[175] Naturally, this blunts the character of conversion as a forced judicial sale. The Act confirms the existence of the court's jurisdiction to award specific relief,[176] but does not affect the way in which the court chooses to exercise it.

Statutory provision is also made in the 1977 Act for the recovery of chattels by way of interlocutory relief,[177] prior to the trial of an action for wrongful interference. In interlocutory proceedings, additional features, relating for example to the strength of the claimant's case and the balance of convenience, complicate the exercise of judicial discretion. As regards the nature of the chattel itself, it remains the case that the claimant must show that it is no mere article of commerce. Thus, in *Howard Perry & Co v British Railways Board*,[178] the recovery of a quantity of steel was permitted under s 4 where industrial action had made it impossible to procure steel in the market ('steel is gold'). The defendant was not claiming an interest in the steel but had refused to release it, fearful of the industrial consequences of such an action.

SELF-HELP

Trespass, the fountainhead of the modern law of torts, evolved initially to preserve peace and public order. It is therefore understandable that the law has been somewhat equivocal about whether individuals may exercise self-help as a remedy instead of pursuing their grievances in court. In the area of wrongful interference with chattels, the law on self-help falls significantly short of standards of clarity and consistency.

Self-help taking the form of the extra-judicial recovery of chattels is technically known as recaption. The right of recaption certainly exists but is constrained by the limitation that reasonable means be employed. This may on the facts compel the owner first to notify the wrongful possessor of the chattel of an intention to recover it if the use of force is to be regarded as within the bounds of reasonable means.[179] It seems that reasonable force may be used, even if the wrongful possessor has not committed a trespass against the owner seeking recaption.[180]

More difficult is the question whether entry upon the land of another is permitted to effect a recaption. It is certainly permissible where the

---

[174] Section 2(1) of the 1977 Act.   [175] Section 3.   [176] Section 3(3)(b).
[177] Section 4.   [178] [1980] 1 WLR 1375.
[179] LRC 18th Report.
[180] *Blades v Higgs* (1861) 10 CB (NS) 713, *per* Erle CJ.

occupier of the land is guilty of a trespassory taking as against the owner[181] and there is support for the view that it is permissible in other cases too.[182] In the latter instance, if the right of recaption exists, it is likely to be dependent upon the making of a prior demand.[183] It is unlikely that legal advice could confidently be given upon the subject of entry and recaption. Any statutory clarification of the right of recaption might have increased the chance of the right being exercised. The continuing obscurity of the right may therefore be seen as evidencing a desire not to encourage recaption. One could, however, offer the practical advice that, if recaption is to be exercised, then it had better be done quickly and effectively, without causing a breach of the peace or incidental damage to the property of the occupier. Furthermore, care should be taken to ensure that the amount at stake is unlikely to make the occupier want to litigate and that the occupier is not someone who derives pleasure from the pursuit of uneconomical litigation.

LIMITATION OF ACTIONS

Apart from cases where the act of conversion leads to the destruction of the chattel, it is one of the tort's curious features that it can be committed on a continuous basis. Since the harm done to the owner's interest is quantified financially in terms of the remedy—the forced judicial sale of the chattel—it follows that the value of the chattel for the time being in no way limits the number of occasions on which the tort may be committed. This is far from saying, however, that the owner can sue repeatedly in conversion and recover in gross a sum far exceeding the value of the chattel at any time. The recovery of damages representing the full value of the chattel serves to transfer the claimant's interest in it to the defendant:[184] the claimant cannot sell the same chattel twice to the same defendant. If another tortious intermeddler is selected as the defendant in conversion proceedings, a claimant who has recovered from one tortfeasor is in no position to sell the chattel again to another tortfeasor.

Consider the following possible chain of involvement with the disputed chattel. A loses a chattel which is later found by B in 1994. B sells the chattel to C in 1995. C in turn sells it to D in 1998 and A traces the chattel to D's possession in 2001. If the ordinary six year rule for tort actions (Limitation Act 1980, s 2) were to apply in this case, then, selecting the latest acts of conversion committed by the relevant parties, A would have

---

[181] *Patrick v Colerick* (1838) 3 M & W 483. [182] *Anthony v Haney* (1832) 8 Bing 186.
[183] LRC 18th Report. [184] See above.

six years from 1995 (the date of the sale to C) in which to sue B; six years from 1998 (the date of the sale to D) in which to sue C; and six years from the date of each and every refusal by D to return the goods, such refusals being made in response to a theoretically infinite series of demands. No limitation period would ever keep A out of court; A could always manufacture a defendant and time would never cease to run.

To prevent the above situation from occurring, the Limitation Act 1980 starts time running as against all of the defendants from the date of the first act of conversion in the disposition chain,[185] provided A does not resume possession of the chattel in the meantime. If the first act of conversion was committed by B in 1995 (the date of the sale to C), then A would be statute-barred as against all defendants in 2001. Furthermore, the Act implements a form of acquisition of absolute title, which brings personal property law into line with land law on the subject of adverse possession. Instead of D, the party in possession, being simply immune from suit after 2001, the Act provides that A's title is 'extinguished' upon the expiry of the limitation period.[186] There is an exception to the above position where the chattel is stolen from A. In effect, the six year period begins to run not from the date of the original conversion but from the date of acquisition of the chattel by the first good faith purchaser, as regards that purchaser and his successors in title.[187] Supposing, in the above example, that C did not act in good faith but that D did, then time, as against D and anyone acquiring the goods from D, would run from 1998 (the date of the sale to D). As regards B and C, however, there would appear to be no statutory period of limitation, since both the six year rule in s 2 and the special rules in s 3 are denied application.[188]

---

[185] Section 3(1).   [186] Section 3(2).   [187] Section 4.   [188] Section 4.

4

The conveyance

INTRODUCTION

We have examined the nature of ownership at common law and the means by which ownership rights are protected. In this chapter, we shall see how ownership rights are transferred (or conveyed). Our primary concern will be with chattels, though from time to time reference will be made to documentary intangibles. Pure intangibles will be dealt with in chapter 6. For the most part, the material in this chapter is devoted to consensual transfers between willing parties to a bilateral transaction, but some attention must be paid to rules of law by which ownership rights pass from one party to another.

The most dominant category of consensual transfers is the passing of property under a contract of sale of goods.[1] Other transactions include gift and the quasi-testamentary transfer known as *donatio mortis causa*. A study of testamentary transfers (bequests by will) goes beyond the scope of this work. Rules of law prescribing transfer apply where chattels become fixtures and where they become inextricably mixed with, joined to or converted into another chattel so as to destroy the separate identity of the original chattel.

CONSENSUAL TRANSFERS: SALE

GENERAL

The modern rules on the subject were first codified in the Sale of Goods Act 1893 and are now to be found in a modern consolidating statute, the Sale of Goods Act 1979.[2] The Act applies only to chattels and not to documentary intangibles.[3] The underlying rule is that the transfer is based upon the intention of the contracting parties, namely the seller and the buyer. According to the classic judgment of Fry LJ in *Cochrane v*

---

[1] For the meaning of 'goods', see chapter 1.   [2] Hereinafter SGA 1979.
[3] SGA 1979, s 61(1).

Moore,[4] this was not always so, for the law in its earlier stages required the observance of forms or the performance of manual delivery before the seller's property rights became vested in the buyer. Until 1954,[5] moreover, the conveyance had to take place under a contract of sale that itself satisfied the writing requirement (to which there were exceptions) contained in the former Sale of Goods Act.[6] Nevertheless, the validity of the conveyance is not inexorably tied to the validity of the contract. Whilst a proprietary transfer takes place pursuant to a contract of sale, it is well settled that the illegality or voidness of the contract will not necessarily undo the transfer.[7] The claimant will succeed who is able to rely upon his property rights rather than upon any illegal contract giving rise to the property right.[8] In this respect, no distinction is to be drawn between legal and equitable property rights since 'English law has one single law of property made up of legal and equitable interests'.[9]

For various reasons, it is important to know at what point the seller's property interest (or ownership) in the goods is transferred to the buyer. The seller's property interest is called the 'general property' (commonly abbreviated to 'property')[10] to distinguish it from the possessory interest of a mere bailee,[11] which is often referred to as a 'special property'. Its transfer affects the performance of the parties' contractual rights and duties. A buyer to whom the property has passed presumptively also carries the risk of loss and so must still pay the seller even if, through an act of God, the goods are destroyed before possession is transferred.[12] If the buyer defaults, the seller may sue for the agreed price, and not just for damages, where the property has passed.[13] Outside the contractual relationship, the passing of property may have various repercussions in connection, for example, with tax and licensing requirements, the law of theft and the law of insolvency.

DEFINITIONS IN THE SALE OF GOODS ACT

To understand the effect of the property rules, it is first necessary to look at the statutory definitions on which they are based. All goods are divided

---

[4] (1890) 25 QBD 57.
[5] Law Reform (Enforcement of Contracts) Act 1954, s 1.
[6] SGA 1893, s 4.
[7] *Singh v Ali* [1960] AC 167; *Bowmakers Ltd v Barnet Instruments Ltd* [1945] KB 65; Goode, R.M., *Commercial Law*, 2nd edn, Harmondsworth: Penguin Books, 1995, pp 136–138.
[8] *Bowmakers Ltd v Barnet Instruments Ltd*; *Tinsley v Milligan* [1995] 1 AC 340.
[9] *Tinsley v Milligan*, *per* Lord Browne-Wilkinson at p 371.
[10] See chapter 2. [11] SGA 1979, s 62(1). [12] SGA 1979, s 20.
[13] SGA 1979, s 49.

by the Act into specific and unascertained goods. Specific goods are those that are identified by the parties at or before the time of the contract[14] as the very goods to be used by the seller in performance of the contract. No substitution, even with goods that are in other respects identical to the contract goods, is permissible. Specific goods may be, for example, a particular self-binder reaper,[15] or the seller's own car which is being sold second-hand.[16]

Unascertained goods, not defined by the Act, are the residuum. The contract goods may, for example, be a stated quantity of Number 1 Oregon winter wheat, the seller being responsible for selecting that quantity from any stocks. Or they may be widgets to be later manufactured by the seller. They may even be an undifferentiated part of a specific bulk, such as a stated quantity of the widgets that the seller currently has in stock or 500 tons out of the 1,000 tons of grain that the seller has in the hold of a ship. If the goods have no physical existence (such as widgets not yet manufactured) or have not been acquired by the seller at the contract date (such as a cargo not yet bought), they may also be described as 'future goods'.[17] Very occasionally, specific goods may also be future goods, as where the seller is going to acquire a particular object before selling it on to the buyer.[18]

PASSING OF PROPERTY IN SPECIFIC GOODS

The starting point is the clear statement that it is up to the parties to determine when the property passes.[19] They may do this by express or by implied choice. If it is the latter, a court may be called upon to interpret the language of a complex commercial document in its search for the parties' intention.[20] Apart from certain contracts where goods are sold on credit,[21] it is relatively rare for parties to stipulate for the passing of property. Consequently, the Act lays down a series of presumptive rules to fill the intention gap, each applicable to a different case involving specific goods. The contracting parties have an unfettered right to depart from the presumptive rules, a right reinforced by SGA 1979, s 19, which has a particular application to the export trade. When the passing of property is held up, the usual reason is that the buyer has not yet paid for

---

[14] SGA 1979, s 62(1).
[15] *Varley v Whipp* [1900] 2 QB 513.
[16] *Beale v Taylor* [1967] 1 WLR 1193.
[17] SGA 1979, s 5(1).
[18] *Varley v Whipp.*
[19] SGA 1979, s 17.
[20] *Re Anchor Line Ltd* [1937] Ch 1.
[21] For example, *Aluminium Industrie Vaassen BV v Romalpa Aluminium Ltd* [1976] 1 WLR 676.

the goods supplied,[22] but the property may be held back until the buyer, for example, pays the seller for all other sums owed, including the price of goods supplied on a previous occasion.[23]

GENERAL PRESUMPTIVE RULE

According to SGA 1979, s 18 *Rule 1*, the presumptive rule is that the property in specific goods passes at the date the contract is made 'and it is immaterial that the time of payment or the time of delivery or both is postponed'. This rule is expressed as applying only where the goods are in a 'deliverable state', such that[24] the buyer is contractually bound to take delivery of them. This would be the case if, for example, the seller had performed final adjustments or alterations or had packed the goods pursuant to the contract.

This presumptive rule has attracted a great deal of criticism over the years, largely because it treats divergent issues, such as the risk of loss and insolvency, in the same way. It was once applied to the auction sale of a car, so that the contract was formed and the property conveyed at the fall of the auctioneer's hammer, even though the successful bidder was some-one of unknown reputation.[25] It should be appreciated, however, that an unpaid seller may exercise a possessory lien[26] to prevent the new owner taking away the goods before payment. Furthermore, in modern times, there is a discernible tendency to find an inconsistent implied intention ousting *Rule 1*, despite the strength of language in the rule.[27] The under-lying rule, it should not be forgotten, is that the intention of the parties governs.[28]

SECTION 18 RULES 2–3

These presumptive rules complement the deliverable state requirement in *Rule 1*. According to *Rule 2*, the property in specific goods does not pass before the seller has put them in a deliverable state if so obliged by the contract. Where it is the buyer who has to do something to the goods before they can be delivered, *Rule 2* does not stand in the way of the property passing,[29] though in most cases a court looking for the parties' implied intention would reach the same conclusion. *Rule 2* was applied in

---

[22] *Romalpa.*
[23] *Armour v Thyssen Edelstahlwerke AG* [1991] 2 AC 339.
[24] See SGA 1979, s 61(5).
[25] *Dennant v Skinner* [1948] 2 KB 164.
[26] See chapter 7.
[27] *R. V. Ward Ltd v Bignall* [1967] 2 QB 534, *per* Diplock LJ.
[28] SGA 1979, s 17.
[29] *Rugg v Minett* (1809) 11 East 210.

a case where a condensing engine had to be detached from the concrete block on which it was bolted prior to its shipment by rail. Property did not pass before the completion of the act of removal.[30] A further requirement of *Rule 2* is that the buyer must receive actual notice once the goods have been put into a deliverable state.

According to *Rule 3*, the property in specific goods will not pass if the seller has to 'weigh, measure, test or do some other act or thing . . . to the goods . . . for the purpose of ascertaining the price'. Notice to the buyer that this has been done is again required. So the property in two lots of turpentine sold at auction did not pass where it remained for the seller to remove a quantity of turpentine (to fill up other lots) before settling the price the buyer had to pay.[31] Where the relevant act was to be performed by a sub-buyer and not the seller, *Rule 3* did not prevent the property passing.[32]

SALE OR RETURN AND SALE ON APPROVAL

As a matter of terminology, sale or return is a bailment transaction by which goods are delivered to a potential buyer with a view to their eventual resale by that buyer. It is a common transaction in the bookselling trade. The potential seller, by dispatching the goods, is offering to sell them to the buyer who may purchase them, when accomplishing a successful resale, or return them, thus rejecting the seller's offer, as the case may be. A sale on approval is the same type of transaction, except that the goods are delivered to a potential consumer buyer, who may retain and then pay for them, if satisfied, or return them to the seller, if deciding instead to reject the offer. Where *Rule 4* applies, not having been excluded by the parties, the formation of the contract of sale and the passing of property occur at the same time. Since the goods will be in the hands of the buyer at the moment of acceptance, they are necessarily specific and not unascertained goods.

According to *Rule 4*, the property passes when the buyer accepts the seller's offer by words or conduct[33] or retains the goods beyond the stated period or (if no period is stated) beyond a reasonable time.[34] Under *Rule 4(a)*, a number of cases deal with conduct of the buyer that evinces an objective intention to accept the seller's offer. They arose out of the Hatton Garden jewellery trade at the turn of the century when it was the

---

[30] *Underwood Ltd v Burgh Castle Brick* [1922] 1 KB 343.
[31] *Rugg v Minett.*   [32] *Nanka-Bruce v Commonwealth Trust* [1926] AC 77.
[33] *Rule 4(a).*   [34] *Rule 4(b).*

practice for jewellery to be sent out with travelling salesmen for resale in the provinces. To limit the risk of dishonesty on the part of the salesmen, they were not employed as agents with a limited mandate[35] but were instead in receipt of the jewellery on sale or return terms. Since they were not agents, they could not bind the Hatton Garden jewellers by their statements or actions. The problem raised in these cases was who bore the risk of a salesman's dishonesty in the following circumstances: A entrusts goods to B on sale or return terms and B, having negotiated a sale to C, disappears with the proceeds of sale without paying A.

In *Kirkham v Attenborough*,[36] the act of the salesman in pledging the jewellery with a pawnbroker was an 'act adopting the transaction' within the wording of the rule. Having to repay the pawnbroker before recovering the goods, the salesman had performed an act inconsistent with his free power to return them, which was an assertion of a personal entitlement to the goods and thus an acceptance of the seller's offer. Consequently, the property passed to the salesman at the same time and he was able, again simultaneously, to pass a special property[37] to the pawnbroker. This special property could therefore be asserted by the pawnbroker against the seller, who would have to redeem the pledge to recover the jewellery.

In *Weiner v Gill*,[38] the seller excluded *Rule 4(a)* by the simple expedient of inserting in the sale or return agreement the words: '[G]oods had on . . . sale or return remain the property of Samuel Weiner until such goods are settled for . . .'. This prevented the property passing to the salesman and thus too a special property to the pawnbroker. We shall see in the next chapter, however, that an attempt to control closely the behaviour of a sale or return buyer could lead to the conclusion that the buyer is in reality an agent, with disastrous results for the seller.

An acceptance, and thus a passing of property, can occur under *Rule 4(b)* by effluxion of time. The notion of a reasonable time was explored in *Poole v Smith's Cars (Balham) Ltd*,[39] where a second-hand car was received by one dealer from another on sale or return terms. In concluding that after two months a reasonable time had expired, the court took account of the seasonal nature of the market in second-hand cars, the rapid depreciation of the car, the 'holiday' character of the arrangement and the failure of the buyer to respond to repeated requests by the seller for the return of the car.

---

[35] See chapter 5 for the reasons. [36] [1897] 1 QB 201. [37] See chapter 2.
[38] [1906] 2 KB 574. [39] [1962] 2 All ER 482.

Since the delivery of goods on sale or return, or sale on approval, terms constitutes an offer to sell them, the offer can be rejected before the events occur or time passes that under *Rule 4* are deemed to amount to acceptance of the goods. In a case involving the bulk delivery of computer games, distributed by the buyer to its various shops, the rejection of the seller's offer before the stated deadline was effective when it gave a generic description of the goods that were being rejected.[40] It was not required of the buyer that it first assemble all of the goods in one place and have them physically ready there and then to be surrendered to the seller. Nor was it necessary to reject all of the goods. The sale or return was on severable terms, so that the seller's offer to sell them could be partly accepted by reference to that quantity of goods actually sold on to sub-buyers. The amount sold on did not have to be quantified at the date the rest of the goods were rejected by the buyer. The ascertainment of quantities could come later.

UNASCERTAINED GOODS: GENERAL

Although the dominant rule is that the intention of the parties governs, this is subject to a rule of law that the property in unascertained goods cannot pass until they have became ascertained.[41] The same goes for the almost identical case of future goods, which must similarly become existing goods before property is allowed to pass.[42] These rules do not apply to the sale of a share of defined goods, for example, a quarter of the contents of a grain silo, as opposed to 1,000 tons from a silo containing 4,000 tons. The property in a share can pass before ascertainment of the goods comprising that share.[43] Furthermore, the rule of ascertainment[44] has been overridden in certain cases by the Sale of Goods (Amendment) Act 1995, implementing changes to the Sale of Goods Act 1979.[45]

Ascertainment means simply the identification of goods by a seller minded to use them in performance of the contract. It does not occur simply because the seller warrants or represents to the buyer that it has taken place when this is not the case.[46] Thus the setting aside of the contractual quantity of widgets in the seller's store room, or the manufacture of a special order of widgets, for example, would amount to an

---

[40] *Atari Corpn (UK) Ltd v Electronic Boutique Stores Ltd* [1998] 1 All ER 1010 (CA).

[41] SGA 1979, s 16.

[42] SGA 1979, s 5(3).

[43] Law Commission, *Sale of Goods Forming Part of a Bulk*, 1993 (Law Com No. 215), paras 2.5–2.6.

[44] SGA 1979, s 16.

[45] See below.   [46] See *Re Goldcorp Exchange Ltd* [1995] 1 AC 74.

ascertainment if accompanied by the necessary intention. Likewise, if the seller is bound to sell 500 tons of grain from a ship's hold containing 1,000 tons, ascertainment could not take place before 500 tons were physically isolated.[47] It has been held that ascertainment occurs when only the contract quantity remains from a specific bulk after all other orders have been separated out.[48] In a similar case, the remaining goods after a number of other contracts had been performed were the commingled sum of two separate sub-cargoes due to the buyer from different sellers.[49] The ascertainment requirement in SGA 1979, s 16 was held to be satisfied. This result has now been confirmed by statute.[50]

ASCERTAINED GOODS

Ascertainment (or the process of future goods becoming existing goods) is not in itself enough to make the property pass. It simply removes an inhibition that prevents a conveyance from taking place. If it cannot be known which goods might be used under the contract, or if the seller does not yet have a property interest in the intended contract goods, it is a simple statement of the possible to say that property can only pass in ascertained, existing goods. Yet this area of law has caused acute difficulty where the buyer has already paid for the goods and the seller then becomes insolvent prior to ascertainment.

In *Re Wait*,[51] the buyer agreed to purchase a cargo of 500 tons of wheat shipped on board the m.v. *Challenger*. The seller held a bill of lading representing 1,000 tons aboard this vessel, all unseparated in one of the ship's holds. Now, the seller did not in fact undertake to supply the 500 tons from this particular batch of wheat; the wheat could have been supplied from any hold on the *Challenger*, though the clear expectation was that it would come from the wheat covered by the bill of lading. In return for a provisional invoice, the buyer paid for the wheat and the seller became bankrupt before the 500 tons became ascertained. The buyer argued that an equitable proprietary interest had been transferred, encumbering the 1,000 ton bulk to the extent of a 500 ton interest in the buyer. While the court recognized that contracting parties could transfer such an interest if they clearly intended, it refused to accept that this had occurred merely because the buyer had paid in advance and because there had been a delay in breaking up the cargo. In Atkin LJ's view, the Sale of

---

[47] *Cf. Re Wait* [1927] 1 Ch 606.
[48] *Wait and James v Midland Bank* (1926) 31 Com Cas 172.
[49] *The Elafi* [1982] 1 All ER 208.
[50] SGA 1979, s 18 *Rule 5 (3), (4)*, as amended.   [51] [1927] 1 Ch 606.

Goods Act 1893 had codified the passing of property and, moreover, commercial uncertainty would arise from the creation of additional rules relating to the passing of equitable proprietary interests. In addition, the court declined to exercise its discretion to order specific performance[52] of the sale contract so as to reach the same result by an indirect route. (Though rejected in sales law, equitable proprietary principles have had a major role to play in the law of security, the subject of chapter 7.)

An alternative approach to the problem would involve the use of the common law concept of tenancy in common.[53] As applied in the context of *Re Wait*, tenancy in common would take on the form of the buyer owning the 1,000 tons covered by the bill of lading in common with the seller (or with anyone else to whom the seller had contracted to sell a portion of the cargo), rateably according to their contributions to the overall quantity. Prior to the Sale of Goods (Amendment) Act 1995, the subject of tenancy in common as it applies to personalty was rather murky. The argument was advanced unsuccessfully in one Court of Appeal decision without being explicitly rejected in the reported judgments.[54] It was applied in *Re Stapylton Fletcher Ltd*,[55] where wines, the subject matter of a contract of sale and separated by the seller from its trading stocks, were then mingled with otherwise identical wines in its warehouse stocks following a storage arrangement with the buyer. The court found a common intention of seller and buyer that the buyer should be a co-tenant of the warehouse stocks (together with other buyers in a similar position). Tenancy in common is one way of dealing with the problem posed by bulk cargo consignments,[56] which has been particularly troublesome in the export trade, especially in view of the modern practice of shipping huge quantities of commodities in bulk. The United States Uniform Commercial Code[57] solves problems of this kind with the aid of the tenancy in common notion.

THE SALE OF GOODS (AMENDMENT) ACT 1995

The Sale of Goods (Amendment) Act 1995 was passed in response to recommendations made by the Law Commission[58] designed primarily to deal with bulk cargoes in international commodity sales. Prior to the Act,

---

[52] SGA 1893, s 52.   [53] See chapter 2.
[54] *Laurie and Morewood v Dudin and Sons* [1926] 1 KB 223.
[55] [1994] 1 WLR 1181. See also *Mercer v Craven Grain Storage Ltd* [1994] CLC 328.
[56] Law Commission Working Paper No. 112, *Rights to Goods in Bulk*, para. 4.7.
[57] See Article 2–105(4).   [58] Law Com No. 215, 1993.

it was common for a buyer to be the agreed purchaser of a stated quantity of goods in a defined bulk (for example, 20,000 tonnes of wheat on a named ship carrying 80,000 tonnes) and to pay against shipping documents representing the contract quantity and yet acquire no property rights at all until the contract quantity was separated at the port of unloading. Such a buyer will now acquire an 'undivided interest' in the bulk provided that the bulk is 'identified', whether in the contract itself or by a subsequent act, to the extent that the buyer makes payment for the goods.[59]

The requirement of an identified bulk would not assist the buyers of bullion in *Re Goldcorp Exchange Ltd*. The seller's promise to hold the agreed quantity of bullion for the buyers would not suffice to identify as a bulk any bullion from time to time in the seller's possession. The undivided interest of a buyer coming within the new statutory provisions amounts to a tenancy in common right to the bulk, to the extent of any payment that has been made. A buyer of 20,000 tonnes in a bulk consisting of 80,000 tonnes, who has paid for 10,000 tonnes, will be a tenant in common only to the extent of those 10,000 tonnes. Any goods removed by the buyer from the bulk will be deemed first to be those for which the part-paying buyer has an undivided interest. Any shrinkage in the bulk will be borne rateably by the various co-tenants according to their respective shares.[60] Nevertheless, the shrinkage principle is not to be applied to permit co-tenants to recover from one of their number to whom delivery has already been made of more than his shrunken share.[61]

SECTION 18 RULE 5

Assuming that there are no difficulties concerning the ascertainment of the goods, the presumptive rule for the passing of property under a contract for unascertained goods is to be found in *Rule 5*. A general statement of the rule is found in para.(1), whilst a particular application of it where a carrier is used to transport the goods is set out in para.(2).

According to the rule, property presumptively passes when goods in a deliverable state[62] are unconditionally appropriated to the contract by one party, usually the seller but sometimes the buyer (for example, a supermarket sale), with the assent of the other. The assent is usually implied and may be given in advance by the buyer to the seller. It will be implied at the moment goods are delivered to a carrier to be transported to the

---

[59] SGA 1979, s 20A as amended.
[61] SGA 1979, s 20B, as amended.
[60] See below.
[62] See above.

buyer, since the carrier (if not an employee of the seller) is presumptively the buyer's agent.[63]

Unconditional appropriation has been said to occur at the time the seller performs his last major contractual responsibility.[64] For practical purposes, this is delivery, though delivery within the context of sale carries the presumptive meaning of the seller making the goods available for the buyer to collect.[65] If an independent carrier is employed, delivery occurs when the carrier is permitted to collect the goods.[66] The word 'unconditional' has been interpreted in modern times in a way that is synonymous with 'physically irrevocable'. This is demonstrated by *Carlos Federspiel*, where the contract was for a quantity of bicycles and tricycles to be sold by a Welsh manufacturer to a Costa Rican buyer. The seller required payment before the goods were shipped to the buyer. It had packed the goods in crates with the buyer's address, awaiting the call of a ship bound for Costa Rica, not a well-travelled route, when its unpaid creditors lost patience and sent in a receiver. The receiver's entitlement to refuse to deliver the goods to the buyer depended upon whether the property had passed. Pearson J held that it had not. The goods had not yet been delivered to the carrier. It did not matter that the seller had reached a clear decision to use the particular goods in the crate in fulfilment of the contract since there was nothing to stop the seller changing its mind and breaking open the crates. The goods had been earmarked for the contract but not in an irrevocable way.

Some decisions do not quite accord with such a strict view of unconditional appropriation. For example, the property has been held to pass as soon as goods have been packed in containers supplied by the buyer, even though delivery has not yet taken place.[67] Moreover, in one case where the buyer was to collect a quantity of rice from the seller's premises, the property was held to pass even before the buyer took delivery of the rice, though it remained for the seller to allow the buyer to enter the premises and to cooperate in the removal of the rice.[68]

The delivery test for the passing of property has also been applied where, at the time of the contract, the goods are held by a third party, such as a warehouse company. In accordance with the bailment rules,

---

[63] *Wait v Baker* (1848) 2 Ex 1.
[64] *Carlos Federspiel & Co v Charles Twigg & Co* [1957] 1 Lloyd's Rep 240.
[65] SGA 1979, s 29(2).
[66] SGA 1979, s 32(1).
[67] *Aldridge v Johnson* (1857) 7 E & B 885; *Langton v Higgins* (1859) 4 H & N 402.
[68] *Pignataro v Gilroy* [1919] 1 KB 459.

delivery occurs when the bailee, the warehouse company, attorns to the buyer,[69] thus effecting a constructive transfer of possession. In one case,[70] attornment took place when, after the seller had contracted to sell 600 out of 1,500 cartons of frozen kidneys, the warehouse company accepted a delivery order[71] and indicated to the carrier the 600 separated cartons standing on the pavement that the carrier was to take away.

Where the buyer acquires an undivided share in an identified bulk pursuant to changes brought about by the Sale of Goods (Amendment) Act 1995, this property entitlement should survive the separation of the buyer's share from the bulk by the seller. To require the buyer to show that the unconditional appropriation test in s 18 *Rule 5* has been satisfied would be tantamount to allowing the seller unilaterally and in his own favour to divest the buyer of a vested property right by the act of separation, which would infinge the very principle of a proprietary right.

RESERVING THE RIGHT OF DISPOSAL

Reference was made earlier to the role of SGA 1979, s 19 in reinforcing the rule[72] that the intention of the contracting parties is the primary determinant of the passing of property. Section 19 is sometimes referred to in support of the conclusion that trade sellers of goods are entitled, by means of *Romalpa* clauses, to delay the passing of property until a stipulated condition, usually payment of the agreed price, has been satisfied. After some initial success, *Romalpa* clauses have proved ineffectual in protecting trade sellers whose goods have been worked into the manufacture of new goods or have been sold off to give rise to money proceeds. Attempts to protect the seller in such an event by means of a property reservation clause have been treated as giving rise to a charge over the newly manufactured goods or the money proceeds as the case may be.[73] Whilst charges of this kind may lawfully be created, they need to be perfected by registration[74] to be asserted against the buyer's other creditors or the buyer's liquidator or trustee-in-bankruptcy. It is not the practice of trade sellers to go through the complex motions that this necessitates.

---

[69] See chapter 2.

[70] *Wardar's (Import and Export) Co v W. Norwood and Sons* [1968] 2 QB 663.

[71] See chapter 2.

[72] See SGA 1979, s 17.

[73] *Re Peachdart Ltd* [1984] Ch 131; *E. Pfeiffer Weinkellerei-Weineinkauf GmbH v Arbuthnot Factors* [1988] 1 WLR 150.

[74] Companies Act 1985, ss 395–396.

The part usually played by SGA 1979, s 19 is to demonstrate the application of the passing of property rules in export sales where a bill of lading is employed. Section 19(1) makes it plain that the right of disposal may be retained even if otherwise there would have been an assented to, unconditional appropriation of the goods sufficient to pass the property under s 18 *Rule 5*. Whilst the use by s 19 of the expression 'right of disposal' instead of 'property' seems odd to modern eyes, it is well settled now that a seller who reserves under s 19 does indeed retain the general property and not some unnamed security.

Section 19(2) enacts a *prima facie* rule that a seller reserves the right of disposal when shipping goods and receiving a bill of lading from the carrier showing the consignee of the goods to be either the seller or an agent of the seller.[75] The normal reason for this is to protect the seller against the risk of future non-payment by the buyer but there are other reasons, such as the desire of oil companies to maintain as long as possible strategic freedom in designating the port of discharge and the eventual recipient of the cargo.[76] The seller may also wish to pledge[77] the bill of lading in order to obtain bridging finance pending payment by the buyer.[78] Instead of the property passing when the seller delivers the goods to the carrier, it will pass at a later date when the s 19 inhibition is lifted, which will occur when the bill of lading is exchanged with the buyer for the price of the goods, in accordance with the underlying intention of the parties.[79] In this way, the seller gets cash (or its equivalent) upon delivery of the bill of lading, which has been described as the 'key' to the floating warehouse.[80]

Sometimes a seller will receive from the carrier a bill of lading naming the buyer as the consignee but will retain possession of the bill of lading until payment, thus making it impossible for the buyer to deal with the cargo. The case law is not clear as to whether the seller is thus retaining the right of disposal or exercising a possessory lien[81] over the bill of lading.[82] For practical purposes, the distinction seems not to matter since the seller is protected against non-payment and the buyer's insolvency in either event.

The effect of s 19(3) is that a seller who dispatches to the buyer the bill

---

[75] See also *Wait v Baker* (1848) 2 Ex 1; *Mirabita v Imperial Ottoman Bank* (1878) 3 Ex D 164, *per* Cotton LJ.

[76] *The Albazero* [1974] AC 774. [77] See chapter 7. [78] *The Albazero*.

[79] SGA 1979, s 17. [80] See chapter 2. [81] See chapter 7.

[82] Contrast *Ladenburg & Co v Goodwin, Ferreira & Co* [1912] 3 KB 275 with *The Kronprinsessan Margareta* [1921] 1 AC 486, *per* Lord Sumner.

of lading together with a draft bill of exchange[83] for the price does not thereby transfer the property in the goods if the buyer refuses to accept the payment obligation set out in the draft. This is consistent with the rule that the transfer of a bill of lading does not necessarily effect a passing of the property: it all depends upon the accompanying intention (a restatement of the SGA 1979, s 17 rule). Thus the transferor may wish merely to confer a special property by way of pledge on the transferee[84] or to give the transferee only the physical freedom to have the goods warehoused upon their arrival at the port of discharge.[85]

GRATUITOUS CONSENSUAL TRANSFERS

GENERAL

This heading is concerned with gratuitous transactions involving the outright transfer of the general property in chattels. We shall deal with gift, as well as with its quasi-testamentary relation, the *donatio mortis causa*. As regards inheritance, it is enough to note the existence of a law of succession by which testators have freedom, when of sound mind and when observing the required forms, to bequeath by will their personal estate. Intestate succession is properly a matter of transfer by operation of law, as is the rule that personalty, even if bequeathed by will, first vests in the testator's personal representatives prior to its distribution among the named legatees.

GIFT AND CONTRACT

In certain continental legal systems, gift is seen as a species of contract. The requirement of consideration in contract prevents us from classifying gift in the same way, though the permissibility of establishing a nominal consideration means that the substance of gift can be concealed in the form of contract. The distinction between gift and contract is not of great significance in the general law once a transaction is executed, whichever of the two it may be. But since an executory promise to give may not be enforced, while an executory promise to perform a contractual duty may, the distinction is of major significance at the executory level. A promise to give is not binding unless it is contained in the form of a deed.[86] If a deed is not executed, a gift promise must be accompanied by physical

---

[83] See chapter 6.
[85] *The Aliakmon* [1986] AC 785.

[84] *Sewell v Burdick* (1884) 10 App Cas 74.
[86] See below.

delivery before the gift becomes a binding legal transaction.[87] In *Re Ridgway*,[88] delivery was not satisfied when a pipe of port was laid by a father in a cellar and known over the years as the son's port.

Contracts for a nominal consideration are usually cast in the form of a unilateral contract: You may have my Rolls Royce if and when you pay me (not promise to pay me) the sum of £1. Since in principle unilateral promises are revocable before acceptance, an executory promise of this kind is no more significant for the purpose of becoming binding than a gratuitous promise. Nevertheless, the form of the contractual exchange may serve a valuable evidentiary purpose, after its execution, in establishing beyond doubt the intention of the promisor and in rebutting the presumption of a resulting trust[89] in favour of the promisor.

REQUIREMENTS OF GIFT OF CHATTELS

An effective gift between a donor and a donee requires that the donor display a clear intention to transfer to the donee his interest in the object that is being given. This alone, however, is not sufficient. There must also occur either physical delivery or the execution and delivery of a deed or an effective declaration of trust. Of these three items, physical delivery is the means most commonly employed in the case of personalty. To a significant extent, the problems raised by gift are of an evidentiary character, namely, were clear words of gift uttered and was there in fact a transfer of possession?

A gift transaction may subsequently be challenged in a variety of circumstances. For example, the donor may later regret an earlier display of generosity, possibly having gone too far in the quest for social and emotional effect. Or the donor's residuary legatee may be seeking to augment the estate available for testamentary distribution by clawing back the subject matter of a disputed gift. Or the donor's trustee in bankruptcy may be on the alert to discover property placed by the donor in the name of a spouse to put it beyond the reach of the donor's creditors. In this last case, one of the weapons in the trustee's armoury is the requirement that delivery take place to complete a gift.

DELIVERY

Delivery means the transfer of possession from the donor to the donee.[90] Courts have not been prepared to let the meaning of delivery be diluted in

---

[87] *Irons v Smallpiece* (1819) 2 B & Ald 551; *Cochrane v Moore* (1890) 25 QBD 57.
[88] (1885) 15 QBD 447.   [89] See below.   [90] See chapter 2.

the context of gift: 'The English law of the transfer of property, domin-
ated as it has always been by the doctrine of consideration, has always
been chary of the recognition of gifts'.[91] For delivery to take place, there
has to be a clear, unequivocal transfer of possession, even clear words of
gift not making up for imprecision in the act of delivery. In this regard,
delivery has posed problems in cases where one spouse seeks to make a
gift of something to the other whilst retaining some measure of use and
enjoyment of the object. In *Re Cole*, a husband introduced his wife to
their new home and, after covering her eyes, removed his hands and said
'Look'. She was then taken around the house, handling certain items in
the process, and then informed 'It's all yours'. Her claim that she had been
effectively given the contents of the home was successfully challenged by
her husband's trustee in bankruptcy. No allowance was made for the fact
that her husband had brought her to the contents of the home, that these
were too many and too bulky to deal with by a physical handing over and
that she had touched some of them on her first visit to the new home.

DELIVERY: SPECIAL CASES

Physical delivery is obviously difficult to accomplish with bulky chattels.
In *Lock v Heath*,[92] a so-called 'symbolical' delivery was recognised when a
chair was delivered to the donee wife coupled with the words of the
husband: 'I give you all the goods mentioned in the inventory.' The
delivery of the chair, a very real act, might more accurately be seen as
representative (rather than symbolical) of the list contained in the inventory. The same approach is evident in *Rawlinson v Mort*,[93] where the
owner of an organ had it installed in a church on terms contained in a
letter from the vicar that it was only lent. The owner decided to make a
gift of it to the church organist and handed him the vicar's letter together
with evidence of the organ's purchase. He also placed the organist's hand
on the organ and declared that he was giving it to him. This was held to
be an effective delivery; it was the nearest thing to a physical transfer of
possession that the nature of the case permitted.

In *Rawlinson v Mort*, it was strictly the bailor's reversionary entitlement that was being transferred by a process that mimicked a transfer of
possession itself. If the goods are held by a bailee at the time the donor
displays a gift intention, the needed transfer of possession can be accomplished by constructive means as and when the bailee attorns to the

---

[91] *Re Cole* [1964] Ch 175, *per* Harman LJ.   [92] (1892) 8 TLR 295.
[93] (1905) 93 LT 555.

donee.[94] Where the donee is already in possession,[95] or has the custody of the thing as an employee in effective occupation of it,[96] the donor's intention is all that is needed to consummate the gift. If words of gift are uttered and the donor, having lost the thing, also gives directions or suggestions as to its recovery, the subsequent discovery of the thing will complete the transaction. This happened in *Thomas v Times Book Co*,[97] where the playwright Dylan Thomas lost the manuscript of 'Under Milk Wood' on a taxi-tour of a string of London public houses. The donee, a BBC producer, provided him with copies of the manuscript made on a previous occasion and was told he could have the manuscript itself if he could find it. The producer followed up leads suggested by the playwright and so discovered the manuscript, which was held to complete the gift.

In unusual circumstances, a purported gift that fails for want of delivery may subsequently be completed if the donee obtains possession of the subject-matter of the gift in another capacity. According to the rule in *Strong v Bird*,[98] an intended donee who subsequently obtains possession as executor of the estate of the deceased donor thereby acquires a perfected title to the thing. The case itself concerned an ineffectual attempt to forgive a debt but the rule is of broader application. The subject-matter vests in the donee in his capacity of executor, but the donor's intention serves to free the title of the donee from the limitations on enjoying the thing that the executorship would otherwise impose.

DEED

As an alternative to physical delivery, the donor may sign and deliver a document called a deed indicating a donative intention. Until the enactment of the Law of Property (Miscellaneous Provisions) Act 1989, a deed had to be executed under seal which, unlike the molten wax impression of old, had latterly taken the form of a red paper disc. Instead of the seal, it is now required that a document be expressed on its face to be a deed.[99] Furthermore, it has become necessary for a witness to attest by signature that the maker of the deed has signed in the witness's presence, or for two witnesses to attest by signature that the deed was drawn up and signed according to the direction and in the presence of its maker.[100] Although a deed has to be delivered to become effective, delivery in the case of deeds

---

[94] See chapter 2.
[95] *Re Stoneham* [1919] 1 Ch 149.
[96] *Winter v Winter* (1861) 4 LT 639.
[97] [1966] 2 All ER 241.
[98] (1874) LR 18 Eq 315.
[99] Section 1(2)(a).
[100] Section 1(3), needed for the case of a maker physically unable to sign for himself.

has acquired the very loose meaning of any act that connotes the intention of the maker of the deed to be bound by it, though it would presumably have to mean more than merely signing the deed since the statute differentiates between signing and delivery.

DOCUMENTARY INTANGIBLES

The gift of certain documentary intangibles (such as share certificates, bills of exchange and bills of lading) must comply with a transfer procedure laid down by contract or statute.[101] This should be read subject to the case of *Re Rose*,[102] which qualifies the maxim that equity will not perfect an imperfect gift. In that case, a question arose as to the effect of a transaction where the owner of shares completed a share transfer form, pursuant to a gift, and was awaiting the registration of the transfer by the company. Although the transfer was only complete upon registration, the owner had done everything in his power to effect a transfer. He had used the proper form and so was to be regarded as a trustee of the shares for the benefit of the donee pending the actual registration of the change of ownership.

An important relaxation of the *Re Rose* principle[103] is evident in *Pennington v Waine*,[104] where the Court of Appeal held that *Re Rose* did not preclude the conclusion that a gift of shares might be completed in equity even before the donor had done everything in his power to effect a transfer.[105] Mindful of the need to protect donors from intemperate benevolence and their creditors from a dissipation of the donor's estate, the Court of Appeal nevertheless concluded that an effective equitable assignment of the shares had occurred when a stock transfer form relating to shares in a family company was handed over by the donor to her solicitor. He received the form as her agent, and not as the agent of the company itself, and took no further steps to complete the transfer prior to the donor's death. For the majority, Arden LJ was prepared to hold that the solicitor, when writing to the intended donee about the gift of the shares and informing him there was nothing further that the donee needed to do, had the effect of rendering the donor and the solicitor himself agents of the donee for the purpose of effecting the transfer by the company. This bold view of the matter was reinforced by the added reason that in the circumstances it would have been unconscionable of the

---

[101] See further chapter 6.   [102] [1952] Ch 499.
[103] Applied in *Trustees of the Property of Pehrsson v Von Greyerz* (PC, unreported 16 June 1999).
[104] [2002] EWCA Civ 227.   [105] *Ibid*, at para. 66 (Arden LJ) and para. 110 (Clarke LJ).

donor's personal representatives to refuse to hand over the share transfers to the donee,[106] just as, it seems, it would have been unconscionable for the donor herself to change her mind. It would have been unconscionable because the donee had been informed of the gift and advised that there was no need for him to do anything, and had taken the necessary steps to become a director of the company, for which position he needed a share-holding qualification.[107] Clarke LJ preferred to rest his decision upon the simple view that the execution of a stock transfer form was, even without delivery of the form, an effective equitable assignment of the shares, given the wording of the stock transfer form ('I/We *hereby* transfer').[108]

Lord Browne-Wilkinson has drawn attention to the limits of the maxim that equity will not perfect an imperfect gift: this does not mean that equity will strive officiously to defeat a gift.[110] The decision in *Pennington v Waine*, however, especially for the way it introduces unconscionability into the inference of an equitable assignment, goes some way beyond abstaining from officious interference and blurs the dividing line between gift and trust.[110]

An interesting feature of gift in the case of documentary intangibles is revealed by *Standing v Bowring*.[111] That case, concerning a transfer of shares into the name of the donee, supports the proposition that the consent of the donee is not needed to effectuate a gift,[112] though an unwanted gift may always be repudiated by the donee upon its discovery. If the absence of any requirement of the donee's consent is of general application, then gift is far removed from contract in the common law tradition. Nevertheless, this point ought not to be overstated. In very many instances, the consent of the donee will necessarily be given by the circumstances of the case: a physical delivery involving a change of possession cannot be accomplished without consent (except possibly if the donee is an infant of very tender years). However, the consent of an intended beneficiary is not required for a valid trust and the absence of consent does therefore appear to be of general application, justifiable perhaps by the fact that the transaction can only be of benefit to the donee.

---

[106] *Ibid*, at para. 67.   [107] *Ibid*, at para. 64.   [108] Original emphasis.
[109] *Choithram (T) International SA v Pagarini* [2001] 1 WLR 1 (PC).
[110] See below.
[111] (1885) 31 Ch D 282.
[112] See also *Shepherd v Cartwright* [1955] AC 432.

INEFFECTIVE GIFTS

The presence of a vitiating factor, such as mistake, duress and undue influence, may vitiate a gift in the same way as it does a contract (see the standard contract texts). Furthermore, some gifts (and one-sided contracts akin to gifts) may be challenged by creditors of the donor to the extent that they diminish the content of an insolvent's estate in the period leading up to the bankruptcy (individuals) or liquidation (companies) of the donor.[113] If the gift is set aside, the subject matter is made available for distribution among the donor's unpaid creditors. In addition, although a gift of personalty need not in general follow a particular form, certain gifts made by individuals (not companies) in writing may be subsequently challenged by creditors of the donor. This will be so if the gift is not followed by delivery or by compliance with the very detailed formal and registration requirements of the Bills of Sale Act 1878. It is unlikely, however, that a gift would nowadays be successfully challenged under this statute.

In addition, though the point normally arises under testamentary dispositions, a gift may be expressed to be subject to restraints (conditions) that are too vague to be enforced or else are invalid because they offend against public policy. If the conditions operate so as to qualify entitlement to the gift, the effect of their unenforceability or invalidity is that the donee may not enforce the gift on any terms. Sometimes, however, conditions are imposed that would divest the donee of a gift that has already vested. The effect of unenforceability or invalidity here is that the gift takes full effect unfettered by the condition.

In *Re Macleay*,[114] a gift 'to my brother John . . . on the condition that he never sells out of the family' was held to be subject to a valid restraint. A general prohibition upon alienation would have been bad, but John had the choice of his family members when it came to sale and could select other means of disposition, such as gift, mortgage or lease, if choosing to go outside the family. On the other hand, a restraint forfeiting a legacy to the testator's daughter if she should marry someone 'not of Jewish parentage and of the Jewish faith' was held to be too uncertain (disjunctive or conjunctive conditions? one or both parents? etc), so the legacy could be enjoyed unimpaired by the restraint.[115] Again, a divesting condition was held to be too uncertain when it permitted the testator's daughter to

---

[113] See the provisions dealing with transactions at an undervalue in the Insolvency Act 1986, ss 238, 240, 339, 341.
[114] (1875) LR 20 Eq 186.   [115] *Clayton v Ramsden* [1943] AC 320.

receive payments from the estate 'only so long as she should reside in Canada'.[116] She was entitled to a precise answer to the question, 'How long may I safely spend outside Canada before I lose my legacy?' and the restraint as formulated did not give it.

PRESUMPTIONS OF A RESULTING TRUST AND OF ADVANCEMENT

Apart from cases where a presumption of advancement arises, the delivery of a thing (or the transfer of a documentary intangible) raises a presumption that it was not intended by way of gift. This accords with the law's reluctance, arising from its commitment to the doctrine of consideration, to recognize gift.[117] If documentary intangibles are transferred, for example company shares on the company register, there is a rebuttable presumption that the transferee holds the shares on a presumed, resulting trust in favour of the transferor. This presumption seems particularly substantial where documentary intangibles are transferred into the joint names of transferor and transferee.[118] As far as chattels go, the physical delivery alone of a thing does not in general appear to be quite so suggestive of an intention to give as to require the obstacle of a presumption of resulting trust to inhibit intemperate benevolence. It is difficult to see what purpose a resulting trust presumption serves here: the recipient will have to prove an intention to give and this will not lightly be established just because delivery has occurred. Delivery, after all, is quite consistent with a short-term loan; the transfer of shares in a company is not.

In certain relations, far from a resulting trust arising to make it difficult to establish a donative intention, a reverse presumption arises that the delivery or transfer of a thing was made with such an intention. This is the presumption of advancement and it occurs where the delivery or transfer operates from father to child[119] or to some other person to whom he stands in *loco parentis*. A weaker presumption arises in other close family relationships where the transfer or delivery moves from the stronger to the weaker individual. Clearly, the presumption of advancement is consistent with hierarchical family units whose junior members do not have the personal autonomy that one finds in the modern, dispersed and emancipated family. In modern times, it is questionable that the presumption of advancement from husband to wife has any real force.[120] Similarly, it has been said that the presumption of advancement

---

[116] *Sifton v Sifton* [1938] AC 656. [117] *Re Cole* [1964] Ch 175, *per* Harman LJ.
[118] *Re Vinogradoff* [1935] WN 68; *Standing v Bowring* (1885) 31 Ch D 282.
[119] *Shepherd v Cartwright* [1955] AC 432. [120] *Pettitt v Pettitt* [1970] AC 777.

between father and son may be rebutted by 'comparatively slight evidence'.[121]

The question of illegality arose in *Tinsley v Milligan*,[122] where A and B made contributions to property conveyed into B's name alone. This was done to facilitate a fraud perpetrated on the Department of Social Security by both A and B. A was nevertheless permitted to claim her share of the property with the aid of the presumption of resulting trust. Far from A relying upon the illegal contract, it was B who sought to do this in defending the action. Had there been a presumption of advancement in favour of B, then A might have been constrained to rely upon the illegal contract in order to rebut this presumption, which would not have been allowed.[123] In cases where the illegal purpose lying behind the conveyance of the property has not in fact been carried out, the transferor will be at liberty to rebut the presumption of advancement. In *Tribe v Tribe*,[124] a father transferred shares to his son in order to avoid paying a bill for dilapidations presented by his landlords. He was able to negotiate a settlement with the landlords without relying upon the transfer of shares, and so was held entitled to rebut the presumption of advancement and recover the shares from his son.

TRUST

As an alternative to delivery, a donor may declare a trust of the thing in favour of the donee, which will serve to transfer the beneficial interest in it to the donee. Alternatively, the donor may settle a thing on a trustee for the benefit of a donee. Equity, however, will not assist a volunteer or perfect an imperfect gift, which means that a trust will not freely be discovered in the ruins of a failed gift by delivery or a failed contract. A gift intended to be effected by one mode will not be carried into effect by another,[125] so for example a trust will not be spelt out of a failed attempt to convey by deed. Explicit trust language is not needed to constitute a trust,[126] so there is scope for a degree of inconsistency in the judicial inference of one. Just as the trust is not easily inferred to solve problems presented in contract by the doctrine of privity,[127] so a trust was not recognised in *Jones v Lock*,[128] where a father, after a lengthy journey,

---

[121] *McGrath v Wallis* [1995] 2 FLR 114.
[122] [1995] 1 AC 340.
[123] See also *Chettiar v Chettiar* [1962] AC 294.
[124] [1996] Ch 107.
[125] *Milroy v Lord* (1862) 4 De GF & J 264, *per* Turner LJ.
[126] *Richards v Delbridge* (1874) LR 18 Eq 11.
[127] See for example *Re Schebsmann* [1944] Ch 83.
[128] (1865) 1 Ch App 25.

briefly placed a cheque for £900 in a baby's hands saying: 'I give this to baby for himself.'

A declaration of trust and a gift are two very different transactions. In the former, which is 'far rarer' than gift, the settlor 'intends to retain his rights but to come under an onerous obligation' whereas a 'giver means to get rid of his rights'.[129] This is one reason why equity has long resisted a movement from the conclusion that a gift has failed to the conclusion that a trust has instead been declared by a settlor. The decision of the Court of Appeal in *Pennington v Waine*,[130] however, shows a modern willingness to leap the gap in exceptional circumstances where a benevolent construction of language is appropriate so that the wind will temper to the shorn lamb (the donee).[131] The same can also be said of the Privy Council in a decision where a donor orally declared a gift of all his wealth to a foundation that he had established by trust deed.[132] He did this on the occasion of his also executing a foundation trust deed between himself as settlor and himself and others as trustees of the foundation. The gift to the foundation was not to be regarded as an outright gift, but rather as a gift for the purposes set out in the foundation trust deed, since the foundation had no other existence apart from that in the deed. Furthermore, the settlor himself was bound by the trust and had to give effect to it by transferring the trust property into the names of all the trustees.

No particular form is required for the creation of a trust of personalty but it should be noted that, if the donor's interest in the thing that is being given is an equitable rather than a legal one, the trust will concern a subsisting equitable interest and so will have to be in writing to satisfy s 53(1)(c) of the Law of Property Act 1925. No such requirement exists when the declaration of trust splits the legal and beneficial interests in the thing for the first time.

DONATIO MORTIS CAUSA

This is a transaction that falls short of the conventional requirements of a gift but is binding because of the circumstances in which it occurs. There must be a delivery of the subject-matter of the gift.[133] A constructive delivery will also suffice where the donee receives the means by which possession can later be taken (such as the key to a bank safety deposit

---

[129] Maitland, F.W., *Equity*, Cambridge University Press, 1909, p 74.
[130] [2002] EWCA Civ 227.
[131] Discussed above.
[132] *Choithram (T) International SA v Pagarini* [2001] 1 WLR 1 (PC).
[133] *Ward v Turner* (1752) 1 Dick 170; *Delgoffe v Fader* [1939] Ch 922.

box). In *Woodard v Woodard*,[134] the delivery of car keys was enough, even though the donee already had a set and was in possession of the car as bailee. Giving a power of attorney to deal with shares, however, is not tantamount to delivery or constructive delivery of the share certificates themselves.[135]

Instead of an intention to make an outright present gift, the law is satisfied if the donor, in contemplation of death,[136] delivers with the intention that a gift will take full effect as from the death of the donor. But there must be some element of present intention to benefit the recipient for otherwise the transaction would be indistinguishable from a testamentary bequest and so would fail for non-compliance with the formal requirements of the Wills Act 1837.[137] In the event of the contemplated death not occurring because the donor makes a happy recovery, the *donatio mortis causa* is not properly constituted[138] and the donee is merely a bailee of the intended gift.

Donatio mortis causa applies not only to chattels and documentary intangibles but also to pure intangibles, such as the indebtedness of a banker to a client with a credit balance in a deposit or other account. The requirements of proprietary transfer in the case of pure intangibles are set out in chapter 6. A transaction effective as a *donatio mortis causa* would fail as an effective assignment because the donor does not fully intend to vest a property interest in the donee. On the face of it, is difficult to see how the requirement of delivery can be satisfied in the case of a species of property with no physical existence such as a debt. Nevertheless, drawing on the idea of *indicia* of title, the courts have recognised a *donatio mortis causa* where documents have been delivered that are sufficiently suggestive of the recipient's entitlement to the pure intangible that they evidence. In *Birch v Treasury Solicitor*, the delivery of various savings account and deposit account pass books was held to satisfy the requirements of a *donatio mortis causa*.

TRANSFERS BY OPERATION OF LAW

The rules regarding the passing of property when chattels become fixtures or lose their identity when attached to, commingled with or transformed into a separate chattel will be dealt with under this head as

---

[134] [1995] 3 All ER 980. [135] *Re Craven's Estate* [1937] Ch 423.
[136] *Cain v Moon* [1896] 2 QB 283. [137] *Birch v Treasury Solicitor* [1950] 2 All ER 1198.
[138] See *Delgoffe v Fader* (1939), *per* Luxmoore J: '[T]he title of the donee is never complete until the donor is dead.'

leading examples of transfers occurring by operation of law. To say that these transfers occur by operation of law is not to deny any role to party intention. Intention has a part to play in the operation of the fixtures rules. It can also play a part in determining the ownership of new chattels to the extent that the parties agree to displace the presumptive property rule. Apart from intention, consent to dealings in chattels may affect the ownership of new chattels coming into existence as a result of those dealings.

FIXTURES

The question here is in what circumstances a chattel becomes so firmly attached to the land that it passes to the owner of the land or other person (such as a mortgagee) with a relevant interest in the land.[139] To answer this question, a related question must be firmly distinguished. In landlord-tenant relations, certain fixtures, known as trade fixtures, may be severed by the tenant from the land at the end of the tenancy.[140] Other fixtures, known as landlord's fixtures, may not. Our concern is with whether a chattel becomes a fixture in the first place.

A number of the cases canvass Roman law principles and reference is sometimes made to the maxim '*quicquid plantatur solo, solo cedit*' (literally, whatever is attached to the soil becomes part of the soil). Nevertheless, the Roman law rules do not as such apply and the maxim clearly goes too far. The authoritative approach to the issue of fixtures is expressed in *Hellawell v Eastwood*[141] as dependent upon the following two-stage test:

> [F]irst the mode of annexation to the soil or fabric of the house, and the extent to which it is united to them, whether it can be easily removed . . . or not, without injury to itself or the fabric of the building; secondly, . . . the object and purpose of the annexation, whether it was for the permanent and substantial improvement of the dwelling . . . or merely for a temporary purpose, or the more complete enjoyment and use of it as a chattel . . .

The two limbs of this test are relative variables. Put simply, strength under one of the limbs, the degree of factual connection for example, may compensate for a lack of evidence as to intention. Conversely, evidence of a clear intention that a chattel shall not become a fixture despite annexation to the soil may offset to a significant degree a strong attachment thereto. In *Hellawell v Eastwood*, machines had been fixed to the ground

---

[139] See Bennett, H. N., 'Attachment of Chattels to Land', in Palmer, N., and McKendrick, E. (eds), *Interests in Goods*, 2nd edn, London and Hong Kong: LLP, 1998.
[140] *Bain v Brand* (1876) 1 App Cas 762.   [141] (1851) 6 Ex 295.

in order to make them 'steadier and more capable of convenient use as chattels'. They were no more fixtures 'than a carpet . . . attached to the floor by nails for the purpose of keeping it stretched out, or curtains, looking-glasses, pictures, and other matters of an ornamental nature, which have been slightly attached to the walls of a dwelling as furniture . . .'. In the same vein, a houseboat has been held to be a chattel despite connected services, moorage to a pontoon, lines to the river wall, and anchorage in the river bed. It could readily be moved into drydock or even moored somewhere else.[142] It will be unusual for a chattel resting on the ground by its own weight to be a fixture, but even an unattached chattel may exceptionally be a fixture if it is vital to the enjoyment of the land.[143] Furthermore, if a chattel resting upon land can be removed from it only by demolition, as was the case with a chalet resting upon concrete pillars, it will be treated as a fixture.[144] Conversely, chattels firmly attached to the land so that their severance would be very difficult may in an exceptional case be a chattel. In *Wake v Hall*,[145] Derbyshire miners exercised customary mining rights, confirmed by statute, on land belonging to others. In order to carry out the mining, they erected on the land machinery and building (engine house, boiler house etc). When the mining ceased, the House of Lords held they were entitled as against the owners of the land to dismantle the buildings and machinery and sell them. The buildings and machinery were clearly accessory to the mining and could be removed without causing great damage to the land. If there had been significant destruction of the land, this would have afforded strong evidence 'that the property in the materials must have been intended to be irrevocably annexed to the soil'.

Ultimately, the matter of intention bulks very large in the application of the *Hellawell v Eastwood* formula. In two cases involving seats in a cinema, the courts reached contrasting conclusions on the fixtures question.[146] In an exceptional case, intention can overcome the fact of chattels merely resting upon land so as to lead to their characterization as fixtures. In *Holland v Hodgson*,[147] Blackburn J gives the examples of blocks placed on top of each to form a dry stone wall (a fixture), when those same blocks

---

[142] *Chelsea Yacht and Boat Co Ltd v Pope* [2001] 2 All ER 409.

[143] *Elliott v Bishop* (1855) 11 Ex 113: house keys.

[144] *Elitestone Ltd v Morris* [1997] 2 All ER 513.

[145] (1883) 8 App Cas 195.

[146] *Lyon & Co v London City and Midland Bank* [1903] 2 KB 135; *Vaudeville Electric Cinema Ltd v Muriset* [1923] 2 Ch 74.

[147] (1872) LR 7 CP 328.

would be treated as chattels if stacked in the same way for storage purposes in a builder's yard. The burden will be on those asserting that chattels resting on land have become fixtures, and on those asserting that chattels even slightly affixed to land remain chattels, to show an intention that counters the presumptive rule.[148] Nevertheless, there are limits to how far intention can be taken, especially where the rights of third parties are at stake. *Hobson v Gorringe*[149] is a good example of this. Hobson delivered an engine to King under a hire purchase contract. The engine was bolted to the floor through iron plates set in newly-poured concrete. A plate was attached to the engine making it clear that it remained the property of Hobson. At a later date, King gave a mortgage over the land, fixed machinery and fixtures in favour of Gorringe and then fell into arrear under the hire purchase contract. Upon the bankruptcy of King, a question arose whether the engine had passed to Gorringe as a fixture under the mortgage. The Court of Appeal held, *inter alia*, that the engine was so firmly fixed to the ground that it had become a fixture. Only where the 'circumstances which shewed the degree of annexation and the object of such annexation . . . were patent for all to see' (the plate being evidently insufficient in this respect) were they germane in determining the issue of intention. So as influential as intention is in settling the fixture question, it cannot be permitted to depart too far from external, observable fact. In a similarly restrictive way, it has been observed that intention can affect the issue only to the extent that it can be presumed from the object and degree of annexation.[150]

ATTACHMENT, COMMINGLING AND ALTERATION

This area of law is so undeveloped at common law that its vocabulary has been borrowed from Roman law, though it should not be assumed that the same goes for the substantive law. The failure of English law to develop systematic answers to the problems raised in these cases probably owes a great deal to the conceptual underdevelopment of personal property law; problems are dealt with as they arise through the medium of the law of torts.[151]

First, *accessio* is the joining of a subordinate thing to a dominant one, so that the identity of the subordinate becomes submerged in the dominant. The impregnation of an animal with the seed of another is a long-standing

---

[148] *Ibid.*
[149] [1897] 1 Ch 182.
[150] *Melluish v B.M.I. (No. 3) Ltd* [1996] AC 454 at p 473 (Lord Browne-Wilkinson).
[151] See chapter 3.

example.[152] Others are the replacement panel welded to a car that has suffered crash damage, and the glue used in repairing the damaged spine of a book. Secondly, there is *specificatio*, where a raw material is altered by labour to produce something of a different identity. The Romans gave examples of grapes converted into wine, and silver fashioned into a jug. We may cite the more recent example of leather that is cut, shaped, and stitched to make handbags.[153] Thirdly, commingling, taking the form of *confusio* (fluid mixtures) or *commixitio* (granular mixtures), occurs where identical (or at least physically compatible) chattels are mixed to produce a volume from which it is impossible to separate the original ingredients.[154] Impossibility here includes impracticability as well as genuine impossibility. Grain may physically be separable in a way that globules of oil are not, but the herculean task of separation means in practice that no distinction can be drawn between fluid and granular mixtures. In neither case is there any prospect of an original contribution being recovered from the mixture in its pristine form. For example, different quantities of Brent crude oil might be poured into the one supertanker (even different qualities whose mixture produces an intermediate quality), or different quantities of amber durum wheat might be poured into the same grain elevator or ship's hold. It is a further characteristic of mixtures, especially fluid ones, that original ingredients of different qualities may be blended to produce a hybrid compound. This process resembles *specificatio* to such a degree as to demand consistency in the rules applicable to the two processes. These various categories of accession, specification and commingling raise questions of ownership of the final product as well as of tort liability where there has occurred wrongdoing.

For accession, the rule is that the owner of the dominant or superior thing retains the thing in its new and enlarged state. Establishing the separate identities of thing and accessory will in many cases be straightforward. In other cases, matters of size, value, and purpose may have to be applied with some sensitivity. The buttons sewed on the clothing of a Pearly King and Queen may be more valuable than the clothing but they function to enhance the clothing. The clothing is not merely the setting for the buttons. An English court should therefore conclude that the buttons accede to the clothing. Likewise, an illuminated manuscript remains a

---

[152] Blackstone, *Commentaries on the Laws of England*, 1765, Book II, chapter 25 'Of Property in Things Personal', p 390: '*partus sequitur ventrem* in the brute creation' since the father is often unknown and the mother, whilst pregnant, useless to its owner.

[153] *Cf. Re Peachdart Ltd* [1984] Ch 131.

[154] See Birks, P., 'Mixtures', in Palmer, N., and McKendrick, E. (eds), *op. cit.*

manuscript regardless of the expense of the gold leaf showered upon it. Apart from this, the young of animals go with the ownership of the mother,[155] except for swans whose young are divided equally between 'the cock and the hen',[156] since 'the father is well-known by his constant association with the female'.[157] According to Blackburn J in *Appleby v Myers*:[158]

> [M]aterials worked by one into the property of another become part of that property . . . Bricks built into a wall become part of the house; thread stitched into a coat which is under repair, or planks and nails and pitch worked into a ship which is under repair, become part of the coat or ship . . .

If, nevertheless, the owner of the coat or ship makes unlawful use of the materials of another, this act will entail liability in the tort of conversion (see chapter 3).

Sometimes, the degree of attachment of one thing to another will be slight enough to allow a reversal of the attachment process without damaging the dominant thing. In this case, the property in the subordinate thing is not transferred to the owner of the dominant. In *Hendy Lennox Ltd v Grahame Puttick Ltd*,[159] a seller supplied diesel engines to a buyer who incorporated them in generator sets in the manufacturing process. The seller retained the general property in the engines but its property right would have been expunged if the accession had been irrevocable. The court held that the seller was entitled to recover the engines under the contract of sale since they remained clearly identifiable and could be removed after several hours' work.[160] It would in many cases defeat commercial expectations to infer too readily that an accession was irreversible. Aircraft engines, for example, are the subject of separate finance leases from the ones governing the airframes in which the engines are incorporated. Similarly, mobile oil drilling platforms (or floating production and off-take facilities (FPSOs)) are composed of connected elements in different ownerships.

There is little authority on the specification issue (which is sometimes dealt with as though it gave rise to issues of accession).[161] Taking first the case of an owner of materials who consents to their being worked upon so as to create a new thing, it is a matter of fine judgement whether and when a new thing comes into existence.[162] If such happens, then first of all

---

[155] Blackstone, above.   [156] *Case of Swans* (1592) 7 Co. Rep 15b.
[157] Blackstone, above.   [158] (1867) LR 2 CP 651.
[159] [1984] 2 All ER 152.   [160] Cf. *Akron Tyre Co v Kittson* (1951) 82 CLR 477.
[161] See *Jones v De Marchant* (1916) 28 DLR 561.
[162] *Chaigley Farms Ltd v Crawford, Kaye & Grayshire Ltd* [1996] BCC 957 (slaughtered cattle).

the ownership of the materials ceases to exist at the point they are consumed in the manufacturing process. Secondly, the ownership of the new thing created by the process of manufacture vests in the manufacturer (or operator),[163] a conclusion that tends to be assumed in the case law rather than justified.[164] Nevertheless, if the owner of the raw materials and the operator agree that the former is to become the owner of the new thing, such agreement will be recognized as having this effect.[165]

Less certain is the case of the operator who unlawfully uses someone else's materials to manufacture a new thing. The operator will certainly incur liability in the tort of conversion for consuming the materials. The question is whether the owner of the materials can go further and claim ownership of the new thing itself so as to ground an action in conversion if the operator refuses to surrender it. On one view, the owner of the materials may not since the operator in this case too becomes the owner of the new thing.[166] The opposite view, consistent with some of the authorities on mixtures,[167] is that the owner of the materials acquires outright ownership of the new thing, at least in cases where the owner's material contribution is the preponderant one and a sharing arrangement is not feasible. This was the outcome in *Jones v De Marchant*,[168] where 18 of the 22 beaver skins used by a man to make a coat which was then given to his mistress had been unlawfully taken from his wife. It was perhaps no accident that the court treated the case as one of accession. An intermediate solution is that the owner of the materials obtains a shared interest in the new thing by way of tenancy in common, along with the operator and the owner of other raw materials used in the process. Similarly to the case of the beaver skin coat, this solution is unavailable if the owner of the materials cannot trace them into the new thing because of the sheer difficulty in quantifying the owner's contribution.[169] The present law on unlawful specification is thus hard to state but, it is submitted, is consistent with the outcome of the mixture cases discussed below. As against a wrongdoer, the owner of the materials is not in principle entitled to the

[163] *Borden (U.K.) Ltd v Scottish Timber Products Ltd* [1981] Ch 25; *Re Peachdart Ltd* [1984] Ch 131.
[164] But it is explained as turning on implied intention in *Glencore International AG v Metro Trading Inc* [2001] 1 Lloyd's Rep 284.
[165] *Clough Mill Ltd v Martin* [1985] 1 WLR 111 (Robert Goff LJ); *Glencore International AG v Metro Trading Inc* [2001] 1 Lloyd's Rep 284.
[166] Holdsworth, W., *History of English Law*, vol III at pp 501–503.
[167] See *Glencore International AG v Metro Trading Inc* [2001] 1 Lloyd's Rep 284.
[168] (1916) 28 DLR 561. See also *Re Oatway* [1903] 2 Ch 356.
[169] *Borden (U.K.) Ltd v Scottish Timber Products Ltd* [1981] Ch 25 (Bridge LJ); see the material on tracing in chapter 5.

new thing, for that would be a penal outcome. Rather, the entitlement will be to a divisible interest in the new thing unless for reasons explained the new thing cannot be divided.

Where chattels are commingled, the basic rule is that the owners of the two chattels share the greater whole as tenants in common according to their individual contributions. If A's 60,000 gallons of oil are mixed with B's 40,000 gallons, they share the 100,000 gallons in the ratio 3 : 2 and suffer any shrinkage occurring through neither party's fault in the bulk in the same proportion.[170]

If, nevertheless, the mixing occurs through the fault of either A or B, it is a different matter. In *F. S. Sandeman & Sons v Tyzack and Branfoot Shipping Co*,[171] certain dicta of Lord Moulton assert that, if the mixing of chattels belonging to A and B occurs through the fault of A (and fault might include negligence), B becomes the owner of the whole. Alive to some of the hardships this rule might cause, he sought to exclude this 'fundamental principle' where 'in extreme cases . . . [it] would lead to substantial injustice', citing this example:

> [I]f a small portion of the goods of 'B' became mixed with the goods of 'A' by a negligent act for which 'A' alone was liable, I think it quite possible that the law would prefer to view it as a conversion by 'A' of this small amount of 'B's' goods rather than do the substantial injustice of treating 'B' as the owner of the whole of the mixed mass.

A further softening of the law's attitude to wrongful mixers is evident in *Indian Oil Corpn v Greenstone Shipping SA*.[172] A consignment of 75,000 tons of Russian crude oil was loaded on a tanker bound for India. Already in the tanker was a quantity of 9,545 barrels of Iranian crude left over from an earlier voyage. The consignees of the Russian oil claimed to be entitled to the Iranian oil on the ground of the carrier's wrongful mixture but the court applied the tenancy in common rule of *Spence v Union Marine Insurance Co*. It was no longer appropriate to have a 'primitive' rule when there were 'modern and sophisticated methods of measurement . . . available'. The new rule was expressed as follows:

> [W]here B wrongfully mixes the goods of A with goods of his own, which are substantially of the same nature and quality, and they cannot in practice be separated, the mixture is held in common and A is entitled to receive out of it a quantity equal to that of his goods which went into the mixture, any doubt as to that quantity being resolved in favour of A. He is also entitled to claim damages

---

[170] *Spence v Union Marine Insurance Co* (1868) LR 3 CP 427.
[171] [1913] AC 680.   [172] [1987] 3 All ER 893.

from B in respect of any loss he may have suffered, in respect of quality or otherwise, by reason of the admixture.

The doubt referred to concerned uncertainty as to how much A had before the wrongful mixing. A more difficult problem would concern, for example, the wrongful mixture by B of B's grade 3 wheat with A's grade 1 wheat to produce a grade 2 blend. One possible solution would be to give A his *aliquot* share of the commingled grade 2 wheat together with damages for the difference in value between grade 2 and grade 1. Another solution would be to give A a larger quantity of grade 2 wheat equal in value to A's grade 1 wheat. The passage in *Indian Oil* quoted above would appear to favour the former of these solutions. Nevertheless, the latter solution is the more likely to be adopted. First, it is consistent with the views of Lord Millett on equitable tracing,[173] where his lordship would give the claimant a choice against a wrongdoer of either a proportionate share of the commingled mass or an equitable lien over that mass to the extent of the claimant's misapplied assets.[174] Secondly, it is favoured by Moore-Bick J in a similar case involving the blending of oil where a preference was stated for proportions that 'reflect both the quantity and the value of the oil' contributed, with 'any doubts about the quantity or value of the oil [to] be resolved against the wrongdoer'.[175] A final difficulty arising out of the *Indian Oil* case is that of shrinkage, not discussed in the case. If *Union Marine Insurance* were simply applied then there would be a rateable sharing of the loss between A and B. This might be the proper result where the mixing in no way contributes to the risk of shrinkage. Otherwise, it might be preferable to charge any shrinkage to B's share until it is exhausted.

FAILED TRANSFERS AND RESULTING TRUSTS

There is considerable doubt about when a resulting trust arises and when it operates to negative the transfer of a proprietary interest. To the extent that a resulting trust does the latter, it includes some of the cases previously examined in which a gift has been held to be incompletely constituted or ineffectual. An increasing awareness that proprietary rights have implications for insolvency distribution[176] and affect third parties,

---

[173] On tracing, see chapter 5.   [174] *Foskett v McKeown* [2000] 3 All ER 97.
[175] *Glencore International AG v Metro Trading Inc* [2001] 1 Lloyd's Rep 284.
[176] *Westdeutsche Landesbank Zentrale v Islington London Borough Council* [1996] AC 669.

suggests a degree of future judicial conservatism in inferring resulting (as well as constructive) trusts.

Resulting trusts are divided into automatic resulting trusts and presumed resulting trusts.[177] An automatic resulting trust arises where property is transferred to a trustee on a trust basis that is ineffectual because either the transfer fails to comply with the requirements of the law or the trusts themselves are never stated.[178] It does not depend for its inference on party intention but arises purely by operation of law. The transferor has in effect failed to divest himself of his property. For this reason, the property subject to the failed transfer should not revert to the Crown as *bona vacantia*.[179] Plowman J once observed that 'a man does not cease to own property simply by saying "I don't want it." If he tries to give it away the question must always be, has he succeeded in doing so or not.'[180] The second type of resulting trust, a presumed resulting trust, arises where the legal interest in property is transferred to another in circumstances where any intent of the transferor to alienate his beneficial interest in the property cannot be sufficiently determined and where there is no presumption of advancement to displace.[181] It also arises where property is transferred for a purpose on trust terms and subsists until that purpose is carried out.[182] It is not clear whether the intentional element takes the form of an unstated intention of the transferor that the property will revert if the transfer fails. It may, alternatively, be simply the absence of an intention to benefit the transferee.[183] The former approach is too artificial to be acceptable but has the merit of retaining strict judicial control over the recognition of resulting trusts. The danger with the latter approach is that it may be too prolific in giving rise to proprietary rights.[184] Nevertheless, one way of containing its proprietary potential is to demand evidence that rebuts any intention at all to benefit rather than

---

[177] Purchase money resulting trusts are a species of the latter.

[178] *Re Vandervell's Trusts (No. 2)* [1974] Ch 269 (Megarry J); *Vandervell v Inland Revenue Commissioners* [1967] 2 AC 291 at p 313 (Lord Upjohn).

[179] *Pace* Lord Browne-Wilkinson in *Westdeutsche Landesbank Zentrale v Islington London Borough Council* [1996] AC 669.

[180] *Inland Revenue Commissioners v Vandervell* [1966] Ch 261 at p 275.

[181] *Re Vandervell's Trusts (No. 2)* [1974] Ch 269.

[182] *Twinsectra Ltd v Yardley* [2002] UKHL 12; Bridge, 'The *Quistclose* Trust in a World of Secured Transactions' (1992) 12 Oxford Journal of Legal Studies 333.

[183] Chambers, R., *Resulting Trusts*, Oxford: Clarendon Press, 1997.

[184] Virgo, G., *The Principles of the Law of Restitution*, Oxford: Clarendon Press, 1999, p 620.

the more easily gathered evidence that rebuts an intention to enter into a specific type of transaction such as a gift.[185]

The role accorded to intention in the case of a presumed resulting trust is of critical importance in determining the number of *in rem* claims that might arise from mistaken gifts, and payments and moneys paid under void contracts. In *Chase Manhattan Bank v Israel-British Bank*,[186] the court found that a party mistakenly duplicating a payment retained a continuing equitable interest in the funds. The reasoning was sparse and no explicit reference was made to a resulting trust. The American authorities cited in support tended towards a constructive trust analysis of the problem. Since it does not treat the constructive trust as a remedial vehicle for the reversal of an unjust enrichment, English law would require the conscience of the payee to be bound in order for a constructive trust solution to be adopted. The *Chase Manhattan* decision came in for stern criticism from Lord Browne-Wilkinson in *Westdeutsche Landesbank Zentrale v Islington London Borough Council*,[187] where his lordship stressed that an equitable interest, separated from the legal interest, cannot be 'retained',[188] and that *Chase Manhattan* should have required knowledge by the payee of the mistaken payment for its conscience to be bound (though such knowledge on the facts arose some time after receipt of payment).

As the above reference to Lord Browne-Wilkinson's speech shows, the *Westdeutsche* case shows how the line between resulting and constructive trusts has not yet been satisfactorily settled. Nevertheless, an intention-driven resulting trust does not require the conscience of a transferee to be bound in order for the transferor to have a proprietary interest in the subject matter of the trust.[189] If conceptual difficulties concerning the one-step transfer of a bare legal interest can be overcome, then the conscience of the transferee becomes irrelevant because there is no need to require the transferee to do anything with a beneficial interest that he never acquired in the first place. Resulting trusts therefore often arise

---

[185] *Westdeutsche Landesbank Zentrale v Islington London Borough Council* [1996] AC 669 (Lord Goff) and Swadling, 'A New Role for Resulting Trusts?' (1996) 16 Legal Studies 110, both critical of Birks, 'Restitution and Resulting Trusts', in Goldstein, S. (ed), *Equity: Contemporary Legal Developments*, Jerusalem: Hamaccabi Press, 1992.

[186] [1981] 1 Ch 105.

[187] [1996] AC 669.

[188] See to similar effect Slade J in *Re Bond Worth Ltd* [1980] 1 Ch 228.

[189] Cf. Lord Browne-Wilkinson's introduction of the payee's conscience when referring to a resulting trust.

more quickly than constructive trusts: the latter may have to attend upon the receipt of information serving to bind the transferee's conscience.

The most important feature of *Westdeutsche* is that it stands as authority for the view that property transferred pursuant to a void contract does not thereby become the subject of a resulting trust. It therefore gives great comfort to those who criticize the proliferation of property rights that comes from the reflex application of equitable maxims, such as 'equity looks on that as done which ought to be done', without thought being given to the competing claims of the transferee's other creditors.[190] Lord Goff in *Westdeutsche* asks 'why should the plaintiff bank be given the additional benefits which flow from a proprietary claim, for example the benefit of achieving priority in the defendant's insolvency', when it already has a personal action for the recovery of money paid under a void contract? He does however appear to recognize that payment can be recovered by means of a resulting trust in cases of fundamental mistake. This concession provides a slender bridge to the intention of the transferor needed for a resulting trust to be inferred. If the decision in *Chase Manhattan* is still sound as an authority on resulting trusts, it is likely to be because the making of the second payment amounted to a fundamental mistake.

The role played in the modern law of resulting trusts by the intention of the transferor, coupled with the conclusion that the transfer of property under a void contract does not as such give rise to a resulting trust, invites a reconsideration of the established rule that non-monetary property transferred under a voidable contract reverts upon rescission to the transferor.[191] If the transferor is treated as having an equitable interest in the property from the beginning,[192] as opposed to a mere equity of rescission, it prompts the question why implied affirmation and delay—factors that prevent rescission—should serve to expropriate the transferor. More importantly, it makes no sense for a proprietary right to be retained, or exercised, under a voidable contract when, in more serious cases, no corresponding property right is retained under a void contract. In the case of a voidable contract, there was a clear intention to pass legal and beneficial title to the transferee.[193] This area of law is ripe for reappraisal.

---

[190] Goode, 'Proprietary Restitutionary Claims', in Cornish, W. R., Nolan, R., O'Sullivan, J. and Virgo, G. (eds), *Restitution: Past, Present and Future*, Oxford: Hart Publishing, 1998.

[191] *Re Eastgate* [1905] 1 KB 465.

[192] See *Daly v Sydney Stock Exchange Ltd* (1986) 160 CLR 371 (Brennan J); *Latec Investments Ltd v Hotel Terrigal Pty Ltd* (1965) 113 CLR 265, 290 (Menzies J); *Lonrho plc v Fayed (No. 2)* [1992] 1 WLR 1 (Millett J).

[193] See Worthington, 'Backdoor Security Devices' [1999] Insolvency Lawyer 153.

5

Transfer of title

INTRODUCTION

In the last chapter we examined the ways in which sellers and donors were able to pass (or convey) to buyers and donees their property interests in chattels. The relationships were bilateral and the property interest was merely transferred from one side of the relationship to the other. We are now going to consider a range of transactions with a tripartite or triangular dimension. The issue here is whether a transferor, seeking to pass a property interest to a transferee, is able to transfer a property interest superior to the one vested in the transferor. When able to do this, the transferor succeeds in derogating from (or overriding) the property interest of the true owner because the transferee is able to oppose that owner's property claim.

For the most part, this chapter will be concerned with the transfer of legal title, usually by way of sale or pledge (see chapter 7), at the expense of the true owner's legal property in the chattel. For the sake of completeness, however, we shall consider also the transfer of legal title at the expense of an equitable property interest. In this instance, many of the issues that could be raised, relating to the doctrine of equitable tracing, are more suitably dealt with in specialist books and courses on trusts.

OVERRIDING LEGAL PROPERTY INTERESTS

GENERAL

All title disputes can be simplified to involve three parties, O, R and T.

O, the owner, is unlawfully dispossessed of a chattel by, or is deceived into surrendering possession of it to, R, a rogue. R later enters into a transaction purporting to confer a legal interest on T, an innocent third party. Having obtained value, R then disappears leaving O and T to fight over entitlement to the chattel, typically by means of an action in conversion brought by O against T.[1] R can either not be found or else has

---

[1] See chapter 3.

dissipated his ill-gotten gains and is not worth suing. The chattel may pass through a series of innocent hands before reaching T, but this is just a further detail of the O–R–T triangle. R may not be a rogue in the true sense (though this is usually the case), but instead someone with mistaken assumptions of personal entitlement or of authority to act. This issue in no way complicates the above simplification of the title chain.

In title disputes, either O or T will lose; there can only be one winner. Furthermore, the law has declined to take losses of this kind and divide them down the middle between O and T.[2] Because of the difficulty this has caused, it is a commonplace observation in title dispute cases for the court to stress how invidious it is to visit a loss caused by a rogue upon one of two innocent parties. Furthermore, the tug of O's and T's competing interests is a particular embodiment of the irreconcilable conflict between two fundamental legal policies. First, there is the protection of private property, essential in any peaceful society. The unrestrained pursuit of this policy would favour O in all title disputes. On the other hand, there is the promotion of security in contractual dealings, essential in any society that has an exchange-driven economy and wishes to encourage the maximization of wealth through exchange. The unrestrained pursuit of this policy would favour T in any title dispute. This clash of opposites was stated as follows by Denning LJ in *Bishopsgate Motor Finance Corpn v Transport Brakes Ltd:*[3]

> In the development of our law, two principles have striven for mastery. The first is for the protection of property: no one can give a better title than he himself possesses. The second is for the protection of commercial transactions: the person who takes in good faith and for value without notice should get a good title. The first principle has held sway for a long time, but it has been modified by the common law itself and by statute so as to meet the needs of our own times.

Irreconcilable interests and policies often produce law that is difficult to justify in purely logical terms. This is particularly true of the body of law under present consideration. The law has started from the policy of property protection, expressed in the Latin principle *nemo dat quod non habet*. According to this, a transferor is able to transfer only such property interest as he himself has. Upon this general rule there has been grafted a series of exceptions designed to create a pragmatic balance with the

---

[2] Law Reform Committee, *Transfer of Title to Chattels*, 12th Report 1966, Cmnd. 2958; *cf. Ingram v Little* [1961] 1 QB 31, *per* Devlin LJ.

[3] [1949] 1 KB 322.

policy of commercial security. As a coherent whole, the law leaves, as we shall see, a great deal to be desired. The rule and exceptions are to be found at common law and in various statutes (notably the Factors Act 1889 and the Sale of Goods Act 1979). The provisions of the Sale of Goods Act 1979[4] cover much of the ground but only apply where at least one of the O–R and R–T transactions is a contract of sale. The common law remains applicable to transactions not explicitly covered in the Sale of Goods Act 1979 and other statutes. This chapter will deal with a selective number of the various exceptions to the *nemo dat* rule.

The legal property interest at risk of being eclipsed by the rogue's dealings is usually ownership. But it is possible for the person duped or dispossessed by the rogue to be a bailee. The bailee (as we saw in chapter 3) is able to rely upon his possession or right to immediate possession in maintaining an action in conversion. The rule of *nemo dat quod non habet*, with its various exceptions, will qualify the success of such an action.

Suppose now that the bailor is the rogue. If, contrary to earlier argument,[5] a bailee's possessory interest does not survive the transfer of ownership by the bailor, the position is as follows. The transferee will obtain ownership of the chattel unencumbered by any right of the bailee to the possession of the chattel. The bailee should look to the bailor for redress, either in contract or in the tort of conversion.[6] Even on this assumption, the bailee may in some cases have a property right that survives the transfer of ownership by the bailor, though it may be imperilled by one or more exceptions to the rule of *nemo dat*. One example is the interest of a pledgee[7] whose common law power of sale makes him more than a simple bailee, which survives the temporary release of pledged shipping documents to the pledgor under the terms of a trust.[8]

COMMON LAW EXCEPTIONS TO THE RULE OF *NEMO DAT*

The Sale of Goods Act 1979 codifies a number of exceptions to the *nemo dat* rule whose origin lies in the common law. Section 21 refers to agency, not an exception at all, since the act of the authorized agent is the act of the principal, who owns the chattel. But agency by estoppel (or apparent authority) is a different matter. The same provision restates in brief form the common law rule that the owner will be estopped from denying the title of a third party where the owner allows an unauthorized individual, who may be exceeding a limited authority or purporting to exercise a

---

[4] Sections 21–26.   [5] See chapter 2.   [6] See *Roberts v Wyatt* (1810) 2 Taunt 268.
[7] See chapter 7.   [8] See chapter 7.

non-existent authority, to appear to be acting with authority. An extension of this rule binds the owner who permits someone else to appear as the true owner in dealings with third parties.

The second common law exception, to be found in s 23 provides that, if title is transferred to a rogue under a voidable contract, the rogue has the power to transmit a good title at any time until the owner avoids the contract. Until its abolition by the Sale of Goods (Amendment) Act 1995, a third common law exception, codified as s 22(1) of the Sale of Goods Act 1979, existed to protect purchasers of goods in market overt. A market overt was a market incorporated by charter, custom or local statute. When this exception applied to protect a purchaser, the circumstances by which the goods came to be in the market were irrelevant. This exception created the closest thing possible to an absolute title.

Apparent authority

The appearance of authority must be created by the owner and not by the supposed agent, the rogue.[9] It is not in practice an easy exception for the third party, who carries the burden of establishing it, to make out. It may consist of a representation made by the owner to the third party[10] or to the world at large. Most often, it will consist of the owner's conduct in placing an agent in a position that in the experience of the commercial world carries a certain authority, without making it outwardly clear that the agent's authority has in the particular case been limited.

Apparent authority is best understood by looking at a number of case law examples. In *Eastern Distributors Ltd v Goldring*, the owner of a van wished to acquire a car but did not have sufficient money to put down a hire purchase deposit. Responding to the dealer's suggestion that the van be used to provide the deposit, the owner colluded with the dealer to create a sham transaction. This involved deceiving the finance company into believing that the owner wished to acquire, on hire purchase terms, both the van and the car. The finance company would then buy both vehicles from the dealer before leasing them on hire purchase terms to the owner. As between owner and dealer, the value of the van would serve as the required deposit for both van and car hire purchase transactions. The owner signed hire purchase proposal forms that represented the dealer to be the owner of the van. The finance company accepted the proposal for the van but turned down the one for the car. It paid the dealer for the

[9] *Colonial Bank v Cady* (1890) 15 App Cas 257.
[10] *Eastern Distributors Ltd v Goldring* [1957] 2 QB 600.

van but the dealer failed to inform the owner of this awkward turn of events. When a title dispute erupted between the finance company and the owner of the van, the former succeeded since the owner was estopped by his representation from denying that the dealer owned the van. In the opinion of Devlin J, the finance company's title was a real one. It could subsequently be transferred by the finance company in the normal way and was not merely a procedural defence that the finance company alone, as opposed to a later transferee from the finance company not privy to the estoppel, could raise against the original owner. A similar decision would have been reached if the owner had represented that someone had an authority to act on his behalf when no such authority in fact existed. For estoppel by representation to succeed, the statement of the owner must be unequivocal. A statement by an agent for the finance company owner of a car, that it has on its books no record of a hire purchase agreement in respect of the car, will not be inflated into a statement that no such hire purchase agreement exists.[11]

Estoppel by conduct generates more problems in practice than estoppel by representation. The basic point here is that an estoppel does not arise merely because the owner permits someone else to possess a chattel so as to take advantage of the practical opportunity thus acquired to deceive others. The law has long been sensitive to the undesirability of finding an estoppel in the simple entrustment of a chattel by a master to a servant.[12] There must be something more on the part of the owner to raise the estoppel. In the Saskatchewan case of *McVicar v Herman*,[13] an owner permitted an employee to keep possession of his car, without taking effective steps to recover it, long after the employment relationship had been terminated. In the meantime, the former employee renewed the car registration in his own name and traded it in with a garage, which verified the registration and found no encumbrances against the car when it conducted a search. All that the owner had done was to put the former employee into a position whereby he was able to deceive others, which was insufficient to constitute an estoppel. This case shows how difficult it is to infer an unequivocal representation from conduct.[14]

Similarly, in *Farquarson Bros and Co v King*[15] the estoppel plea failed. A

---

[11] See *Moorgate Mercantile Co Ltd v Twitchings* [1977] AC 890.

[12] See Lord Macnaghten in *Farquarson Bros and Co v King and Co* [1902] AC 325.

[13] (1958) 13 DLR (2d) 419.

[14] See also *Jerome v Bentley* [1952] 2 All ER 114.

[15] *Cf.* the Canadian Supreme Court decision in *Canadian Laboratory Supplies Ltd v Englehard Industries Ltd* [1980] 2 SCR 450 and *Henderson & Co v Williams* [1895] 1 QB 521.

firm of timber merchants gave their confidential clerk authority to complete sales with their established customers and informed the warehouse where the timber was stored that the clerk's delivery orders were to be honoured, but the warehouse was not informed that the clerk's authority was a limited one. Assuming the identity of 'a phantom broker [with] the plain and unpretentious name of Brown', the rogue ordered the warehouse to transfer a quantity into the name of Brown by issuing a delivery order in Brown's favour. Using the name of Brown, the clerk then sold the timber to the defendant company and endorsed the delivery order, using his fictitious name of Brown, in favour of the defendant. There was nothing said or done by the claimant firm of timber merchants amounting to a representation that the clerk or someone called Brown had authority to transfer the timber to the defendant so the latter's estoppel plea failed.

Indicia of title

Attempts have been made to bolster the estoppel plea by asserting that the owner has not merely delivered the chattel to the rogue but has also surrendered possession of an indefinable extra called an *indicium* of title. We saw earlier[16] that only a very limited number of documents passed the common law test of a document of title in order for their delivery to be tantamount to delivery of the chattel itself. We shall see later that various statutory exceptions to the *nemo dat* rule have extended the meaning of document of title for this purpose. In each of these two cases, the question is to what extent a document can serve as a substitute for the chattel. If delivery of the chattel is not sufficiently suggestive of ownership or authority of the person to whom it is delivered, the delivery of a document instead will be no more effective to create an estoppel.[17]

When it comes to *indicia* of title, however, we are concerned with documents that pass neither the common law nor the extended statutory test of a document of title, yet are so suggestive of ownership that their transfer, along with the chattel itself, is considered by some to create an appearance of ownership or authority that a bare delivery of the chattel itself would not produce. In *Central Newbury Car Auctions Ltd v Unity Finance Ltd*,[18] a rogue obtained possession from the claimant garage of a

---

[16] See chapter 2.

[17] *Mercantile Bank of India v Central Bank of India* [1938] AC 287; cf. *Commonwealth Trust Ltd v Akotey* [1926] AC 72.

[18] [1957] 1 QB 371.

car, along with its logbook, when he traded in his own vehicle as the deposit on a proposed hire purchase of the car. The finance company declined the hire purchase proposal for the car and the garage subsequently discovered that the rogue's own vehicle was stolen. The rogue later sold the car to a dealer who in turn sold it to the defendant finance company in connection with a hire purchase agreement. The rogue's actions were undoubtedly assisted by the fact that the logbook contained the name of the previous owner, who had supplied the car to the garage. This previous owner had not signed his name in the logbook, so it was a simple matter for the rogue to sign on his behalf and later pass himself off as this previous owner. By a majority decision, the Court of Appeal ruled that the garage was not estopped from denying the authority of the rogue to sell the car. The logbook, though often associated in the lay mind with ownership, was not in any sense a document of title and its delivery to the rogue, along with the car, made no difference. In dissent, Denning LJ was of the view that the behaviour of the claimant garage, in delivering this *indicium* of title at the same time as it intended to divest itself of the car (though in favour of a finance company under the first abortive hire purchase agreement), created a sufficient appearance of authority to give rise to an estoppel.

Estoppel by negligence

In the past, unavailing attempts have been made to assert that the negligence of an owner is so peculiarly suggestive of apparent ownership or authority as to tip the balance in favour of the innocent purchaser. Sometimes reliance has been placed in vain on a worn *dictum* of Ashhurst J in *Lickbarrow v Mason*[19] that 'whenever one of two innocent persons must suffer by the acts of a third, he who has enabled such third person to occasion the loss must sustain it'. This is too serious a threat to private property to be tolerated in a legal system that creates rather circumscribed exceptions to a strong *nemo dat* rule. In any case, it is not easy to see what the negligence of the owner adds to the appearance created by the delivery of the chattel.

In *Moorgate Mercantile Co Ltd v Twitchings*,[20] the House of Lords, by a bare majority, held that a failure to register a hire purchase agreement under a voluntary trade registration scheme did not involve a breach of duty on the part of the finance company owner of a car towards persons

---

[19] (1787) 2 TR 63.
[20] [1977] AC 890; see also *Mercantile Credit Ltd v Hamblin* [1965] 2 QB 242.

dealing with the rogue in possession. The great majority (though not quite all) of hire purchase agreements were registered, since most finance companies belonged to the registration scheme. Developments in the tort of negligence occurring in the last decade, striking at the heart of economic loss liability, make the innocent purchaser's prospects for a change in the law look exceedingly bleak. Estoppel has proved to be a rather weak source of protection for such purchasers. It should also be noted that the claimant's own contributory negligence is no defence to an action for conversion.[21]

Voidable title

If a rogue fraudulently assumes the identity of someone else when buying a chattel, it is a question of some importance to know if the contract thus concluded is void for unilateral mistake or merely voidable for misrepresentation (see the standard contract texts). If the contract is void, it is wholly ineffective to transfer title to the rogue and thence to the innocent third party.[22] If the contract is voidable, the rogue will have title to the chattel (assuming the owner's general property passed under the contract of sale to the rogue).[23] The effect of rescission, however, is that title will revest in the owner. Nevertheless, it is one of the conventional bars to rescission that it will not be permitted if, in the meantime, a third party has acquired an interest in the subject matter of the contract. This position is expressed in s 23 of the Sale of Goods Act 1979:

> When the seller of goods has a voidable title to them, but this title has not been avoided at the time of the sale, the buyer acquires a good title to the goods, provided he buys them in good faith and without notice of the seller's defect of title.

Apart from the distinction between voidness and voidability, the most troublesome issue arising from this *nemo dat* exception concerns the steps that the defrauded owner must take to demonstrate an intention to rescind the contract. On the one hand, anything that falls short of notifying third parties, coming into contact with the rogue, of the rescission deprives them of the effective means of protecting themselves. On the other hand, the rogue will usually have disappeared without leaving a forwarding address, thus making it impossible to inform those who deal

---

[21] Torts (Interference with Goods) Act 1977, s 11(1).

[22] *Cundy v Lindsay* (1878) 3 App Cas 459; *Hudson v Shogun Finance Ltd* [2001] EWCA Civ 1000.

[23] *Lewis v Averay* [1972] 1 QB 198.

with the rogue. Furthermore, third parties dealing with the rogue will be unaware of the circumstances in which the rogue acquired possession of the chattel: it is not easy to see how they have been any more deceived by outward appearances than those third parties who claim that surrendering possession to a rogue raises an estoppel.

The authoritative view is that any outward act by the third party that reveals an intention to disavow the contract with the rogue will suffice to rescind the contract. Apart from the general judicial discretion in the Misrepresentation Act 1967[24] to order damages in lieu of rescission, rescission is a self-executing remedy. It certainly does not depend upon the consent of the rogue. If the owner is able to confront the rogue, anything that suggests the rogue is being given a second chance to pay will negative rescission. This happened in an Albertan case where the owner told the rogue at a police station that all he wanted was his money.[25]

A clear intention to rescind the contract will be shown if the owner succeeds in recovering the goods.[26] The owner, however, was unable to do this in *Car and Universal Finance Co v Caldwell*.[27] In that case,[28] as soon as the rogue's worthless cheque was dishonoured, the owner sought the help of the police and a motoring organization in finding the car. This behaviour was seen, with little discussion, as evidencing the owner's election to rescind the contract. Though the court accepted the rule that an election to rescind should normally be communicated to the other contracting party, this requirement of communication was dispensed with when a rogue put it out of the owner's power to communicate. This appears to be a type of estoppel. What is perhaps curious, though it is entirely consistent with other strands of *nemo dat* law, is that the rights of the third party are defined in terms of the contractual rights and duties of owner and rogue.[29]

The Law Reform Committee[30] was of the view that the protection given to purchasers by the voidable title exception to *nemo dat* had largely been destroyed by the decision in *Car and Universal Finance Co v Caldwell*. It recommended that the owner should have to communicate an election to rescind to the rogue, which would for practical purposes

---

[24] See s 2(2).   [25] *Jim Spicer Chev Olds Inc v Kinniburgh* [1978] 1 WWR 253.

[26] *Re Eastgate* [1905] 1 KB 465.

[27] [1965] 1 QB 525.

[28] See also *Newtons of Wembley Ltd v Williams* [1965] 1 QB 560.

[29] See also *Lewis v Averay*, *per* Megaw LJ.

[30] 12th Report, *Transfer of Title to Chattels*, Cmnd 2958, 1966.

convert the rogue's voidable title into a fully effective one. Once again, this recommendation was not enacted.

A final point concerns the third party's good faith. The Court of Appeal in *Whitehorn Brothers v Davison*[31] held that the burden of demonstrating the absence of good faith should, in accordance with the normal forensic rules of proof, fall on the claimant owner. This is strangely inconsistent with the general law on *nemo dat* which would put the burden on the third party of showing why the owner's title ought in the special circumstances to be displaced. The third party, moreover, is in possession of the information relating to his dealings with the rogue. The *Whitehorn Brothers* approach might not work if the police, in possession of the goods, interpleaded when faced with competing claims, and should not work if the owner has already repossessed the goods so as to be the defendant in the action. It is not obvious, public policy considerations apart, why there should be a requirement of good faith at all. Section 23 of the Sale of Goods Act 1979 requires it, but that provision applies only to cases where the transaction between rogue and third party is one of sale (as opposed to pledge). The rogue's title, while liable to be avoided, is a real, common law title. That is what the third party gets, not an equitable title that needs to be supported by clean hands.

SPECIAL STATUTORY EXCEPTIONS TO THE RULE OF *NEMO DAT*

A number of exceptions that had to be created by statute, having no prior common law existence, need to be considered. The major general exceptions are mercantile agency,[32] the seller in possession[33] and the buyer in possession.[34] A detailed treatment of these exceptions is best left to specialist texts on commercial law, likewise a number of other statutory exceptions to the *nemo dat* rule.

Mercantile agency

In the nineteenth century, legislation was passed which had the practical consequence of providing a statutory extension to the common law estoppel exception. The present text is s 2(1) of the Factors Act 1889 which provides:

Where a mercantile agent is, with the consent of the owner, in possession of

---

[31] [1911] 1 KB 463; see also *Thomas v Heelas*, 27 November 1986 (CAT No. 1065).
[32] Factors Act 1889, s 2.
[33] Factors Act 1889, s 8; Sale of Goods Act 1979, s 24.
[34] Factors Act 1889, s 9; Sale of Goods Act 1979, s 25.

goods or of the documents of title to goods, any sale, pledge, or other disposition of the goods, made by him when acting in the ordinary course of business of a mercantile agent, shall, subject to the provisions of this Act, be as valid as if he were expressly authorised by the owner of the goods to make the same; provided that the person taking under the disposition acts in good faith, and has not at the time of the disposition notice that the person making the disposition has not authority to make the same.

A number of points in this provision (for example, good faith) are common to all the *nemo dat* exceptions; others (such as 'documents of title' and 'disposition') are common to a number of the special statutory exceptions. Each element that is relevant to more than one *nemo dat* exception will be discussed under the most convenient exception for this purpose. The nub of s 2(1) is that a transaction entered into by the mercantile agent will, where the requirements of the provision have been satisfied, be deemed to have been authorized by the owner of the goods who has entrusted them to the mercantile agent's possession. Where the agent acts in accordance with the principal's mandate, there is of course no need to invoke a *nemo dat* exception at all.

A mercantile agent is 'a mercantile agent having in the customary course of his business as such agent authority either to sell goods, or to consign goods for the purpose of sale, or to buy goods, or to raise money on the security of goods'.[35] The word 'factor', a type of nineteenth-century purchasing agent who has in the twentieth century been transmuted into a financier, appears only in the title of the Act. Instead, the Act attempts to encompass, under the broad heading of 'mercantile agent', a number of different commercial intermediaries in established positions whose possession of goods is suggestive of authority or ownership. The category comprises for the most part established selling agents like brokers and auctioneers. It excludes carriers[36] and warehousemen[37] since, though both take possession of goods in a commercial capacity, they do not perform any of the functions listed in s 1(1). It also excludes employees.[38]

The definition of mercantile agent includes retail sellers and car dealers,[39] provided they do not make it a practice to sell exclusively their own goods.[40] It has also been held that someone can be a mercantile agent who

---

[35] Factors Act 1889, s 1(1).   [36] *Monk v Whittenbury* (1831) 2 B & Ad 484.
[37] *Cole v North Western Bank* (1875) LR 10 CP 354.
[38] *Lamb v Attenborough* (1862) 1 B & S 831.
[39] *Folkes v King* [1923] 1 KB 282.
[40] *Belvoir Finance Co v Harold G Cole & Co* [1969] 1 WLR 1877.

is acting as such for the first time.[41] Thus in *Lowther v Harris*,[42] an established antiques dealer took on a special commission to show potential purchasers antique furniture and tapestry belonging to his principal and displayed in his principal's home. In so acting, he was a mercantile agent. Nevertheless, a person with no settled commercial occupation is not a mercantile agent merely because he is entrusted with jewellery to solicit offers from people in his social circle.[43]

It is not enough that a mercantile agent be given possession of goods. A well established judicial gloss requires that the goods be possessed by the mercantile agent in his capacity as a mercantile agent.[44] Thus a car hire company receiving a car for the purpose of hiring it out does not receive it as a mercantile agent:[45] receipt for the purpose of hiring out is not one of the functions of a mercantile agent listed in s 1(1). This qualification is designed to protect owners entrusting goods to someone with a dual capacity, only one of which fits the definition of a mercantile agent. An owner is therefore not at risk in entrusting a car for repair to a car repairer, or a watch to a watch repairer, because the car repairer and the watch repairer are also dealers in second-hand cars and watches, whether the owner knows this or not.[46]

Consent to mercantile agent's possession

The owner must consent to the mercantile agent's possession of the goods. Fraud on the part of the agent will not destroy the validity of the consent.[47] Consent was not even destroyed for the purpose of the Factors Act 1889 when the agent committed the old offence of larceny by a trick[48] since it was not the owner's intention to pass the property in the goods to the agent.[49] The same was true for other exceptions to *nemo dat* based upon the possession of the rogue.[50]

In establishing the owner's consent for the purpose of s 2 of the Factors Act 1889, the third party is assisted by a number of statutory presumptions: first, that a mercantile agent with the actual custody of goods is in possession of them;[51] and secondly, that the possession of the mercantile

---

[41] *Heyman v Flewker* (1863) 15 CB(NS) 519.   [42] [1927] 1 KB 393.
[43] *Jerome v Bentley* [1952] 2 All ER 114.   [44] *Cole v North Western Bank.*
[45] *Astley Industrial Trust v Miller* [1968] 2 All ER 36.
[46] *Cole v North Western Bank*, *per* Blackburn J.
[47] *Cahn v Pockett's Bristol Channel Co* [1899] 1 QB 643, *per* Collins LJ.
[48] *Folkes v King* [1923] 1 KB 282.
[49] *Cf.* voidable title under s 23 of the Sale of Goods Act 1979.
[50] Buyers and sellers in possession: *Du Jardin v Beadman Bros* [1952] 2 QB 712.
[51] Section 1(2).

agent is with the owner's consent.[52] In addition, the consent once given is irrebuttably deemed to continue despite the owner's retraction of it, provided that the third party dealing with the rogue does so in good faith and without notice of the retraction.[53] Thus mercantile agency departs significantly from voidable title.[54] It is not easy to make actual contact with the third party once the rogue disappears.

Mercantile agent's dealing with the goods

The third party dealing with the mercantile agent obtains good title under any 'sale, pledge, or other disposition of the goods' if the agent was 'acting in the ordinary course of business of a mercantile agent'. The nature of the transaction will be discussed under a later *nemo dat* exception. The issue for the moment is the nature of an ordinary course disposition.

The expansion of mercantile agency to cover a wide range of commercial activities and occupations has made it difficult to apply this test. This difficulty has been compounded by the application of the test to certain categories of agent who transact business, sometimes on their own account and sometimes for a principal, named, unnamed or even undisclosed. It follows that a third party may be protected who believes that he is dealing with the owner of the goods. This aspect of the matter, and the interpretation of s 2 of the Factors Act 1889 that it compelled the court to adopt, is brought out in the leading case of *Oppenheimer v Attenborough & Son*.[55] The owner of certain diamonds entrusted them, for the purpose of showing to potential purchasers, to a diamond broker who had in the past conducted business on his own account as a diamond merchant. The broker fraudulently pledged the diamonds with the defendant pawnbroker, who had had prior dealings with the broker in his earlier capacity of merchant and believed that he was dealing with a merchant. It was well known that diamond brokers did not in normal cases possess authority to pledge their principals' goods for advances; this was, however, a common enough practice for diamond merchants seeking short-term finance. The question was whether 'acting in the normal course of business of a mercantile agent' referred to the business of that type of mercantile agent who was a diamond broker. If this were so, the owner would win in his title dispute with the third party since the latter

---

[52] Section 2(4).   [53] Section 2(2).
[54] See *Car and Universal Finance Co v Caldwell* [1965] 1 QB 525.
[55] [1908] 1 KB 221.

could not reasonably expect the broker to have authority to act in the way he did. The Court of Appeal, faced with this intractable problem, decided that the ordinary course of business referred in a non-specific way to business-like behaviour common to agents in general, such as attendance at places of business and the observance of normal business hours. The transaction in the present case satisfied this very bland test.

The ordinary course requirement, however, will not be satisfied if the agent sends a friend into the pawnbroker's premises,[56] for commercial agents do not behave like this. Similarly, the third party failed in one case[57] where the agent allowed the price paid by the purchaser to be set off against a debt owed personally by the agent to the purchaser.

Documents of title

We saw earlier[58] that the common law took a rather narrow view of documents of title, limiting the concept to certain bills of lading. For the purposes of mercantile agency (and of the seller and buyer in possession exceptions to *nemo dat*), the expression 'documents of title' is more broadly understood to include a wide array of documents whose possession is suggestive of authority or ownership. Thus s 1(4) of the Factors Act 1889 defines the expression as including:

> any bill of lading, dock warrant, warehouse-keeper's certificate, and warrant or order for the delivery of goods, and . . . any other document used in the ordinary course of business as proof of the possession or control of goods, or authorising or purporting to authorise, either by endorsement or by delivery, the possessor of the document to transfer or receive goods thereby represented.

There would appear to be no need that the document be made out in negotiable form;[59] the question whether any particular document passed the test would appear to depend heavily upon commercial usage and context. Once a mercantile agent is entrusted with the document of title, this entrustment will continue even if the agent surrenders the document of title to the bailee for a fresh document—as where a delivery order is handed in for a delivery warrant—or obtains the goods from the bailee. Similarly, an agent has consent to the possession of a document of title if possession of goods was given and thus the means of depositing the goods with a bailee in return for a document of title.[60]

---

[56] *De Gorter v Attenborough and Son* (1904) 19 TLR 19.
[57] *Lloyds and Scottish Finance v Williamson* [1965] 1 All ER 641.
[58] Chapter 2.
[59] Cf. *Mercantile Bank of India v Central Bank of India* [1938] AC 287.
[60] Section 2(3).

Good faith and notice

The Factors Act 1889 does not define good faith but it would be most strange if it did not attract the Sale of Goods Act 1979 definition of honesty in fact. It is likely that good faith is the same thing as the absence of notice that the mercantile agent is exceeding the authority conferred by the owner, since in commercial matters the law has resisted the bringing in of equitable doctrines of constructive notice.[61] Notice, however, may exist where there had been wilful blindness and might arise where an unusually low price is paid for a car.[62] Care should be taken in applying this approach to goods whose value is notoriously imprecise, such as second-hand cars.

Seller in possession

When it was held that the mercantile agency exception did not include the seller left in possession of goods after the sale,[63] Parliament was prompt in responding with a new *nemo dat* exception to fit the case. This new provision later became s 8 of the Factors Act 1889 as well as, coincidentally, the almost identical s 24 of the Sale of Goods Act 1979.

According to s 24 of the Sale of Goods Act 1979, a seller who 'continues or is' in possession of goods or documents of title to goods, after selling them to the buyer, is able to deliver or transfer them to a third party, as though authorized by the owner to do so. The goods have to be sold, which means that the seller's property will have passed to the first buyer under the sale contract.[64] If the transaction with the first buyer is only an agreement to sell, the seller will be able to transmit title to the second buyer in accordance with the *nemo dat* rule itself for no exception to the rule is needed where the seller is still the owner. The reference to owner in s 24 itself means that first buyer, who has become the owner.[65] Although the provision merely deems the authorization of delivery of the goods or transfer of documents of title by the owner (the first buyer), the better view is that these actions have to be read as pursuant to the transactions under which they occur. A second buyer would get very little relief under s 24 if it only amounted to immunity from liability in conversion for receipt of the goods. This would fall well short of the acquisition of

---

[61] *Manchester Trust v Furness* [1895] 2 QB 39; *cf. Macmillan Inc. v Bishopsgate Trust (No. 3)* [1995] 1 WLR 978, at p 1000.
[62] *Heap v Motorists' Advisory Agency* [1923] 1 KB 577.
[63] *Johnson v Credit Lyonnais* (1877) 3 CPD 32.
[64] Sale of Goods Act 1979, s 1.   [65] See below.

title; the second buyer would be vulnerable to a demand for the return of the goods made by the first buyer.

Consequently, the second buyer taking delivery under a sale acquires full title to the goods at the expense of the first buyer (but not of course at the expense of the true owner if the seller had no right to sell in the first place). Going beyond s 24 of the Sale of Goods Act 1979, s 8 of the Factors Act 1889 protects this second buyer if the goods are received under an agreement to sell. If, subsequently, the property passes to the second buyer under the contract with the seller, then a sale has occurred to the second buyer who therefore is protected by s 8. But what if the second buyer is paying for the goods on an instalment basis, the property being retained by the seller until payment in full, when the first buyer appears? If this instalment contract is deemed to be authorized by the first buyer, as it should be, then the second buyer may continue paying the instalments to the seller in the normal way. Nevertheless, the result of proceedings brought by the first buyer against the seller for converting the goods may well include a garnishee order directing the second buyer to make the payments to the first buyer.

The seller's possession

Apart from actual possession, the seller is deemed to be in possession of the goods for the purpose of s 8 of the Factors Act 1889 when they are held by a third party 'subject to his [i.e. the seller's] control, or for him or on his behalf'.[66] In one case,[67] the second transaction was a pledge of certain furs, accomplished when the warehouse in possession of the goods surrendered them directly to the pledgee at the seller's direction. The court upheld the pledgee's title at the expense of the first buyer. In many such instances, the seller will make use of a document of title (as defined by s 1(4)), such as a delivery warrant.

The leading case on s 24 of the Sale of Goods Act 1979 is *Pacific Motor Auctions Ltd v Motor Credits Ltd*,[68] which makes two critical points about the seller's possession. Under the terms of a 'floor plan', a car dealer sold its stock-in-trade to a finance company, repaying the finance company the price of individual cars when these were sold to consumer buyers, as the dealer was at liberty to do under the plan. The cars did not leave the dealer's possession until delivery was taken by the consumer buyers. The

---

[66] Factors Act 1889, s 1(2).
[67] *City Fur Manufacturing Co v Fureenbond Ltd* [1937] 1 All ER 799.
[68] [1965] AC 867.

dealer got into financial difficulties and its licence to dispose of the cars was revoked by the finance company. Before the cars were repossessed, however, the dealer sold a number of the cars to one of its creditors, an auction company. The cars were paid for by cheque, which was then indorsed back to the auction company in settlement of the debt owed to it. The Privy Council held that the auction company had acquired a good title to the disputed cars. First of all, the Board rejected the finance company's argument that the seller had to hold in the capacity of seller in order to transmit title under s 24 (declining to follow the earlier case of *Staffs Motor Guarantee Ltd v British Wagon Co.*[69] It had been the finance company's contention that the dealer was holding the cars as bailee under a financing plan. As Lord Pearson expressed it: 'The object of the section is to protect an innocent purchaser who is deceived by the vendor's physical possession of goods or documents and who is inevitably unaware of legal rights which fetter the apparent power to dispose'. The mercantile agency authorities, requiring the mercantile agent to hold in his capacity as such,[70] were not followed.

The second major point about possession concerned the continuity of the seller's possession. The Privy Council, in contrast with its holding that the nature of the seller's possession did not matter, held that the seller had to remain continuously in possession in order to be able to transmit title under s 24. Consequently, the buyer of a car taking it back to the dealer for servicing or warranty repairs does not run a risk under s 24. Since the section refers to a seller who 'continues *or is* in possession' (emphasis added), the words 'or is' had to be explained away as referring to a case where the first sale occurred at a time when the seller was not yet in possession,[71] for it cannot be said there that the seller 'continues' in possession after that sale and up to the date of the second transaction.

Sale, pledge or other disposition

If the second transaction is a pledge,[72] then the pledgee acquires against the first buyer the special property of a pledgee since that is all that the seller purportedly transfers. The real difficulty here is the meaning of 'other disposition'. At first glance, it could include a gift, an almost unimaginable conclusion given the conservative way that the law has allowed exceptions to *nemo dat*. Furthermore, s 5 of the Factors Act 1889,

---

[69] [1934] 2 KB 305. See also *Michael Gerson (Leasing) Ltd v Wilkinson* [2001] 1 All ER 148 (CA).

[70] See above.

[71] See also *Mitchell v Jones* (1905) 24 NZLR 932.   [72] See chapter 7.

though contained in a part of the legislation headed 'Dispositions by Mercantile Agents', and not in the part headed 'Dispositions by Sellers and Buyers of Goods', defines, in accordance with normal contractual principles, the 'consideration [that is] necessary for the validity of a sale, pledge, or other disposition'. One way or another, there will be a need for consideration under the second transaction.

The meaning of 'other disposition' was considered on the unusual facts of *Worcester Works Finance v Cooden Engineering Co.*[73] A car was sold by the respondent company to a rogue who paid for it with a cheque that was later dishonoured. Before the respondent could avoid the transaction, the rogue sold the car to the appellant finance company in pursuance of a transaction by which a confederate of the rogue was supposed to receive the car from the appellant on the usual hire purchase terms. Unknown to the appellant, however, the transaction was a sham; the car never left the possession of the rogue, who for a time kept up the confederate's hire purchase payments before defaulting. Before the appellant could repossess the car, a representative of the respondent traced the car and, with the rogue's consent, repossessed it in return for an undertaking not to pursue the rogue on the cheque. The Court of Appeal held that the second transaction between the respondent and the rogue was a Sale of Goods Act 1979, s 24 disposition that overrode the appellant's title acquired on the sale to it by the rogue. According to Megaw LJ, a disposition occurred where there was 'some transfer of an interest in property, in the technical sense of the word "property," as contrasted with mere possession'. Lord Denning would have found a s 24 disposition ('a very wide word') whenever 'a new interest (legal or equitable) in the property is effectually created'. The reference to equitable interests is controversial, since it is a fundamental principle of title transfer (see below) that equitable interests do not override legal interests.

Buyer in possession

As in the case of the seller in possession, there are parallel, though slightly different, *nemo dat* exceptions in the Factors Act 1889[74] and the Sale of Goods Act 1979.[75] Where the seller permits someone who has bought or agreed to buy goods to take possession of them, then any sale, pledge or other disposition of the goods entered into by the buyer in possession will be treated as authorized by the seller. Where the transaction entered into by the buyer is itself only an agreement to sell, the

---

[73] [1972] 1 QB 210.   [74] Section 9.   [75] Section 25.

sub-buyer receiving the goods on reservation of title terms until payment is made, then the sub-buyer will not obtain title as against the seller.[76] The party dealing with the buyer must do so in good faith and without notice of the seller's interest and, besides actually providing value,[77] must take delivery of the goods (a transfer in the case of documents of title, which includes their delivery). At first sight it is not easy to see why the section should apply if the buyer has 'bought' the goods, for surely the buyer ought to be able to transfer title under the normal *nemo dat* rule. It is possible, however, for an unpaid seller's lien to persist despite a temporary release of the goods[78] and s 25 would defeat this lien. Furthermore, a buyer would be able to transmit title under s 25 even if the seller has avoided a sale for fraudulent misrepresentation. The consequences of this distinction between ss 23 and 25 will be considered below.

Delivery by the buyer

For a third party dealing with the buyer to be protected, the buyer must voluntarily[79] deliver the goods or transfer the documents of title, as the case may be, to a transferee receiving the same. The question here is whether a delivery and receipt of the goods may take place by constructive means. Suppose that the buyer warehouses the goods and the warehouseman attorns to a third party purchasing the goods from the buyer in possession. In *Nicholson v Harper*,[80] a seller in possession case, the second transaction was a pledge of the goods to the warehouse that was already holding them to the seller's order. The court held that a delivery for the purpose of s 24 had not taken place. A different and, it is submitted, preferable view is taken in the Australian buyer in possession case of *Gamer's Motor Centre Ltd v Natwest Whole Australia Ltd*.[81] It concerned a floor plan for financing cars already in a dealer's possession under an agreement to sell. The question was whether the dealer, the buyer in possession, transmitted a good title to a floor plan financier that bought the goods from the dealer and bailed them back to him. The cars did not leave the dealer's possession under the floor plan. The Australian High Court held that in these circumstances a constructive transfer of possession to the financier, sufficient to satisfy s 25, had taken place. The same

---

[76] *Re Highway Foods International Ltd* [1995] BCC 271.

[77] See *Shaw v Commissioner of Police of the Metropolis* [1987] 1 WLR 1322, a case of apparent ownership.

[78] *Cf. Langmead v Thyer Rubber Co* [1947] SASR 29 and see chapter 7.

[79] See *Forsyth International (UK) Ltd v Silver Shipping Co Ltd* [1994] 1 WLR 1334.

[80] [1895] 2 Ch 415.   [81] (1987) 163 CLR 236.

approach has recently been adopted by an English court.[82] The requirements of s 25(1) were also held to be satisfied in a case where goods were
delivered directly by seller to sub-buyer without passing through the
hands of the buyer.[83] There had been a constructive delivery to the buyer.

Acting as a mercantile agent

In order for the transferee from the buyer in possession to obtain a good
title under a sale, pledge or other disposition, the transfer must take place
in the ordinary course of business of a mercantile agent. Since the buyer
in possession does not have to be a mercantile agent, it has to be asked
what this can possibly mean. The argument has been advanced in the past
that the transfer is to be given the same effect as though it had taken place
in the ordinary course of business as a mercantile agent.[84] This approach,
however, was decisively rejected by the Court of Appeal in *Newtons of
Wembley Ltd v Williams*.[85]

In that case, a rogue obtained possession of a car with the aid of a
cheque. Property was not to pass until the buyer's cheque had been
cleared but the cheque was subsequently dishonoured. The seller publi-
cised his avoidance of the sale, for the purpose of the voidable title exception in s 23, but the rogue was subsequently able to sell the car in a
London street market (Warren Street) to an innocent purchaser to whom
the defendant in the present action traced his title. The sale by the rogue
was held to take place in the ordinary course of business of a mercantile
agent because the street market in question was one where cars were
regularly sold. Consequently, the formal test for business behaviour, laid
down for s 2 of the Factors Act 1889, in *Oppenheimer v Attenborough &
Son*,[86] was satisfied. Furthermore, the bringing in of mercantile agency
imported also the rule in s 2(2) of the Factors Act 1889 that the owner's
consent to a mercantile agent's possession was deemed to continue if the
relevant third party had not been notified of its revocation. Since the
purchaser in the street market was not in fact aware of the revocation of
consent, it followed that the rogue was still in possession of the goods
with the consent of the owner notwithstanding the latter's avoidance of
the contract.

---

[82] See *Forsyth International (UK) Ltd v Silver Shipping Co Ltd*.
[83] See *Four Point Garage Ltd v Carter* [1985] 3 All ER 12.
[84] *Langmead v Thyer Rubber Co* [1947] SASR 29—s 25 is an 'as if' provision.
[85] [1965] 1 QB 560 (followed reluctantly in *Forsyth International (UK) Ltd v Silver
Shipping Co Ltd*, at p 1351).
[86] [1908] 1 KB 221.

A-B-C-D transactions

Market overt apart, all the *nemo dat* exceptions under consideration require the owner's consent to the rogue's possession. Where that consent is absent, all subsequent transactions are in principle defective. This is subject to the special limitations rule,[87] barring all conversion actions six years after the commission of the first 'innocent' conversion in the chain,[88] which would apply if the goods were lost by the owner but not if they were stolen. The orthodox position that the rogue must have the owner's consent has, however, been challenged on the ground that s 25 of the Sale of Goods Act 1979 carefully differentiates the owner and the seller and deals with them as though they were separate entities. Applying this argument to a chain of transactions, it reads as follows. Where a buyer (C) is in possession of goods with the consent of the seller (B), any sale etc by the buyer to a transferee (D) is deemed to have occurred with the consent of the owner (A). This reasoning ignores altogether the incidents of the relationship between A and B, which might be based upon theft; it assumes that even a thief might be the seller for the purpose of s 25.

If the above reasoning were adopted, the law would provide a laundering facility for defective titles once the requisite number of actors were involved. The *nemo dat* rule would lie in ruins, for the same type of argument could be made under s 24 of the Sale of Goods Act 1979. Somewhat surprisingly, the argument, which owes a lot to a literal reading of s 25 and absolutely nothing to an informed understanding of the law's development, made its way as far as the House of Lords in *National Employers' Assurance v Jones*,[89] where it was roundly rejected.[90]

Bought or agreed to buy

A hundred years ago, the Court of Appeal held in *Lee v Butler*[91] that a buyer under a conditional sale, to whom the property in the goods would automatically pass once all the instalments had been paid, was someone who had agreed to buy the goods for the purpose of s 9 of the Factors Act 1889. Two years later, however, the House of Lords in *Helby v Matthews*[92] held this provision to be inapplicable to a genuine hire purchase transaction where the property would only pass if the hirer in possession

---

[87] See chapter 3.   [88] See chapter 3.   [89] [1988] 2 All ER 245.
[90] See also *Brandon v Leckie* (1972) 29 DLR (3d) 633 (Alberta) and *Elwin v O'Regan* [1971] NZLR 1124.
[91] [1893] 2 QB 318.   [92] [1895] AC 471.

exercised an option to purchase after paying all the instalments. It did not matter that, when the option matured, it could be exercised for a nominal sum and that it made overwhelming economic sense to do so. The hirer never gave a commitment to exercise the option and so could not be said to have 'agreed' to buy. On similar grounds, the potential buyer who receives goods on the terms of a sale or return or sale on approval, and is thus not at the time committed to their purchase, lacks the power to transmit title under s 25 of the Sale of Goods Act 1979.[93]

The emergence of hire purchase created a rift between it and conditional sale, s 25 being applicable only to the latter. The current law has now approximated consumer conditional sales to hire purchase in that the relevant conditional buyer is not empowered to transmit a good title under s 25.[94] The agreements in question are conditional sales as defined by the Consumer Credit Act 1974. A conditional sale that does not pass the consumer credit test continues to carry the buyer's power to transmit title under s 25. This piecemeal approach is hard to justify in rational terms, but the law of *nemo dat* and its exceptions is replete with irrationality and pragmatic, incremental reform in the cause of establishing an acceptable balance between warring principles. It has to be added that the bulk of *nemo dat* problems arising out of hire purchase and conditional sale are created by motor vehicles. Since the Hire Purchase Act 1964 (Part III), there has been a special *nemo dat* exception in the case of unlawful dispositions of motor vehicles covered by hire purchase and conditional sale agreements (but not leases). According to this exception,[95] a good title is transmitted to the first *bona fide* private purchaser— provided he is the first private purchaser in the chain extending from the rogue—and, in accordance with familiar principle, to all his successors in title (including subsequent trade or finance purchasers). An earlier trade or finance purchaser, denied protection under the Act, may be driven to argue that what looks like a hire purchase contract is in fact a non-consumer conditional sale with the result that the 'hirer' is in fact a buyer in possession with the power under s 25 of the Sale of Goods Act to transmit a good title to bona fide purchasers whether or not they are engaged in trade or finance.[96]

---

[93] *Percy Edwards Ltd v Vaughan* (1910) 26 TLR 545; see also *Shaw v Commissioner of Police of the Metropolis* [1987] 1 WLR 1322.

[94] Section 25(2); Factors Act 1889, s 9(2) as added by the Consumer Credit Act 1974, Sched 4.

[95] See further commercial law texts.

[96] *Forthright Finance Ltd v Carlyle Finance Ltd* [1997] 4 All ER 90 (CA). See chapter 2.

OVERRIDING EQUITABLE PROPERTY INTERESTS

The rule of *nemo dat* should be seen as just part of a complex rule structure that, in title disputes, prefers the first in time. Indeed, it would be difficult to see any substance in a property entitlement if its holder were generally vulnerable to the subsequent claims of others. Nevertheless, there are circumstances in which an equitable interest in personalty is liable to be displaced in favour of a subsequent transferee thereof. This successful transferee may sometimes acquire a legal interest in the personalty; in other cases, it may even be an equitable interest.

CONFLICTING EQUITABLE AND LEGAL INTERESTS

It is a maxim of equity that, where the equities are equal, the law prevails. The maxim achieves concrete form in the rule that the *bona fide* purchaser of the legal estate, for value and without notice, takes clear of earlier equitable interests (*a fortiori* defeats later equitable interests) in the same property.[97]

The legal purchaser must have provided valuable consideration and so may not be a donee.[98] Actual notice has the same meaning here as it does for the *nemo dat* exceptions.[99] In principle, the purchaser ought not to have constructive notice of the earlier equitable interest. Constructive notice arises where there is a failure to make the inquiries, that would have revealed the earlier interest, which a prudent purchaser would have made. Yet there is a considerable reluctance to import the doctrine of constructive notice into commercial dealings[100] and thus into dealings with personal property, where it is not a practical matter to investigate title in fast-moving transactions. Hence, the registration of an interest as a bill of sale[101] will not amount to constructive notice of it to subsequent transferees of the property.[102] Similarly, it is no bar to the attainment of the status of holder in due course of a negotiable instrument that the holder might on inquiry have discovered the transferor's title to be defective.[103]

---

[97] *Pilcher v Rawlins* (1872) 7 Ch App 259; *MCC Proceeds Inc v Lehman Bros International (Europe)* [1998] 4 All ER 675 (CA).
[98] *Re Diplock* [1948] Ch 465, affirmed [1951] AC 251.
[99] See above.
[100] *Manchester Trust v Furness* [1895] 2 QB 39; *Greer v Downs Supply Co* [1927] 2 KB 28.
[101] See chapter 7.
[102] *Joseph v Lyons* (1884) 15 QBD 280.
[103] *London Joint Stock Bank v Simmons* [1892] AC 201.

SUCCESSIVE EQUITABLE INTERESTS

A mere equity, such as a right to have a conveyance rescinded or rectified,[104] is liable to be defeated by a later equitable interest.[105] There is one exception: the assignee of a chose in action takes subject to earlier equities whether the assignee has notice of them or not.[106]

Apart from the special priority rule for competing assignments of the same chose in action,[107] the rule for competing equitable interests in personal property is that the first in time prevails.[108] Nevertheless, there will be many instances involving personalty where the first interest is postponed to the second, particularly where the first interest is taken on terms permitting the owner of the legal interest to carry on dealing with the property in the ordinary course of business. This occurs, for example, where a floating chargee[109] impliedly authorises the chargor company to grant a prior-ranking fixed[110] or even floating[111] charge over a narrower range of assets than are covered by the floating charge.

In certain cases, a second equitable interest holder will be able to vault ahead of the first. This will occur if the second holder, after acquiring an equitable interest in property without notice of the first, is able to purchase the legal interest. It will not matter that, at the time the legal interest is purchased, the second holder is fixed with notice of the first holder's equitable interest.[112]

TRACING

In this chapter, we have been examining the cases in which both legal and equitable interests in chattels may be overridden as a result of subsequent dealings with those chattels. Stepping back from these priority conflicts and dealing with events preceding them, it is convenient at this point to summarize the complex law on tracing, beginning with some general observations. The emphasis will be placed upon tracing in aid of a proprietary remedy.

---

[104] *Shiloh Spinners Ltd v Harding* [1973] AC 691, *per* Lord Wilberforce.
[105] *National Provincial Bank v Ainsworth* [1965] AC 1175.
[106] See chapter 6.
[107] *Dearle v Hall* (1828) 3 Russ 1: see chapter 6.
[108] *Phillips v Phillips* (1862) 4 De GF & J 208.
[109] See chapter 7 for the floating charge.
[110] *Re Castell & Brown Ltd* [1898] 1 Ch 315.
[111] *Re Automatic Bottle Makers Ltd* [1926] Ch 412.
[112] *Taylor v Russell* [1892] AC 244; *Bailey v Barnes* [1894] 1 Ch 25.

To take a very general example, suppose that assets belonging to A are sold by B to C. The money proceeds in B's hands are then deposited in a bank account. B later makes a withdrawal from this account which he uses to purchase some shares. As a matter of vocabulary, A may seek to *follow* his original assets into C's hands. A may also seek to *trace* his assets, or rather their value, into new assets. This latter process involves identifying the proceeds of (or substitutions for) A's original assets as first the credit in B's bank account produced by the payment in, followed by the shares purchased with the fruits of the withdrawal from that account. The two processes of following and tracing are often broadly described as tracing. References below to tracing are to tracing in this broad sense, unless a specific reference to tracing in the narrower sense is made. Tracing is a physical process and not a remedy.[113] It seeks to locate assets and their substitutes. The remedy will come afterwards when A, upon completing the tracing process, *claims* a proprietary entitlement in the traced asset, as against the person who either holds or previously held it, and then selects a cause of action in furtherance of that claim. There is no guarantee that A's cause of action will be successfully maintained. A may for example be defeated by C in the type of priority conflict discussed earlier in this chapter.

The process of tracing, together with the claims that arise as a result of it, is essentially a proprietary one. A person seeking to recover his own asset in this way is not seeking relief on the ground that the ultimate holder of that asset, or any intermediate person in the holding chain, has been unjustly enriched at his expense.[114] Merely because the law of tracing is of such abiding interest to restitution lawyers is no reason to classify it as a branch of the law of restitution. Nevertheless, the tracing or following process may also serve a restitutionary purpose if used in aid of establishing the requisite causal connection between a claimant's loss and a defendant's enrichment.

Over time, the common law and equity have developed different approaches to tracing.[115] As with so many other issues, it is hard to justify the continuing existence of separate rules of common law and equity a century and a quarter after the administrative fusion of the courts of equity and common law. Lord Millett has stated forcefully: 'Given its

---

[113] *Boscawen v Bajwa* [1996] 1 WLR 328 (Millett LJ).

[114] *Foskett v McKeown* [2000] 3 All ER 97, at pp 101–102 (Lord Browne-Wilkinson), 119–120, 124 (Lord Millett).

[115] For an example of statutory tracing that has its own rules, see s 15(4) of the Insolvency Act 1986.

nature, there is nothing inherently legal or equitable about the tracing exercise. There is thus no sense in maintaining different rules for tracing at law and in equity. One set of tracing rules is enough.'[116] Although such common sense may represent the likely future, account must yet be taken of the present. The real difficulties are posed by proceeds (or substitutions), the province of tracing in the narrow sense of the expression.

Taking first the common law, the orthodox proposition is that the traced asset must be the direct successor of the claimant's original asset or of an earlier traced asset, itself the successor of the claimant's original asset. One consequence of this view is that the common law cannot trace into a mixed fund.[117] Therefore, if a claimant's widgets are mixed with other widgets so that it is physically impossible to identify them in the commingled fungible mass, the common law tracing claim will fail. For the same reason, the property in goods may not pass under a contract of sale to the extent that the goods remain unascertained, even within a larger ascertained bulk. Similarly, if money is paid into an account already in surplus, it will be impossible at common law to identify that precise portion of the bank's indebtedness attributable to the payment in of the claimant's money. At common law, the property in money is lost when it is mixed with other money.[118]

Now, this may be the long-established position, entirely in accordance with the absence at common law of a remedy in the nature of a charge or non-possessory lien over the larger whole to the extent of the claimant's interest. Nevertheless, it neglects important developments, fuelled by statute, in the law of tenancy in common by which a claimant might hold assets at law in common with other persons in the proportions of their respective entitlements.[119] This is true enough for tangible widgets, though it would require an expansion of the tenancy in common idea for it to be extended to intangible assets, such as an entitlement arising under a bank account. The importance of common law tracing is dependent to a large extent upon any limitations on equitable tracing. Common law tracing will give the claimant a legal property right, as opposed to a mere equitable property right, which, though no more effective in insolvency distributions than an equitable right, is yet stronger for priority purposes in conflicts with third-party purchasers.

---

[116] *Foskett v McKeown* [2000] 3 All ER 97, at p 121.

[117] *Agip (Africa) Ltd v Jackson* [1991] Ch 547; *Banque Belge pour l'Etranger v Hambrouck* [1921] 1 KB 321.

[118] *Lipkin Gorman v Karpnale Ltd* [1991] 2 AC 548 (Lord Goff).

[119] Sale of Goods (Amendment) Act 1995.

A claimant successfully tracing money at common law will be able to recover a money sum in an action for money had and received. In the case of chattels, an action in conversion may be maintained. In claiming the traced chattel, the claimant will have to surrender his claim to the original chattel.[120] It is not clear how much time the claimant has to elect in favour of the substitute asset, a matter that could have implications for limitation purposes.[121] The action for money had and received is a personal action,[122] and so is effectively pursued only against a solvent defendant.[123] The conversion action, though conventionally yielding a personal remedy, is treated as a proprietary action so that the claimant is not to be treated as an unsecured creditor in the defendant's insolvency.[124] Until the forced judicial sale that results from a satisfied judgment in favour of the claimant, the claimant has a good title to the chattel. Consequently, if that title is wrongfully denied by a liquidator or trustee-in-bankruptcy, that party will in his personal capacity incur liability in conversion to the claimant. The use of conversion when tracing in the narrow sense, whether in insolvency proceedings or otherwise, is somewhat untested but there is no reason why the action should not be maintained, though the rule preventing common law tracing through mixtures will give the action relatively little scope in practice.

The conventional view is that it is easier to trace in equity, the processes of which are not impeded by difficulties with mixtures or with precise substitutes. Moreover, a tracing claim in equity may lead to a proprietary claim for the recovery of money unhampered by difficulties in the nature of following the precise passage of money through a bank clearing system.[125] But equitable tracing does have the formidable drawback that a fiduciary relationship has long been seen as a necessary requirement for tracing to take place. There is also the smaller point, in relation to chattels, that a claimant with an equitable entitlement may not have the necessary right to immediate possession to ground an action in

---

[120] *Lipkin Gorman v Karpnale Ltd* [1991] 2 AC 548 (Lord Goff).

[121] See chapter 3.

[122] *Lipkin Gorman v Karpnale Ltd* [1991] 2 AC 548. But see Millett LJ in *F. C. Jones & Sons v Jones* [1996] 3 WLR 703.

[123] Since the process yields only a personal liability, tracing difficulties arising out of the transfer of money in electronic banking systems (e.g., *Agip (Africa) Ltd v Jackson* [1990] Ch 265 (Millett J)) will not be dealt with here.

[124] For the distinction between proprietary claim and personal remedy, see Millett LJ in *F. C. Jones & Sons v Jones* [1996] 3 WLR 703.

[125] *F. C. Jones & Sons v Jones* [1996] 3 WLR 703 (Millett LJ).

conversion,[126] which could prove troublesome if the defendant is an intermediate holder of assets.

In equity, the tracing rules apply to assets disposed of by a trustee or person in a fiduciary position such as an agent.[127] Somewhat controversially, the existence of a fiduciary relationship has been found in the fact of receiving mistaken payment,[128] but this conclusion cannot stand in the light of Lord Browne-Wilkinson's assertion in *Westdeutsche Landesbank Girozentrale v Islington London Borough Council*[129] that the conscience of a recipient of money cannot be bound—a necessity for a fiduciary relationship—until that recipient retains the money with notice of the mistake. The trust or fiduciary relationship having been established, the claimant will have a proprietary claim after tracing into the proceeds of the disposition whether or not the disposal in question took place lawfully or wrongfully.

In the event of tracing into proceeds, the claimant may as against the trustee or fiduciary elect to take the proceeds purchased[130] or take instead an equitable lien over those proceeds to the amount of his assets used for their purchase.[131] Where, however, the proceeds have been acquired out of a mixed fund that includes the trustee's own assets, and the proceeds are capable of division, the claimant is not entitled to all the proceeds. Instead, he may claim a lien on the proceeds, electing between the amount of his assets traceable therein and the proportion of the value of the proceeds attributable to his assets,[132] a measure obviously more favourable to the claimant where the proceeds have appreciated. In respect of the mixed fund or any proceeds thereof, the claimant is entitled, as against a wrongdoing trustee, to charge any depletion in the fund against the wrongdoer's interest in it.[133] In one case the tracing claimant will recover the whole proceeds even if his assets do not account for the whole, namely where the proceeds cannot be divided because the process by which they arose is physically irreversible.[134]

---

[126] See chapter 3.

[127] *Re Hallett's Estate* (1880) 13 Ch D 696; *Boscawen v Bajwa* [1996] 1 WLR 328 (Millett LJ). See also *Agip (Africa) Ltd v Jackson* [1990] Ch 265 (senior accountant of employer as fiduciary).

[128] *Chase-Manhattan Bank v Israel British Bank* [1981] 1 Ch 105.

[129] [1996] AC 669.

[130] The wrongdoer will hold them on the terms of a constructive trust: *Boscawen v Bajwa* [1996] 1 WLR 328, at pp 334–335.

[131] *Re Hallett's Estate* (1880) 13 Ch D 696.

[132] *Foskett v McKeown* [2000] 3 All ER 97.

[133] *Re Oatway* [1903] 2 Ch 356.

[134] *Jones v De Marchant* (1916) 28 DLR 561; *Foskett v McKeown* [2000] 3 All ER 97.

The right to trace will fail as and when the claimant's assets come into the hands of a *bona fide* purchaser for value without notice of the legal estate. In the hands of a volunteer providing no consideration for the acquisition of the assets, however, the right to trace will endure as effectively as against the trustee.[135] Nevertheless, where the claimant's assets have been mixed with assets of the volunteer, then, contrary to the rule that applies to wrongdoers, any depletions in the mixed fund will be shared rateably by the claimant and the volunteer.[136] If there is a mixed fund and more than one tracing claimant, then the likely result, given the interests of justice and forensic simplicity, is that the fund will be shared by all claimants on a rateable basis, ignoring the precise dates on which their contributions were made to the fund and investments were made out of that fund.[137]

---

[135] *Re Diplock* [1948] 1 Ch 465.

[136] *Re Diplock* [1948] 1 Ch 465. As with the case of wrongdoers, the rule in *Clayton's Case* (1816) 1 Mer 572, by which payments out of a fund are charged against payments into that fund in the order of payment in, is excluded.

[137] *Barlow Clowes International Ltd v Vaughan* [1992] 4 All ER 22.

6

Transfer of intangible property

INTRODUCTION

We saw in chapter 4 how ownership rights in tangible personal property were transferred (or conveyed). In the case of intangible property (or things in action), simple physical delivery and a consensual intention to effect a conveyance have never been feasible methods of transfer. Furthermore, the influence of equity, rather insubstantial where personalty is tangible, has been more pronounced for intangible property. Consequently, the transfer of ownership rights in intangible property merits a separate chapter. In this same chapter, we shall also consider priority conflicts between two or more persons claiming an entitlement to the thing, which was dealt with in chapter 5 in the case of tangible personal property.

As its alternative name 'things (or choses) in action' plainly indicates, intangible property cannot be physically enjoyed in and of itself. It consists of an entitlement arising from obligations that are enforceable by legal action. As an item of value, intangible property commands a certain price when it is sold to a purchaser. A creditor, for example, has the right to receive payment of a debt from the debtor. Payment will take the form of legal tender (coin and banknotes). Where the debtor is unwilling or unable to pay, or there is a risk of this occurring, the value of the debt in the market place obviously has to be discounted when it is sold to a purchaser. To take another example, a shareholder in a company has the right to participate as a member of that company in its profits. The corresponding shares will command a price commensurate with the value of that right.

Intangible property must for present purposes be divided into pure intangibles and documentary intangibles[1] Where it is pure intangible property whose ownership is to be transferred, the rules are to be found in the law relating to the assignment of things in action, largely a matter

---

[1] A division propounded by Goode, R.M., *Commercial Law*, 2nd edn, London: Penguin Books, 1995, chapter 2.

of case law but with a statutory addition (notably, the Law of Property Act 1925, s 136). As we shall see, the common law was resistant to the notion that such rights could be transferred, so it was left to equity to repair this deficiency. The best example of a pure intangible for our purposes is a debt. It will be used throughout this chapter in examples, but it should be remembered that many other types of intangible exist, such as patent rights, shares in a partnership, and copyright. The rules for documentary intangibles, a mixture of common law and statute, recognize that the intangible right is so firmly locked up in the document embodying it that it can be dealt with at common law only through the medium of that document. In consequence, the transfer in due form of the document is necessary if the legal property right that it embodies is to be transferred. In certain circumstances, nevertheless, it is possible to transfer equitable rights in the documentary intangibles by means falling short of those required to transfer legal rights therein. Good examples of documentary intangibles are share certificates, bills of lading, and bills of exchange. The bulk of this chapter is concerned with the transfer of pure intangibles. When this has been dealt with, brief consideration will be given to the transfer of documentary intangibles, a subject that can be left to more detailed texts for a fuller treatment.

ASSIGNMENT OF THINGS (OR CHOSES) IN ACTION

GENERAL

Under this heading we shall consider the equitable rules that were developed to deal with the transfer of rights in intangible property, together with the statutory overlay (now the Law of Property Act 1925, s 136) that was first introduced in 1873 (Supreme Court of Judicature Act 1873, s 25(6)) with the fusion of the courts of common law and equity. These rules apply to pure intangibles. In the case of rights embodied in documentary intangibles, the rules on assignment will not normally have a significant part to play. This is because contract (bills of lading) or statute (company share certificates) prescribes a different method of transfer of rights than that required for an assignment. In the case of bills of exchange, there is a statutory method of transferring the document that gives the transferee more extensive rights than those flowing from an assignment of the debt embodied in the bill.

DEFINITION OF ASSIGNMENT

This is best done by means of a simple example involving a debt. Suppose that A, a householder, owes money to B, a department store, for furniture supplied. The householder may have been given a period of credit so that the price of the furniture may not be due for some time. Meanwhile, B, needing finance, decides to assign A's debt to C, in return for payment from C. When payment from A falls due, A pays C instead of B. In this example, A is the debtor, B the assignor and C the assignee. Assignment means that B may transfer the debt, owed by A, to C without obtaining the prior permission of A; C may then call upon A to pay him instead of B; and C may then give A a good discharge for payment of the debt initially owed to B. The effect of assignment is to transfer B's payment entitlement to C. In consequence, a relationship of debtor and creditor between A and C is substituted for the earlier relationship between A and B. The debt owed previously by A to B has been transferred by B to C in the same way as B might have sold to C an antique clock or a second hand car earlier acquired from A. The debt is just as much a piece of property as the clock or the car. Once paid, however, the debt ceases to exist.

DEVELOPMENT OF ASSIGNMENT

The common law set its face against assignment, principally because debts and similar things in action were regarded as personal obligations.[2] Allowing C to sue on a debt incurred by A to B was regarded as a form of champerty or maintenance; it was seen as contrary to public policy to allow C to press, or interfere in the assertion of, B's claim against A. Even today, the assignment of a cause of action may fail, on the ground that it is tantamount to maintenance,[3] if it cannot be seen as part of a larger transaction such as the sale of a business together with its assets. The assignment of causes of action by companies to individuals eligible for legal aid has been upheld despite the opportunistic motive,[4] but certain actions, because of their penal or public character, on public policy grounds may not be assigned.[5] When the common law incorporated from the law merchant jurisdiction over bills of exchange, and other negotiable instruments, it came to recognize exceptionally an assignment taking the

---

[2] *Fitzroy v Cave* [1905] 2 KB 364, *per* Cozens-Hardy LJ.
[3] *Trendtex Trading Corporation v Credit Suisse* [1982] AC 679.
[4] See *Norglen Ltd v Reeds Rains Prudential Ltd* [1996] 1 All ER 945.
[5] *Re Oasis Merchandising Services Ltd* [1997] BCC 282 (CA) (liquidator's action against directors for wrongful trading).

particular form of a negotiation of the instrument, which has consequences going beyond those flowing from ordinary assignment.

Equity, however, gave effect to assignments in two ways. First of all, if the thing in action assigned was enforceable only in, or was subject to the exclusive jurisdiction of, courts of equity, then the assignee could initiate proceedings directly against the debtor in a court of equity. Examples of such items include legacies and the interests of beneficiaries in trust funds. Secondly, if the thing in action was enforceable at common law, for example a debt, the assignee could bring proceedings in a court of common law against the debtor in the name of the assignor. An assignor unwilling to cooperate in this way can be compelled in equity to permit the assignee to use his name.[6] This joinder of the assignor in the proceedings, either as a willing co-plaintiff, or as an unwilling co-defendant, which occurs 'save in special circumstances',[7] ensures that all relevant parties are before the court and that the details of each relationship (A-B, B-C, A-C) in the A-B-C triangle can be worked out in an harmonious way. For example, the debtor (A) might be able to assert that the assignor (B) had already been paid at the same time as the assignor disputed as against the assignee (C) the validity of the assignment. The form of legal entitlement was thus preserved at the same time as the conscience of the assignor was bound in the time-honoured way in equity. Just as an equitable assignee cannot proceed without joining the assignor to the action, so too the assignor wishing to sue (a rare case) must join the assignee.[8]

The fusion of the courts of common law and equity brought with it a new form of statutory assignment. In respect of certain things in action, and provided certain formalities were observed, an assignee could bring an action directly against the debtor without having to join or use the name of the assignor. This new procedure did not replace equitable assignment. The latter remained wider than the statute in that it covered a greater range of assignments. It also continued to be relevant to those assignments falling within the purview of the statutory procedure. When the parties to an assignment failed to obey the statutory forms, the assignment might yet take effect as a valid equitable assignment.

---

[6] *Re Westover* [1919] 2 Ch 104, *per* Sargant J.
[7] *Three Rivers District Council v Bank of England* [1996] QB 292, at p 313.
[8] *Three Rivers District Council v Bank of England.*

REQUIREMENTS OF EQUITABLE ASSIGNMENT

We shall see what constitutes a valid equitable assignment before we turn our attention to the further requirements needed for the assignment to qualify as a statutory assignment.

Equitable assignment and form

The first point to note is that no particular form of words is required for there to be an effective assignment, merely sufficient to establish a clear intention to transfer an item of intangible property to the assignee. In a well-known passage in *Brandt's Sons & Co v Dunlop Rubber Co*,[9] Lord Macnaghten said of an assignment:

> It may be addressed to the debtor. It may be couched in the language of command. It may be a courteous request. It may assume the form of mere permission. The language is immaterial if the meaning is plain.

The assignee must consent to the assignment for it to be effective[10] but there is no need for the account debtor to be informed of the assignment. It might make business sense, however, for the assignee to ensure that this is done. First, if the assignor has assigned the debt to more than one assignee, we shall see that the rights of the competing assignees may depend upon which is the first to notify the account debtor. Secondly, until notified of the assignment, the debtor is able to pay the assignor and receive a good discharge for the debt. The assignee would then have to recover the payment from the assignor. It has been held, nevertheless, that the debtor need not do anything so onerous as stop a cheque that has already been sent or given to the assignor.[11] The debtor in a case of this nature may wait for the discharge that comes when payment reaches the assignor.

The case of *Gorringe v Irwell India Rubber Works*[12] illustrates when an equitable assignment is complete. The assignor, B, was indebted to the assignee, C, for a bill of exchange for £660 drawn by C on B and accepted by B. On 11 January, B wrote to C in these terms: '[W]e hold at your disposal the sum of about £425 due to us from [A] for certain goods supplied . . . until balance of our acceptance . . . in your favour . . . has been paid.' C notified A of the assignment on 5 February. Meanwhile, B had gone into liquidation with effect from 2 February. It was important therefore to know whether the equitable assignment had been completed

---

[9] [1905] AC 454.   [10] *Standing v Bowring* (1885) 31 Ch D 282.
[11] *Bence v Shearman* [1898] 2 Ch 582.   [12] (1886) 34 Ch D 128.

before notification to A, for, if it had not been, the debt could have been taken over by B's liquidator for the benefit of B's general creditors. The Court of Appeal held that the letter of 11 January effected an immediate equitable assignment. Consequently, the debt was no longer the property of B and did not therefore vest in B's liquidator.

Writing

An equitable assignment need not be in or evidenced by writing. Purely informal means will suffice. Nevertheless, it will not often make business sense for an assignee to be content with an oral assignment. Prudence would dictate something in writing for evidential purposes. Furthermore, while there is no legal requirement for an equitable assignment to be in writing, suppose that the assignee, C, sub-assigns A's debt to D. According to s 53(1)(c) of the Law of Property Act 1925, dispositions of 'subsisting' equitable interests in personalty 'must be in writing signed by the person disposing of the same or by his agent thereunto lawfully authorised'. The assignment from B creates C's equitable interest in the debt owed by A to B, so there is no need for writing here. That interest, however, is a subsisting one by the time C comes to sub-assign it to D. As regards satisfying the writing requirement, it should be enough if C defines the property to be assigned, which will involve identifying A as the debtor (if the assignment is of an individual debt) and B as the creditor, and names himself and D in language showing an intention to transfer the debt to D.

Absolute, conditional or by way of charge

We saw earlier that an equitable assignment of an equitable thing in action permitted the assignee to take proceedings against the debtor without using the name of the assignor. It would be more accurate to say that this is true of absolute assignments, and not of conditional assignments or assignments by way of charge. The definitions of these differing types of assignment, however, are more important in the context of statutory assignment and will therefore be treated later.

Consideration

The starting point is that consideration is not necessary to support a valid equitable assignment. Once completed—and we have seen that the requirements for a completed assignment are simple and undemanding —the assignment is as effective in divesting the assignor of the debt as the gift of a chattel is in transferring the donor's property rights to the donee. Thus, in *Holt v Heatherfield Trust*,[13] there was a question as to whether consideration had been given for the assignment of a debt. A garnishee creditor of the assignor claimed an entitlement to charge the debt and was refused on the ground that the assignor could no longer honestly deal with the debt, which had become the property of the assignee. Consideration was not necessary to complete the equitable assignment.

Re McArdle[14] carries the consideration theme further. The trustees of a residuary estate promised the wife of one of them a sum of money '[i]n consideration of your carrying out certain improvements to the property'. This money was to come from the estate upon its distribution and therefore concerned an equitable thing in action. The wife's action to recover the money failed in contract because she had already performed the work before the promise was made: past consideration is no consideration.[15] Moreover, the promise could not be regarded as a valid equitable assignment because its language was consistent with something to be done in the future and not with a present transfer. Similarly, a promise to convey a future thing, such as a debt that has not yet come into existence, cannot constitute an effective present assignment. Even if expressed as a purported present assignment, it will be treated as a promise to assign when the debt arises.[16] Because equity will not perfect an imperfect gift, the Court of Appeal in *Re McArdle* refused in the absence of consideration to enforce the promise to make a future assignment. The wife therefore had the misfortune to fall between the two stools of contract and equitable assignment. Evershed MR expressed his attitude to executed assignments by way of gift in these terms:

> [I]f what is done amounts to a gift, complete and perfect of a subject-matter which is an equitable chose in action, there is no reason in principle and in authority why the done should not take the benefit just as much as he will if the donor gives him a pound note and puts it in his hand. Since the transaction is thus perfect, the question of consideration becomes irrelevant, for consideration is only necessary to support the assertion of a right to have made perfect something which is not yet perfect—for example, a contractual right.

If Evershed MR meant that consideration was dispensed with only in the case of equitable assignments of equitable choses in action, no such

---

[13] [1942] 2 KB 1.   [14] [1951] 1 Ch 669.
[15] *Roscorla v Thomas* (1842) 3 QB 234.
[16] *Tailby v Official Receiver* (1888) 13 App Cas 523.

limitation is present in the words of Jenkins LJ in the same case.[17] Certainly, there is no stated need for consideration in the case of statutory assignments and therefore no justification for importing it into the statute. There seems no good reason to restrict equitable assignment in the way that Evershed MR's dictum would impliedly suggest. The important thing is that the assignor has done everything required of him for an effective assignment: it is not a case of equity perfecting an imperfect gift because consideration has nothing to do with gift and the assignment is as complete as an executed gift.

STATUTORY ASSIGNMENT

The scope and requirements of the statute are contained in the opening words of s 136(1) of the Law of Property Act 1925:

> Any absolute assignment by writing under the hand of the assignor (not purporting to be by way of charge only) of any debt or other legal thing in action, of which express notice has been given to the debtor, trustee or other person from whom the assignor would have been entitled to claim such debt or thing in action, is effectual in law (subject to equities having priority over the right of the assignee) to pass and transfer from the date of such notice:
>
> (a) the legal right to such debt or thing in action;
>
> (b) the legal and other remedies for the same; and
>
> (c) the power to give a good discharge for the same without the concurrence of the assignor . . .

The meaning of this provision is best brought out by analysing some of the key words and phrases therein. In contrast with equitable assignment, an assignment that fits the statutory provision enables the assignee to bring an action directly against the debtor without involving the assignor in the proceedings.

Absolute assignments

The first point to note here is that absolute assignments have to be contrasted with assignments by way of charge[18] and conditional assignments.[19] The latter two types do not come within the statute. In the case of an assignment by way of charge, the thing in action is subjected to a security taking the form of an encumbrance. No actual transfer of the

---

[17] And see to similar effect *Holt v Heatherfield Trust*; *6 Halsbury's Laws of England* (4th edn), 'Assignment of Choses in Action', para. 37 note 2.

[18] See chapter 7 for the meaning of a charge.

[19] See *Durham Bros v Robertson* [1898] 1 QB 765.

property in the thing takes place. For example, suppose B owes C £1,000 to be paid by a certain date. B in turn is owed £5,000 by A and charges this debt in favour of C as security for the £1,000 owed to C. If in due course C is paid by B, the charge over the A-B debt is released. But if B fails to pay C, C may enforce the charge by seeking payment of the £1,000 from the £5,000 owed by A to B. C having been satisfied, A will then pay the balance of the £5,000 to B.

Suppose, however, that B is owed £5,000 at a future date and does not wish to wait for payment. B may decide to sell or discount that debt to C. This will involve an absolute assignment of the debt and the payment by C to B of an amount equivalent to the debt but reduced to take account of two matters: first, the risk of default by A when payment falls due; and secondly, the value to B of getting in early the money owed by A, which corresponds broadly to the burden borne by C in paying B and then having to wait for payment from A. This latter item approximates to interest on the amount advanced by C to B, though the law classifies such transactions, not as loans, but as sales of intangible property.[20] Absolute assignments of this kind are a common form of financing arrangement. The role of B may be taken by a company, which needs cash flow to keep its business going, and that of C by a factor, which is also in the business of debt management. A may or may not be aware that the debt has been assigned to C: this is the difference between notification and non-notification financing. Where A is not aware, then one of the require-ments of s 136(1) of the Law of Property Act 1925 (written notice to the debtor) has not been met so the transaction between B and C will have to be treated as an equitable assignment only. The assignment to C may involve a guarantee by B that A will pay (recourse financing) or it may not (non-recourse financing).

We have seen that the granting of a charge over a debt does not involve an absolute assignment. What about other forms of security, for example a mortgage[21] given by B to C over a debt owed by A to B? The issue is explored in *Tancred v Delagoa Bay Railway Co*[22] where a mortgage of certain debts owed by A to B, as security for an advance made by C to B, provided that the mortgage would be redeemed and the debts reassigned back to B in the event of the advance being repaid. Denman J held that the mortgage was an absolute assignment, in contrast with a charge which 'only given a right to payment out of a particular fund or particular

---

[20] *Re Charge Card Services Ltd* [1987] Ch 150.
[21] See chapter 7 for the meaning of a mortgage.   [22] (1889) 23 QBD 239.

property, without transferring that fund or property'. Prior to their reassignment to B, the debts in question had been transferred in their entirety to C.

An example showing the need to distinguish a mortgage from a charge on the facts is *Hughes v Pump House Hotel Co.*[23] B, a builder, assigned to C 'all moneys due, or to become due, . . . from [A, a hotel] by virtue of a [particular] contract'. C was also empowered to manage the account arising from that contract, which included the giving of 'effectual receipts' to A. Even though B's indebtedness to C was for an uncertain amount, and even though the assignment was expressed to be 'by way of continuing security', the Court of Appeal held the assignment to be absolute. As a result of the assignment, A could pay C without concerning itself with the state of the underlying account between B and C and could also resist a claim by B for payment under the building contract. According to Mathew LJ: '[T]hough a mortgage is only a security for the amount which may be due, it is nevertheless an absolute assignment because the whole right of the mortgagor in the estate passes to the mortgagee.' The absence of an express provision for reassignment of the debt, in the event of payment by B to C of the sum owed, did not affect the position, since such a provision would be implied in any event. Until notified of the redemption of the mortgage, itself an assignment of the debt back to the original assignor, the debtor could safely pay the mortgagee and obtain a good discharge.

In *Durham Bros v Robertson*,[24] one of the reasons the assignment was not regarded as absolute was that it was expressed to endure only 'until' the sum owed by assignor to assignee had been paid off. The assignment was therefore a conditional one, the assignor retaining an interest of a contingent nature in the debt. The court stressed the need for the account debtor to know the precise state of affairs between the assignor and assignee for an assignment to be regarded as absolute. If the assignment was clearly absolute, the debtor could go on paying the assignee until notified that the debt had been reassigned. Otherwise the debtor needed the assurance of all relevant parties appearing before the court for a true balance to be struck amongst the three of them.

A similar need for certainty in the mind of the debtor explains why the law has settled on the view that the assignment of only part of a debt does not amount to an absolute assignment.[25]

---

[23] [1902] 2 KB 190.   [24] [1898] 1 QB 765.
[25] See *Hughes v Pump House Hotel Co*, *per* Mathew and Cozens-Hardy LJJ; *Williams v Atlantic Assurance Co* [1933] 1 KB 81.

Writing

To qualify under s 136(1) of the Law of Property Act 1925, the assignment must be 'by writing under the hand of the assignor'. This is the
same for practical purposes as the writing requirement for disposition of
subsisting equitable interest under s 53(1)(c) of the Law of Property Act
1925,[26] minus the complicating element of the sub-assignment.

The notice given to the debtor must be written notice: no particular
form of words is prescribed. It need not be given by the assignor; notice
from the assignee will suffice.[27] We shall examine later other aspects of
notice to the debtor.

Legal thing in action

Section 136(1) of the Law of Property Act 1925 is confined to assignments of 'any debt or other legal thing an action'. On the face of it this
would exclude equitable things in action, such as the interests of trust
beneficiaries and would significantly reduce the reach of the statutory
provision. In *Torkington v Magee*,[28] the defendant agreed to sell his reversionary interest in certain property to a purchaser who assigned it to the
claimant. Despite having received written notice of the assignment, the
defendant refused to perform. Channell J held that the section applied
equally to legal and equitable things in action:

> I think the words 'debt or other legal chose in action' mean 'debt or right which
> the common law looks on as not assignable by reason of its being a chose in
> action, but which a Court of Equity deals with as being assignable'.

By watering down the meaning of 'legal' to 'lawfully assignable', Channell J made the section workable at the expense of rendering the word
'legal' redundant. Other aspects of the section made it plain that the
equitable rule of assignment was in substance being adopted by statute, so
the result in *Torkington* is in harmony with the statute. It should also be
observed that the section refers to written notice of the assignment,
where relevant, being given to trustees, which supports the view taken by
Channell J.

SUBJECT TO EQUITIES

The statutory assignment in s 136(1) of the Law of Property Act 1925 is
stated to be effectual 'subject to equities having priority over the right of

---

[26] See above.
[27] *Re Westover* [1919] 2 Ch 104; *Holt v Heatherfield Trust* [1942] 2 KB 1.
[28] [1902] 2 KB 427.

the assignee'. The same rule applies in the case of equitable assignments falling outside the statute. Equities might include, for example, the right of the debtor to rescind the contract for mistake or for misrepresentation. The assignment rule is therefore less generous to the assignee than the corresponding rules for things in possession. If A sells goods to B who then transfers them to C, a *bona fide* purchaser for value without notice, before A is able to rescind the contract for misrepresentation, then title to the goods passes to C and A is unable to recover them or their value from C.[29] But if B sells goods to A and then assigns the benefit of A's payment obligation to C before A discovers B's misrepresentation about the goods, A will be able to oppose against C the same misrepresentation claim that could have been opposed against B.

Although s 136(1) states that the assignee takes subject to 'equities', the assignee's vulnerability extends beyond equities in the narrow sense to include defences and certain claims of the debtor against the assignor that fall within the limits of the rules concerning set off, regardless of whether the assignee has or has not notice of these at the time of the assignment. As the Privy Council observed in *Government of Newfoundland v Newfoundland Railway Co*:[30]

> It would be a lamentable thing if it was found to be the law that a party to a contract may assign a part of it, perhaps a beneficial portion of it, so that the assignee should take the benefit, wholly discharged of any counter-claim by the other party in respect of the contract, which may be burdensome.

Suppose that a builder is engaged to do work for a householder. The builder fails to do the work that is prescribed in the contract as a pre-condition for payment. The builder is in no position to claim payment and an assignee from the builder is no better off. If the builder had done sufficient to claim payment, but the work was done badly so that the householder had a counterclaim in damages against the builder, the builder's action for the agreed sum would be abated to the extent of the damages.[31] Likewise, the householder would be allowed to set off the damages claimed for the defective work by way of defence to the assignee's action for the agreed sum.

An example of an assignee being met by a successful defence is *Roxburghe v Cox*.[32] Ker assigned by mortgage to the Duke of Roxburghe

---

[29] See chapter 5.
[30] (1888) 13 App Cas 199.
[31] See *Gilbert-Ash (Northern) Ltd v Modern Engineering (Bristol) Ltd* [1974] AC 689.
[32] (1881) 17 Ch D 520.

all moneys that should be realised at a future date on the sale of his army commission. When Ker later resigned, the moneys in question were lodged by the Army Commissioners in a special account with Cox & Co, who also happened to be Ker's bankers. Ker was overdrawn on his personal account and Cox then took the decision to combine the two accounts into one, as bankers are entitled to do.[33] Consequently, the debt that Cox owed to Ker for the commission moneys was reduced by the amount of Ker's indebtedness on his personal account. This was done after the mortgage to the duke but before Cox was given notice thereof. The court held that Cox's equity, for the overdrawn amount of Ker's personal account, could be offset against the duke's claim, since it had come into existence before notice of the assignment had been received by Cox. James LJ went on to say that 'after notice of an assignment of a chose in action the debtor cannot by payment or otherwise do anything to take away or diminish the rights of the assignee as they stood at the time of the notice'. Thus a later advance by Cox to Ker could not have been offset against the duke's claim.[34]

Another example is *Young v Kitchin*.[35] A builder assigned to the claimant a sum owed under a building contract by the defendant. When sued by the claimant assignee for the sum owed, the defendant pleaded certain breaches of contract by the assignor builder in failing to complete the work on time. To the extent that the sum claimed did not exceed the amount of the debt, the defendant was held entitled to deduct the damages claim from the debt. (Since the debtor's rights are defensive, an assignee cannot be subjected to a counterclaim to the extent that it exceeds the debt.) It should be emphasized that the position of the assignee would not have been improved if notice of the assignment had been given before the building work had been done or before any damage attributable to the work already done had manifested itself. The debtor's equity to hold back payment arises as soon as the building contract is concluded, even though it may not then be known how much damage has been caused or even if any damage will be caused at all.

A controversial case is *Stoddart v Union Trust Ltd*.[36] The defendant debtors agreed to buy a newspaper ('Football Chat') from its owner. A portion of the price, made payable in instalments at future dates, was assigned by the owner to the claimant. Later, the defendants discovered that the sale had been induced by fraudulent misrepresentations, though

---

[33] *Garnett v M'Kewan* (1872) LR 8 Ex 10.
[34] See also *N. W. Robbie & Co v Witney Warehouse Co* [1963] 3 All ER 613.
[35] (1878) 3 Ex D 127.   [36] [1912] 1 KB 181.

the claimant assignee had no notice of the fraud at the time of the assignment. Whilst the Court of Appeal would have been prepared to recognize the defendant's equity in the form of a rescission of the contract of sale, which the defendant was not seeking, it refused to allow damages for the owner's fraud to be set off against the claimant's claim for the sums due under the assignment. According to Vaughan Williams LJ, the fraud was not something 'flowing out of, and inseparably connected with, the contract which gave rise to the cause of action', which seems to put the matter rather narrowly. The fraud claim was inseparably connected with the purchase of the newspaper since it induced that purchase. It seems anomalous not to permit a defence against the assignee based upon fraud when there would have been a defence if the fraudulent statements had become contractual warranties or if the contract of sale had been rescinded.

COMMON LAW SET OFF

The debtor may have a defence to the assignee's claim outside the words of the statute. Common law set off goes beyond equities since it is available whenever the claim and counterclaim are for debts or liquidated sums, regardless of whether there is a contractual or other material connection between the two. The equitable rule allows set off even if one or both of the claim and counterclaim is for unliquidated damages, but requires there to be such a close connection between the two that it would be inequitable not to grant relief to the defendant.[37] The point of view of the common law, however, is that set off is merely a matter of accounting so that, if both sums are at least liquidated, it will be permitted in order to avoid circuity of litigation. Nevertheless, to apply in the context of assignment, the account debtor's claim against the assignor must have fallen due at the time notice of the assignment is received if it is to be opposed to the assignee as a matter of common law set off. This is illustrated by *Business Computers Ltd v Anglo-African Leasing Co.*[38] The debtor, A, owed money to the assignor, B, for computers that it had purchased from B. Under a quite separate contract between the same two parties, A supplied B with a computer on hire purchase terms, B to pay hire purchase instalments in the usual way. When B got into financial difficulties, C, a secured creditor of B, sent in a receiver under a floating charge.[39]

---

[37] *Bim Kemi v Blackburn Chemicals Ltd* [2001] 2 Lloyd's Rep 93 (CA); *Government of Newfoundland v Newfoundland Railway Co; Hanak v Green* [1958] 2 QB 9.

[38] [1977] 2 All Er 241.

[39] See chapter 7 for the meaning of a floating charge.

This action had the effect of assigning to C property of B embraced by the floating charge. This property included B's right to payment for the computers that it had supplied to A. Furthermore, A had notice of the appointment of the receiver and thus of the assignment of its indebtedness to C. At a later date, A decided to terminate its hire purchase contract with B as a result of B's failure to keep up payment of the instalments. Under the hire purchase contract this action had the effect of collapsing all future instalments into one presently owed and liquidated lump sum. The question, in proceedings brought by C against A, was whether A could set off against C's claim the amount that B owed it under the hire purchase contract. This could have been done by means of equitable set off had it not been for the lack of a material connection between the sale and the hire purchase contracts. The Court of Appeal, moreover, held that common law set off could not help A since notice of the assignment to C had occurred before B's obligation to pay the lump sum had fallen due.

A final point to note about the debtor's defences is that they may be excluded by contract. This is commonly done in company debenture instruments to facilitate sales by holders (assignors) to buyers (assignees) who are freed from the burden of inquiring into the underlying relations between the holder and the company debtor.[40] The ease of transfer this produces obviously encourages investors to take up company debenture issues.

NO-ASSIGNMENT CLAUSES

It was earlier stated that the consent of the debtor was not needed to effect an assignment. Where A, B and C combine by contract to transfer the debt, the transaction is more appropriately termed a novation and C has a direct contractual right against A to receive payment, rather than a right transferred from B. Novation is the appropriate transaction to employ if burdens under the A-B contract are to be transferred to C[41] since the rule of privity of contract prevents burdens from being imposed on strangers to a contract.

Although the debtor's consent may not be needed for an assignment, suppose that the contract giving rise to the debt prescribes the method of assignment or even prohibits it altogether. An example of a prescribed

---

[40] *Palmer's Company Law*, 25th edn, London: Sweet & Maxwell, 1992, chapter 13.049.
[41] *Tolhurst v Associated Portland Cement Manufacturers (1900) Ltd* [1902] 2 KB 660, *per* Collins MR; *Linden Gardens Trust Ltd v Lenesta Sludge Disposals Ltd* [1994] 1 AC 85.

method of assignment concerns shares in a company. Section 183 of the Companies Act 1985 states that a proper instrument of transfer must be used and regs. 23–28 of Table A deal as a matter of contract with the conditions governing the registration by the company of the shares' new owner. Greater difficulties are presented in cases where the contract prohibits assignment. It is a standard condition of hire purchase agreements that the hirer shall not assign the benefit of the option (though the finance company will agree a settlement figure with, for example, a car dealer taking a hire purchase vehicle as a trade-in). Such clauses are recognized as effective.[42] Large organizations, such as universities and local authorities, commonly incorporate no-assignment clauses in their standard terms of trading. The reasons for this are not hard to find. The organization wishes to guard against the possibility of a junior employee inadvertently paying the assignor, despite having received notice of the assignment, with the result that a good discharge for payment is not given. Furthermore, notice of an assignment prevents the debtor from raising fresh equities and defences against the assignee. In the absence of an assignment, the debtor could raise them against the assignor in their continuing mutual dealings.

The effectiveness of a no-assignment clause was recognized in *Helstan Securities Ltd v Hertfordshire County Council*.[43] A contract for road works stipulated that the contractor should not 'assign the contract or any part thereof or any benefit or interest therein or thereunder' without the local authority's written consent. An assignment of the moneys due having been made without this consent, the claimant assignee brought an action against the authority for payment. The action was unsuccessful despite the claimant's argument that the debt was not caught by the language of the prohibition. If the court had stopped there, the result would have been unexceptionable.[44] Croom-Johnson J, however, went beyond holding that the debtor had a complete defence to the assignee's action; he stated that the assignment itself was invalid.

The significance of this distinction is as follows. Suppose that the assignor becomes insolvent after the assignment. It is one thing to say that an assignment that flouts a no-assignment clause is ineffective as between debtor and assignee; it is another to go on and say that it is also ineffective as between assignor and assignee. Suppose for the moment that the

---

[42] *United Dominion Trust Ltd v Parkway Motors Ltd* [1955] 1 WLR 719.

[43] [1978] 3 All ER 262.

[44] See the similar dictum of Bramwell LJ in *Brice v Bannister* (1878) 3 QBD 569, expressing a common lawyer's hostility to the equitable rule in the immediate post-fusion years.

no-assignment clause affects only relations between the debtor and the assignee. It is likely, as a matter of contractual construction, that an assignor will be in breach of contract if the debtor refuses to pay, but an action for breach of contract is worth very little against an insolvent assignor. If, however, the assignment is effective as between assignor and assignee to transfer the property interest in the debt, the assignee's proprietary interest will prevail against a liquidator or trustee in bankruptcy representing the unsecured creditors of the insolvent assignor. Any moneys coming into the hands of the assignor or the liquidator or trustee will be impressed with a trust in favour of the assignee.[45]

The reasoning of Croom-Johnson J would deny effect to the assignment between assignor and assignee on the ground that the contract decides whether a right to payment may be treated as an item of property (see the contrary view of the court in *Re Turcan*).[46] In view of the importance of trade debts in the raising of finance, the width of language in the decision is regrettable, despite Lord Browne-Wilkinson's observation in *Linden Gardens Trust Ltd v Lenesta Sludge Disposals Ltd* that 'there is no public need for a market in choses in action'.[47] It is not practicable for a factor or mortgagee to make inquiries about each individual debt when blocks of debts are being assigned. No hardship as between debtor and assignee arises from the assignee having a property entitlement against the assignor.

The House of Lords in *Linden Gardens Trust* affirmed the ruling in *Helstan Securities Ltd v Hertfordshire County Council* that a debtor could invoke a no-assignment clause against the assignee, but affirmed too that 'in the absence of the clearest words' the clause would not invalidate the contract between assignor and assignee.[48] There seems, however, no good reason to allow a no-assignment clause in the underlying contract between debtor and assignor to affect the contractual relations of assignor and assignee at all, for that would impose on the assignee the burden of a contract to which he was a stranger. If notwithstanding a no-assignment clause the assignor undertakes to effect an assignment, the assignor should be contractually bound to do so, just as a seller of goods who contracts to transfer a full title to the buyer is in breach of contract when

---

[45] See *Barclays Bank plc v Willowbrook International Ltd* [1987] 1 FTLR 386; *International Factors Ltd v Rodriguez* [1979] QB 351 (where there was an express clause in the assignment to that effect).

[46] (1880) 40 Ch D 5.

[47] [1994] 1 AC 85, at p 107.

[48] *Linden Gardens Trust Ltd v Lenesta Sludge Disposals Ltd* [1994] 1 AC 85, at p 108.

failing to bring this about.[49] The House of Lords also noted without disapproval the possibility of the assignor's conduct amounting to a declaration of trust of the proceeds of the debt in favour of the assignee.[50]

No-assignment clauses together with trusts arising from assignments were given an extended treatment in *Don King Productions Inc v Warren*.[51] The case arose out of a contractual undertaking on the part of a boxing promoter to assign to a partnership 'the full benefit and burden of all existing promotional and management contracts'. Because the contracts concerned personal services, they could not be assigned. Some of them, furthermore, contained no-assignment clauses. Nevertheless, the court held that the agreement was effective in making the promoter trustee not only of the contracts but also of the benefit of being a contracting party. The meaning of this extension was that not just the fruits of these non-assignable contracts, but also rights to renew them upon expiry, were the subject matter of the trust. Apparent recognition was given to the underlying contract effectively prohibiting not merely assignment but also a declaration of trust of the benefit of a contract, though it was noted that a court would not lightly construe the contract to this effect.[52] Just as a no-assignment clause ought not to invalidate the contract between assignor and assignee, so too there seems no good reason to allow it to invalidate a trust. The account debtor, nevertheless, may have legitimate concerns about being drawn into contact with the assignee, a possibility that might arise where the beneficiary of a trust takes proceedings in respect of trust property in default of action by the trustee.[53] A response to this comes in the form of an assurance that '[r]ules and procedures designed to enable a beneficiary to sue in respect of a contract held in trust for him would not be applied so as to jeopardise trust property'.[54] Traditional trust rules of a specialist and non-fundamental kind ought not to be applied in commercial matters if this would be inappropriate.

To conclude the above discussion, apart from the difficulties arising out of very extensive no-assignment clauses, a no-assignment clause will prevent the assignee from suing the account debtor, who has a defence or an equity based upon that clause. It will not however prevent the assignee from claiming the proceeds of the debt in the hands of the assignor under

---

[49] Sale of Goods Act 1979, s 12.　　[50] [1994] 1 AC 85, at p 106.

[51] [1998] 2 All ER 608, affirmed [1999] 2 All ER 218 (CA).

[52] [1998] 2 All ER 608, at pp 632–633.

[53] *Vandepitte v Preferred Accident Insurance Corpn* [1933] AC 70. See Tettenborn [1998] LMCLQ 498.

[54] [1999] 2 All ER 218, at p 234.

the terms of an express trust, if there is one, or on the terms of a constructive trust if there is no express trust.

Finally, there is a curious, but potentially significant, decision of the Court of Appeal to consider.[55] This case concerned a debenture creating security over future contract rights, which was followed by a contract containing a no-assignment clause. The court held that the decision in *Linden Gardens* on no-assignment clauses extended only to assignments in breach of such clauses and not to antecedent assignments which could not infringe a clause not yet in existence. If this is correct, which must be doubted, no-assignment clauses will be largely ineffective against banks providing medium- to long-term finance, though they will still be effective against factors purchasing existing accounts.

PRIORITIES

Suppose that the same debt or other thing in action is assigned to two or more assignees. Which of them has priority? the basic priority rule where there are successive transfers of either legal or equitable property, real or personal, is that the first in time prevails, but an exception is made to this in the case of assignment of things in action. According to the rule in *Dearle v Hall*,[56] the first of two or more assignees for value to give notice of the assignment to the debtor will have priority. This rule of priority includes an assignment by way of charge, even though the assignment in such a case is a partial one.[57] A proviso to the rule is that the assignee did not have notice (which may be the constructive notice that comes from being put on inquiry[58]) of an earlier assignment. Notice may be given to the debtor, trustee (if the property is equitable) or other person whose duty it is to make payment in respect of the assigned property.[59] When given to trustees, it need not be given again merely because those trustees are subsequently replaced by others.[60] If the competing assignees give notice on the same day, priority between them will depend upon the date of creation of the assignments.[61] Though the notice that has to be given may generally be informal for present purposes,[62] a special statutory

---

[55] *Foamcrete (UK) Ltd v Thrust Engineering Ltd* (CA, unreported 21 December 2000).
[56] (1828) 3 Russ 1.
[57] *Colonial Central Mutual Insurance Co Ltd v ANZ Banking Group (New Zealand) Ltd* [1995] 3 All ER 987.
[58] *Spencer v Clarke* (1878) 9 Ch D 137.
[59] *Stephens v Green* [1895] 2 Ch 148.
[60] *Ward v Duncombe sub nom. Re Wyatt* [1892] 1 Ch 188.
[61] *Re Dallas* [1904] 2 Ch 385, *per* Buckley J.
[62] *Ex p Agra Bank* (1868) LR 3 Ch App 555.

provision requires written notice to the trustee in the case of dealings in equitable property.[63] This same section[64] extends the rule in *Dearle v Hall* to successive dealings in equitable interests in land.

The priority rule in *Dearle v Hall* appears to have been influenced by the companion rule that the debtor is discharged on payment to the assignor unless notified of the assignee's superior entitlement. Nevertheless, a review of the authorities shows that the reasoning behind the rule is hard to find and may not now be the same as that supporting its initial formulation in the early nineteenth century. As stated by Lord Macnaghten in *Ward v Duncombe*[65] (see also the summary of his reasons by Buckley J in *Re Dallas*), the rule stemmed from early bankruptcy authorities laying down the steps that had to be taken by an assignee if the property in question were not to be regarded as within the order and distribution of a (subsequently) bankrupt assignor and thus available for distribution to the bankrupt's general creditors. The giving of notice was seen as removing the appearance of the assignor's continuing ownership of the property, though it is hard to see why, and as amounting to the nearest thing to the taking of possession as was possible in the case of intangible property. The modern view is that notice is not needed in order to complete or perfect the assignment.[66] Furthermore, the requirement that notice be given is not based upon the idea that an assignee who fails to give notice is in neglect of a duty to do so, or upon a comparative evaluation of the conduct of the competing assignees.[67] Hence, the rule in *Dearle v Hall* was held applicable even though one of the assignees of an expectant interest in a legacy was unable at the relevant time to give notice, because no qualified trustee had been appointed to receive it.[68]

Lord Macnaghten[69] has roundly criticized the rule in *Dearle v Hall*, claiming that it has caused as much injustice as it has prevented. There has been a modern tendency not to extend the rule. Thus it was not applied between competing creditors, each with a floating charge over property of the debtor company covering debts owed to it by the Crown.[70] It was also excluded where a landlord, exercising a statutory right akin to distress, and the receiver of the tenant company each claimed an

---

[63] Law of Property Act 1925, s 137(3).
[64] See subsection (1).
[65] [1893] AC 369.
[66] *Ward v Duncombe*; *Gorringe v Irwell India Rubber Works* (1886) 34 Ch D 128.
[67] *Ward v Duncombe*.   [68] *Re Dallas*.
[69] In *Ward v Duncombe*.   [70] *Re Ind Coope & Co* [1911] 2 Ch 223.

entitlement to sub-rental income owed to the tenant.[71] The rule has no application to successive dealings in company shares. The company itself is not the owner of the shares[72] and in any event would be prevented by statute from entering notice of assignments on the company register.[73]

Nevertheless, the view has recently been taken that the rule in *Dearle v Hall* applies to competing assignments even if one (or more) of them is a legal, in the sense of statutory, assignment. In *E. Pfeiffer Weinkellerei-Weineinkauf GmbH & Co v Arbuthnot Factors*,[74] a contract for the sale of a quantity of German wine contained a clause that was held to amount to an assignment by way of charge over the proceeds of resale of the wine by the buyer. Those same proceeds were the subject of an assignment of book debts made by the buyer in favour of a factor. Though the case went in favour of the factor on another ground, Philips J rejected the factor's argument that its later assignment prevailed because, in complying with the formal requirements of s 136 of the Law of Property Act 1925, it had acquired a legal title to the proceeds of resale overriding the seller's mere equitable title. The s 136 statutory assignment was a matter of machinery;[75] it only altered the procedure by which the assignee could take proceedings against the debtor. Furthermore, the rule subjecting the assignee to defences and equities that the debtor could have raised against the assignor showed that the equitable rules of assignment served as the model for the statutory assignment. Consequently, the rule in *Dearle v Hall* applied. It is likely too that the rule would also apply as between an assignment, on the one hand, and an equitable right to trace, on the other.[76] Such a conflict would have arisen in *Pfeiffer* if the contest had been between the factor's assignment and the seller's retained equitable interest in the wine without a further assignment of the proceeds of its resale in the seller's favour.

---

[71] *Rhodes v Allied Dunbar Pension Services Ltd* [1989] 1 WLR 800.

[72] *Société Génerale de Paris v Walker* (1885) 11 App Cas 20.

[73] Companies Act 1985, s 360.

[74] [1988] 1 WLR 150.

[75] See also *Torkington v Magee* [1902] 2 KB 427; *Compaq Computers Ltd v Abercorn Group Ltd* [1991] BCC 484.

[76] See Goode, R.M., *Legal Problems of Credit and Security*, 2nd edn, London: Sweet & Maxwell, 1988, p 121; *cf.* McLauchlan (1980) 96 LQR 90.

NEGOTIABILITY

MEANING OF NEGOTIABILITY

The word 'negotiability' is a very misleading one. It means one thing for bills of exchange and quite another for bills of lading. These two instruments may be taken as illustrative examples of the different meanings of 'negotiability'. Their negotiation, moreover, may also be compared with the assignment of things in action.

BILLS OF EXCHANGE

In chapter 5, we saw that the rule of title transfer in the case of currency (cash and banknotes) was more generous to the transferee than the rule of *nemo dat quod non habet* together with its various exceptions. A transferee for value and without notice obtains title to currency even at the expense of a previous owner from whom it was stolen.[77] Briefly, the bona fide purchaser for value without notice of a bill of exchange, known as the holder in due course, gets the protection of the currency rule and is not subjected to equities and defences arising out of the transaction that gave birth to the bill of exchange. (For the protection of borrowers acquiring, for example, goods on hire purchase terms, the use of bills of exchange (and promissory notes) is severely curtailed in regulated consumer credit agreements.[78]) According to Denning LJ in *Arab Bank v Ross*:[79] 'A bill of exchange is like currency. It should be above suspicion.' The holder in due course is therefore better off than an assignee, who takes subject to equities and defences arising under the contract between the debtor and the assignor even if unaware of them.

The law relating to bills of exchange, as well as to other negotiable instruments known as promissory notes, is laid down in a codifying statute, the Bills of Exchange Act 1882. In the case of those bills of exchange that are cheques, there is also the Cheques Act 1957 and the Cheques Act 1992, which fall outside the scope of this work.

A bill of exchange is an unconditional order in writing addressed (and signed) by a drawer to a drawee to pay a sum of money to a named person or to bearer.[80] The named person may even be the drawer or the drawee.[81] The bearer is anyone who happens to be in possession of a bill of exchange,[82] so a bill made out in this form can be informally circulated by

---

[77] *Miller v Race* (1758) 1 Burr 452.
[79] [1952] 2 QB 216.
[81] Section 5(1).

[78] Consumer Credit Act 1974, s 123.
[79] Bills of Exchange Act 1882, s 3(1).
[82] Section 2.

being passed from hand to hand. To take a simple case, suppose that B wishes to sell goods to A for £1,000. B may draw on A for the price by ordering A to pay C, B's banker. B may already have received advances from C and have incurred a commitment to draw on A in favour of C. A unilateral order of this sort will not bind A. For A to become liable on the bill, A must accept the bill by writing on it that it has been accepted and then must sign the bill.[83]

The sum payable by the bill must be a sum certain.[84] This, together with the requirement that it must be an unconditional order,[85] emphasizes that the bill is a financial instrument as divorced (so far as is practicable) as a banknote from an underlying contract for the sale of goods, to name one example. According to Ashhurst J in *Carlos v Fancourt*:[86] 'Certainty is the great object in negotiable instruments, and unless they carry their own validity on the face of them they are not negotiable'. Furthermore, the bill must be payable either 'on demand' or 'at a fixed or determinable future time'.[87] A demand bill drawn on a bank is a cheque.[88] It is common for future bills to be drawn at intervals (or usances) of thirty days and larger denominations of thirty day periods. In this way, the drawee, the buyer of goods in our example, obtains credit before being called upon to pay.

Once a bill has been drawn, and even before it has been accepted, it may be negotiated, in the sense of being transferred, down a chain of holders. This process is started by the payee, if a named person, indorsing the bill in favour of and delivering it to another named person,[89] who may then subsequently do the same for another and so on. At any time in the process, the bill can become a bearer bill by being made out to bearer in the first place, or being indorsed in favour of bearer or simply being signed in blank by the holder,[90] whereupon it passes from hand to hand.[91] Each person signing the bill (but not a mere bearer) undertakes that payment will be duly made by the drawee and may be sued by the holder if payment is not forthcoming.[92] The negotiable character of the bill can be removed by its being restrictively indorsed so as to prevent further transfer or allow it only within certain limits.[93]

To return to our example of the sale of goods, suppose that the

---

[83] Section 17(2).
[84] Bills of Exchange Act 1882, sections 3(1) and 9(1).
[85] Sections 3(1) and 11.
[86] (1794) 5 TR 482.
[87] Section 3(1).
[88] Section 73.
[89] Section 31(3).
[90] Section 34(1).
[91] Section 31(2).
[92] Section 23.
[93] Section 35(1).

eventual holder presents the bill to the drawee-buyer, who has previously accepted it. The buyer argues that the goods sold were defective. If this were simply a case of an assigned debt, the assignee would be subject to the buyer's equities and defences against the seller. But if the holder of the bill is a holder in due course, the buyer will be required to pay on the bill. The holder in due course is one who takes it in good faith and for value without notice of any defect of title on the part of the person who negotiated it.[94] A defect of title arises when the bill or its acceptance was obtained 'by fraud, duress, or force and fear, or other unlawful means etc', which is all very broad. A forged or unauthorized signature on the bill, however, is wholly inoperative[95] and results in an absence of title rather than a mere defect. A drawee paying out on a stolen bearer cheque, however, without notice of its theft, is discharged from further liability on the instrument,[96] which illustrates the risk involved in carrying bearer bills.

The other type of negotiable instrument in the Bills of Exchange Act 1882 is a promissory note, defined as an unconditional promise in writing signed by the maker of the note in favour of a named person or bearer.[97] It is quite hard to produce a bill of exchange by accident, but much easier to do in the case of a promissory note. Given that lay persons may not understand the significance of what they are signing, courts have declined to recognize as promissory notes mere receipts and IOUs and similar informal documents.[98]

BILLS OF LADING AND OTHER CARRIAGE DOCUMENTS

In international sales the carrier of goods bridges the gap between the seller and the buyer. It is common for the seller to contract with an ocean-going carrier for delivery to the buyer. Since the buyer has a practical interest in the successful outcome of the carriage, it is commercially necessary to devise a means of substituting the buyer for the seller in the contract with the carrier. This involves not merely transferring the seller's contractual rights to the buyer, as would be so for a simple assignment; the seller's contractual liabilities (for example, for unpaid freight charges) need to be transferred too.

The classical method for transferring such rights and liabilities may be seen in the following example. Suppose that a seller of goods has them loaded on an ocean-going vessel and makes a contract for their carriage to

---

[94] Bills of Exchange Act 1882, s 29(1). [95] Section 24.
[96] *Charles v Blackwell* (1876) 1 CPD 48. [97] Section 83(1).
[98] *Akbar Khan v Attar Singh* [1936] 1 All ER 545; *Claydon v Bradley* [1987] 1 WLR 521.

an overseas port with the carrier (an owner or charterer of the vessel). The carrier issues a document called a bill of lading attesting to the fact that the goods have been shipped on board the vessel and naming either the seller of the goods or some other person as consignee to collect the goods at the port of discharge. During the voyage the goods are damaged in circumstances engaging the contractual responsibility of the carrier. Suppose further that the current holder of the bill of lading (to whom the bill has been negotiated in a way similar to that employed for bills of exchange) is the buyer. Does the buyer have the benefit of the carrier's delivery obligation undertaken to the seller?

The answer is not quite straightforward. The common law rule was that the negotiation of the bill did not transfer to the new holder the benefit of the carrier's obligation to deliver.[99] Starting from the position that 'by the Custom of Merchants . . . all Rights in respect of the Contract contained in the Bill of Lading continue in the original Shipper or Owner' (preamble), the now repealed Bills of Lading Act 1855 (in s 1) went on to state, by way of exception, a statutory procedure for the transfer of rights and liabilities. This provision was replete with problems because it referred only to bills of lading and because it tied the negotiation of the bill to the contemporaneous passing of property in the cargo. Particular difficulties arose in the case of bulk cargoes.[100] A holder obtaining the bill of lading in circumstances outside the section, or someone relying on an equivalent carriage document, did not acquire contractual rights or incur contractual liabilities under the statute. The effects of such a transfer, however, were produced outside the statute by inferring artificial contracts between the holder of the bill of lading and the carrier on the basis of behaviour like the payment of freight by the holder and the delivery of the goods by the carrier.[101] Such contracts had read into them the terms of the original contract of carriage set out in the bill of lading. As a result of the Carriage of Goods by Sea Act 1992, the position is now much simpler. The use of a number of specified documents, such as sea waybills, received for shipment bills of lading and ship's delivery orders, and not just the on board bill of lading, may serve to transfer rights and liabilities under a marine carriage contract. Furthermore, the process of transfer will no longer depend upon the passing of property.

---

[99] *Thompson v Dominy* (1845) 14 M & W 403.
[100] See for example *The Aramis* [1989] 1 Lloyd's Rep 213; Law Commission (No. 196), *Rights of Suit in Respect of Carriage of Goods by Sea* (1991).
[101] *Brandt v Liverpool Brazil and River Plate Steam Navigation Co* [1924] 1 KB 575; *Cremer v General Carriers* [1973] 2 Lloyd's Rep 366.

7

Security interests in personal property

INTRODUCTION

In this chapter we shall be looking at the use of property concepts, discussed in earlier chapters, to perform a security function. The security function will exist to reinforce the performance of a personal obligation, typically but not invariably the payment of a sum of money. If A owes B £500 and A defaults, B has a personal action on the debt but may also have recourse to any property that secures payment of the debt. When A gives security in this way, A's incentive to repay is heightened, especially if the property secured is worth more than the amount of the debt, or has a value to A in excess of its market value or would, if disposed of by B, seriously inconvenience the conduct of A's affairs. Besides the incentive given to A to perform, B has a further advantage whose importance can scarcely be overestimated in troubled economic times. As someone with a security interest, B may be able to resort to the secured property in order to seek payment without having to join all of A's unsecured creditors in the queue for a dividend payable upon A's liquidation (if A is a company) or upon A's bankruptcy (if A is an individual).

The above example is only one of many different types in which security is granted. For present purposes, security in the case of chattels may take one of four different forms. It may take the possessory form of a lien or a pledge (or pawn). The former is a security that arises at common law in defined circumstances and the second is one whose usefulness is strictly limited. In addition to lien and pledge, there are the (usually) non-possessory securities of mortgage and charge, the latter of which may exist in either a fixed or a floating form. Lien and pledge are based purely upon the common law idea of possession,[1] though there is such a thing as an equitable lien, to which reference will later be made. Mortgage, driven by the idea that ownership is transferred, may be either legal or equitable. A charge, recognized only in equity, is a type of encumbrance on property and may exist in either a fixed or a floating form.

[1] See chapter 2.

Property concepts may also be used in a way that does not, in the eyes of the law, involve the grant of security rights. We saw in chapter 2 the nature of a hire purchase contract by which a finance company could retain the general property in goods pending the payment of all the agreed instalments and the (usually nominal) option fee. It has been held at the highest level that such a transaction does not involve the grant of security by the hirer but rather the reservation of ownership by the finance company.[2] Consequently, the finance company would not have to register its interest under bills of sale (individuals and partnerships) and company charges legislation since these provisions apply only to a nominate list of mortgages and charges. Moreover, the finance company would be able to invoke the general rule of *nemo dat quod non habet* to repel the claims of transferees from the hirer, whether this occurs absolutely or by way of security (subject to the *nemo dat* exception contained in Part III of the Hire Purchase Act 1964). In a similar fashion, it has become common in recent years for trade suppliers of goods to avail themselves of their rights to retain the general property in goods supplied when an application of the presumptive rules in s 18 of the Sale of Goods Act 1979 would otherwise have recognized the passing of property to the buyer.[3]

POSSESSORY SECURITY

LIEN

Lien may be defined in general terms as a passive right to retain a chattel (in certain cases, documentary intangibles and papers) conferred by law. The party entitled to assert the lien may be called the lienee and the party surrendering the possession, which gives rise to the lien, the lienor. Lien is therefore not consensual, is not conferred by the lienor and is confined to cases where the right has historically been established. It seems fair to say that the modern law is content to leave the existence of a lien to legal history without making any real attempt to rationalize its existence in modern conditions. According to Diplock LJ in *Tappenden v Artus*,[4] a lien is a 'self-help remedy' like 'other primitive remedies such as abatement of nuisance, self-defence or ejection of trespassers to land'. There is a general confluence between the conferment of a lien and the exercise of a common calling (though liens are not confined to the common callings). In mediaeval times, the exiguous nature of services in an underdeveloped

---

[2] *McEntire v Crossley Bros* [1895] AC 457.   [3] See further chapter 4.
[4] [1964] 2 QB 185.

economy led to the imposition of a duty to render them to members of the public on demand in defined circumstances, such as the common callings of innkeepers, ferrymen and common carriers, who were entitled in return to a lien for their services. It is hard to imagine this common law entitlement being extended to new relationships. Nevertheless, statute from time to time creates similar rights. The Civil Aviation Act 1982[5] permits an airport to detain an aircraft for unpaid airport charges and aviation fuel supplied. This was treated as a lien for the purpose of insolvency legislation in *Bristol Airport plc v Powdrill*.[6]

Possession and the lienee

The lien will usually involve a possessory relationship between the lienee and the object in question. Thus a garage exercising the repairer's lien can retain a vehicle in its possession pending payment of its repair charges. The lien may be exercised in such cases only in so far as the chattel is improved; it may not extend to the cost of servicing or maintenance,[7] which is perhaps an artificial line to draw. Sometimes, the lienee will not have possession as such, but rather the right to impede the party in possession from exercising in full the rights that normally accompany possession. One example of this is the right of detention, as opposed to seizure and detention, of an aircraft in *Bristol Airport plc v Powdrill*. Another is the innkeeper's right to detain the luggage of a guest[8] against unpaid charges. The personal baggage of a guest in a hotel bedroom can hardly be said to be possessed by the hotel.[9]

General and special liens

Liens may be divided into general and special (or particular) liens. The former is the rarer case. It is to be found, for example, in the case of solicitors (bankers, accountants and stockbrokers too) who have a lien over their clients' papers for all sums owing for professional services rendered. The effectiveness of the lien will depend upon the extent to which the retention of papers impedes the client's personal or business dealings.[10] The lien may not, however, be exercised in circumstances

---

[5] Section 88.

[6] [1990] Ch 744. See also *The Freightline One* [1986] 1 Lloyd's Rep 266 (detention of ship under Port of London Act 1968, s 39).

[7] *Hatton v Car Maintenance* [1915] 1 Ch 621.

[8] But not vehicles: Hotel Proprietors Act 1956, s 2(2).

[9] See Fletcher Moulton LJ in *Lord's Trustee v Great Eastern Railway Co* [1908] 2 KB 54.

[10] *Eide UK Ltd v Lowndes Lambert Group Ltd* [1998] 1 All ER 946 (CA).

where statute requires the papers to be kept in a particular place or surrendered to an insolvency office-holder.[11] The lien is general in the sense that it is not confined to services connected with the papers in question. A special lien, on the other hand, requires a close connection between the chattel and the services rendered. The repairer's lien, for example, can only be exercised in respect of charges arising out of the instant transaction. If the repairer has performed work in the past and released the chattel to the owner, the lien thereby lost cannot be revived by attaching the unpaid bill to a later lien arising as a result of future services.[12] A special lien, however, may be expanded by contract so as to amount to a general lien. This is common in the case of carriers.[13] It appears to be uncontroversial that a general lien thus created is not an equitable charge.

Limitations of lien

A lien cannot be transferred;[14] in this respect it is weaker than a pledge interest.[15] It cannot be asserted by a third party to whom possession of the goods is given, without the bailor's authority, by a bailee to perform services that should by agreement have been performed by the bailee.[16] If the chattel is surrendered to the lienor, the lien entitlement is lost[17] unless, by agreement with the lienor, the lien is to persist despite a temporary release of possession by the lienee.[18] A lienee who releases possession of a chattel without authority thereby surrenders any lien entitlement.[19] A lien does not carry with it a power of sale at common law,[20] a matter of some embarrassment to the lienee if the chattel is awkward or expensive to maintain. A lienee who unlawfully sells the chattel commits the tort of conversion and also surrenders the lien.[21] In certain cases, however, a power of sale is explicitly conferred by statute.[22]

---

[11] See *Re Anglo-Maltese Dry Dock Co Ltd* (1885) 54 LJ Ch 730; *Re Aveling Barford Ltd* [1989] 1 WLR 360; *DTC (CNC) Ltd v Gary Sargent & Co* [1996] 1 WLR 797.

[12] *Hatton v Car Maintenance*.

[13] *George Barker Ltd v Eynon* [1974] 1 WLR 462.

[14] *Legg v Evans* (1840) 6 M & W 36.

[15] *Donald v Suckling* (1866) LR 1 QB 585.

[16] *Pennington v Reliance Motors Ltd* [1923] 1 KB 127.

[17] *Hatton v Car Maintenance*.

[18] *Albemarle Supply Co v Hind* [1928] 1 KB 307: car released 'in pawn'.

[19] *Ibid*.

[20] *Thames Iron Works Co v Patent Derrick Co* (1860) 1 J & H 93; *Somes v British Empire Shipping Co* (1859) 28 LJQB 220.

[21] *Mulliner v Florence* (1878) 3 QBD 484.

[22] For example, the Innkeepers Act 1878; Torts (Interference with Goods) Act 1977, Schedule 1, Part II (uncollected goods).

In the case of an unpaid seller of goods, the exercise of a lien,[23] or the essentially similar right of retention where the property has not yet passed to the buyer,[24] is often the prelude to the termination of the contract and resale of the goods for the seller's own account in the way prescribed by the Act.[25] A power of sale may arise as a result of a contractual provision. It may also be permitted by statute in the case of a statutorily conferred lien.[26]

A lien may not be expanded to cover also the cost of its exercise and in any event will be lost if execution is levied against the chattel to enforce a judgment against the lienor.[27] It is in this sense that a lien is a passive right of retention.

Lienor, lienee and owner

Suppose the lienor granting the lienee possession of the chattel is not its owner. May a lien be asserted against the true owner? Certain statutes amplify the right of a lienee at the expense of the owner (a particularly striking example being the Civil Aviation Act 1982, s 88). The position at common law is best dealt with by considering separately the cases of repairers and innkeepers, since they raise different considerations. Of the two, only the repairer adds value to the chattel, while only the innkeeper has a duty to deal with members of the public.

It would not be a practicable requirement for a repairer to inquire into the ownership of each and every chattel presented for repair. A number of cases have involved cars, the leading one being *Tappenden v Artus*.[28] This case responds to the thorny question of why a repairer's lien binds an owner who has not specifically consented to the repair transaction. The owner of a van allowed a prospective purchaser (the lienor) to use it on condition that he licensed and insured it. When the van was being driven by the lienor in connection with his work, it broke down. The lienor called in a repairer who took possession of the van imagining the lienor to be its owner and making no inquiries to that effect. When the owner tracked down the repairer, the repair work had already been done. The owner refused to pay and the repairer's lien was upheld by the Court of Appeal. The lien was a 'right to continue an existing actual possession of goods' and was thus dependent on that possession (*viz*, the repairer's possession) being 'lawful at the time at which the lien first attached'

---

[23] Sale of Goods Act 1979, s 39(1)(a).   [24] Section 39(2).   [25] Section 48.
[26] Civil Aviation Act 1982, s 88.
[27] *Thames Iron Works Co v Patent Derrick Co.*   [28] [1964] 2 QB 185.

rather than when the repairs were later done. The lienor had an implied authority, defined by the terms of the contract and the purposes of the bailment, to give possession of the car to the garage for repairs 'necessary to render [the van] roadworthy' since this was 'reasonably incidental' to his use of it. The question was not whether the lienor had authority to confer a lien: liens are conferred by operation of law once a particular relationship has arisen between the parties.

Tappenden v Artus does not state the position where the lienor has repairs done that go beyond roadworthiness, or otherwise acts beyond the authority conferred by the owner, as might happen where the owner forbids the lienor to give possession of the chattel to a repairer. (If the owner forbids the granting of a lien, this would not be sufficient to withdraw the lienor's implied authority to give possession.) It is well settled, however, that if the lienor has apparent authority to surrender possession for repair, this will be sufficient to permit the repairer to assert the lien.[29] A restrictive clause not drawn to the attention of the repairer (how could it have been?) by the owner will not detract from this apparent authority.[30]

An innkeeper's lien extends to all chattels brought as baggage to the inn by the guest and is not confined to chattels that are the subject of the innkeeper's services.[31] Where the chattel comes later, for example a courtesy piano supplied by a manufacturer for the use of a travelling virtuoso,[32] it falls outside the lien since it is 'not brought to the inn by a traveller as his goods' but rather is sent later for a defined purpose. The principle of the matter was expressed by Parke B who put it in terms of the duty owed by innkeepers, engaged in a common calling, to those travelling the roads of the realm. An innkeeper would not be bound to accept a piano as part of his guest's baggage any more than an innkeeper, with space in his stable only for a horse, would have to accept a carriage. No clear guidance is given by the court as to what the position would be if the guest had brought the piano with him and the hotel had willingly received it. Nor is a clear response given to the rather more important question whether the lien could be asserted even if the innkeeper knew that his guest did not own the goods in question, whether at the time the guest arrived in the inn or at some later date. If the innkeeper does not extend credit on the faith of the guest's apparent ownership of the

---

[29] *Albemarle Supply Co v Hind* (1928); *Bowmaker Ltd v Wycombe Motors Ltd* [1946] KB 505.
[30] *Albemarle Supply Co v Hind.*   [31] *Mulliner v Florence* (1878) 3 QBD 484.
[32] *Broadwood v Granara* (1854) 10 Ex 417.

baggage and does not add value to it, this is an argument for construing narrowly the lien right if it conflicts with the right of a third party owner.

The difficult issue of the third party owner is carried further in *Robins & Co v Gray*.[33] An innkeeper had advance notice that sewing machines, the baggage of a commercial traveller, belonged to his employer. The court held that the innkeeper had a lien upon the machines which, in accordance with the custom of the realm, he had to receive as his guest's baggage, when the salesman left without paying his bill for board and lodging. The innkeeper is under no obligation to inquire as to the ownership of such baggage but he need not accept 'something exceptional' (Lord Esher: 'a tiger or a package of dynamite'). If he does accept such goods, then the lien would extend to them. According to Lord Esher, 'the question of whose property they are, or of the innkeeper's knowledge as to whose property they are, is immaterial'. This very wide reading of the innkeeper's rights is justified by reference to the strict liability of the innkeeper under the custom of the realm, which goes beyond the ordinary negligence standard. At common law, the innkeeper guarantees the safety of the goods against thieves, except where the goods are lost through the fault of the traveller and the innkeeper proves that this is the case. Nevertheless, where this common law liability is routinely limited in accordance with legislation,[34] it is questionable how strong the liability argument is today.

PLEDGE

Pledge is an ancient form of security that takes the form of the pledgor, a debtor, transferring possession of the pledge (the property serving as security) to the pledgee creditor. It is therefore a type of bailment.[35] Since pledge involves the pledgee retaining possession of the pledge whilst the loan remains outstanding, it is not at all a suitable security to use in connection with productive assets. A manufacturer cannot pledge machinery needed on the production line. As we shall later see, however, a variant of pledge can be used in a flexible way in connection with shipping documents used in the export trade. By and large, it would be accurate to substitute indifferently the words pawn, pawnor, and pawnee for pledge, pledgor, and pledgee. The word pawnbroker, nevertheless, connotes someone who carries on the business of making small advances against pledges. Formerly regulated by pawnbroker legislation (the

---

[33] [1895] 2 QB 501.   [34] Hotel Proprietors Act 1956.
[35] See *Coggs v Bernard* (1703) 2 Ld Raym 909.

Pawnbrokers Acts of 1872 and 1960) and now by the Consumer Credit Act 1974,[36] the occupation of pawnbroker is very much associated with consumer as opposed to trade credit, and moreover with debtors who are unable to obtain advances from conventional sources of lending.

Security aspects of pledge

Unlike a lienee, a pledgee is considered as acquiring a special property in the pledge.[37] For practical purposes, the pledgee's interest is therefore capable of being transferred[38] and the pledgee is also invested with a common law power of sale in the event of default by the pledgor in repaying the loan.[39] Pledge is considered as a security of intermediate strength between a lien and a mortgage.[40] A pledgor has an absolute entitlement to redeem the pledge unless this is constrained by the contract giving rise to the pledge. In the absence of a stated time for repayment, the pledgee may give the pledgor reasonable notice of repayment (but a pawnee has a minimum six months to redeem under the Consumer Credit Act 1974[41]) in default of which the pledgee may sell the pledge. This power of sale[42] is considered to turn upon an implied authority granted by the pledgor. The pledgor therefore retains the general property in the pledge and may transfer it during the currency of the pledge agreement, with the result that the pledgee is liable in conversion for refusing to permit the pledgor's transferee to redeem the pledge.[43] Furthermore, the pledgee must account to the pledgor for any surplus realized after the debt (for pawn see the Consumer Credit Act 1974[44]) and the costs of selling have been reimbursed.[45] It has been held that a fiduciary relationship exists between pledgor and pledgee so that, if this surplus is not paid to the pledgor, the pledgee will be bound in equity to pay interest to the pledgor.[46] Where a deficiency has been realized, notwithstanding the sale being a provident one, the pledgor can be sued by the pledgee for this balance.[47]

---

[36] Sections 114–121.
[37] *Carter v Wake* (1877) 4 Ch D 605; *Sewell v Burdick* (1884) 10 App Cas 74.
[38] *Donald v Suckling* (1866) LR 1 QB 585.
[39] *Ex p Hubbard* (1886) 17 QBD 699.
[40] *Halliday v Holgate* (1868) LR 3 Ex 299.
[41] Section 116.
[42] See Consumer Credit Act 1974, s 121, for the case of pawn.
[43] *Franklin v Neate* (1844) 13 M & W 481.
[44] Section 121(3).
[45] *Halliday v Holgate.*   [46] *Mathew v T. M. Sutton Ltd* [1994] 4 All ER 793.
[47] *Jones v Marshall* (1889) 24 QBD 269.

Wrongful disposition by pledgee

It is certainly the case that a pledgee who sub-pledges the chattel without the authority of the pledgor,[48] or who disposes of the pledge without giving the bankrupt pledgor notice of the intention to sell,[49] may commit a wrong in the nature of a breach of contract in so doing and so be liable in damages based on the cost of redeeming or recovering the pledge as the case may be. The courts, however, have been reluctant to treat such behaviour as repudiating the bailment underlying the pledge,[50] given that the pledgee has a property right that is capable of being transferred. They have thus avoided the imposition on the pledgee (or on the transferee for that matter) of liability for the full value of the chattel in the tort of conversion.[51] It should be understood that the pledgee will be successful in transferring the special property in the chattel; the pledgor can always recover the pledge from a sub-pledgee by tendering the amount owed under the sub-pledge agreement.[52] In *Halliday v Holgate*, the pledgor's assignee in bankruptcy tried unsuccessfully to maintain a conversion action without tendering the balance of the debt[53] secured by the pledge, failing because he did not have the requisite entitlement to immediate possession. It is unlikely that the pledgee will be able to transfer outright title to a *bona fide* transferee under one of the exceptions to the rule of *nemo dat quod non habet*.[54]

Pledge or mortgage

It sometimes happens that a documentary intangible is deposited with a creditor as security for the repayment of a debt without the parties to the transaction characterizing the nature of the security. In such a case, the question is whether a pledge agreement or an equitable mortgage by deposit of the document has been concluded. In the case of a mortgage, the mortgagee has a drastic remedy available which may not be exercised by a pledgee: the mortgagee may foreclose,[55] thus treating the security as his outright property and retaining any surplus realised on a subsequent sale of the security. It seems that, where a transaction of this nature can be reasonably interpreted as a pledge, a sense of judicial minimalism will

---

[48] *Donald v Suckling.*   [49] *Halliday v Holgate.*
[50] *Cf. Fenn v Bittleston* (1851) 7 Ex 152: see chapter 2.
[51] *Halliday v Holgate; Donald v Suckling.*
[52] *Sewell v Burdick* (1884).
[53] Similarly, see *Donald v Suckling.*
[54] See chapter 5.
[55] But note that the pawnee may foreclose where the amount owed is small: Consumer Credit Act 1974, s 120(1)(a).

result in the agreement being so characterized. In *Carter v Wake*, the documents in question were Canada railway bonds in bearer form. Since they could be manually transferred, the pledgee's power of sale adequately protected the interests of the creditor. Similarly, the deposit of a bill of lading with a bank as security for an advance will, in accordance with normal commercial understanding, be treated as a pledge, though there is nothing to stop the parties from structuring the transaction as a mortgage.[56] In contrast, the deposit of share certificates that are not in bearer form, and thus less easy to dispose of without the cooperation of the depositor, will be interpreted as an equitable mortgage by deposit of title deeds giving rise to the remedies of a mortgagor rather than a pledgor.[57]

Trust receipt

Though fundamentally different from a lien, pledge is similar to it in another respect in addition to its being possession-based: it can be expressed to endure despite a temporary transfer of possession back to the pledgor. *North Western Bank Ltd v Poynter*[58] deals with a transaction common in the export trade. Goods in transit are dealt with through the medium of a bill of lading, which serves as a document of title to the underlying goods. This bill is sometimes pledged by the buyer with a bank as security for the bank's payment of the seller on the buyer's behalf. In order to obtain the goods from the carrier when the cargo is discharged, the buyer needs possession of the bill of lading and, to effect this, the bank releases the bill of lading to the buyer under the terms of a 'trust receipt'. The pledge of the bill is considered, in the light of the terms of the trust receipt, as continuing despite the release. The buyer takes delivery of the goods from the carrier as agent for the bank and has in that capacity to account to the bank for the amount of the advance out of the proceeds of sale of the goods.

NON-POSSESSORY SECURITY

Many of the authorities on charges and mortgages involve land. They may usefully be considered in dealing with personalty apart from certain instances where the rules of personalty and realty diverge.

---

[56] *Burdick v Sewell* (1884) 13 QBD 159, *per* Bowen LJ.

[57] *Harrold v Plenty* [1901] 2 Ch 314.

[58] [1895] AC 56. See also *Lloyds Bank v Bank of America National Trust* [1938] 2 KB 146 and *Re David Allester Ltd* [1922] 2 Ch 211.

MORTGAGE

A mortgage is the conveyance or assignment of property by a mortgagor to a mortgagee as security for the repayment of a debt or the performance of some other obligation.[59] Whilst the mortgagor will normally remain in possession, there is no requirement that this should be so. The security may be redeemed once the debt has been paid or the obligation performed as the case may be.[60] This entitlement to redeem, or equity of redemption, may not be prevented by any term or condition in the mortgage agreement, for 'once a mortgage always a mortgage'. Such an impediment to the right of redemption is known as a 'clog' on the equity of redemption. It follows that the law will be astute to see that the mortgagee does not introduce artificial terms into the agreement to deny its character as a mortgage, but there is a fine line to be drawn between freedom of contract, which involves the right to be legally creative and to choose legal forms that best advance one's interests, and the enforcement of paramount legal policy, whether it be the compulsory registration of security granted by a company[61] or the particular tenderness extended by equity to mortgagors and expressed in the form of the equity of redemption. That equity intervenes notwithstanding form is borne out by the classical way in which the mortgage is drafted: an outright conveyance or assignment with a provision that this proprietary transfer will become null and void once the debt or obligation has been paid or performed.

Personalty and land

This way of expressing a mortgage is still perfectly proper and common in the case of personalty but it has not been possible in the case of land since 1925,[62] where the mortgage of an estate in fee simple can only take effect as 'a demise for a term of years absolute subject to a provision for cesser on redemption' or as 'a charge by deed expressed by way of legal mortgage'. Since the form of an outright legal conveyance or assignment is prohibited, these statutory provisions reflect equity's maxim 'once a mortgage always a mortgage' in a way that is not the case with personalty.

---

[59] *Keith v Burrows* (1876) 1 CPD 722.

[60] *Santley v Wilde* [1899] 2 Ch 474; *Carter v Wake* (1877) 4 Ch D 605—payment puts a 'stop' on the conveyance.

[61] Companies Act 1985, ss 395–396.   [62] Law of Property Act 1925, ss 85–86.

Legal and equitable mortgages

Mortgages may be either legal or equitable. An equitable mortgage arises in two different forms. First of all, it may be the conveyance or assignment of property recognized only in equity, such as the interest of a beneficiary in a trust. Secondly, it may arise as a result of a failure to comply with the forms of a legal mortgage, for example, not using a deed where the law demands that a deed be executed (as it does with a mortgage of land: Law of Property Act 1925[63]). A similar case is where the parties agree by contract that a valid legal mortgage will be executed at a future time. In the case of both the defective execution and the binding agreement, equity looks on that as done which ought to be done and decrees that a valid equitable mortgage has been granted which can, by the equitable remedy of specific performance, be inflated into a legal mortgage. It makes a difference, of course, whether the mortgagee's interest is legal or equitable; the interest of an equitable mortgagee is liable to be defeated by the *bona fide* purchaser of the legal estate without notice. Sometimes, a mortgagee may not be greatly concerned to exact a legal mortgage. Where there is an equitable mortgage by deposit of title deeds, it must of course be treated as equitable if the relevant legal form (for example, the registration of a transfer of shares in a company) has not been used, but it will be difficult for the mortgagor to enter into dealings with a subsequent purchaser if not in possession of the title deeds.

Future property

Returning to the equitable mortgage that arises where the property in question is equitable, an important case to consider is future property. It is not so much that equity and not the common law will recognize future property; rather, only equity will give effect (eventually) to conveyances (by mortgage or otherwise) of future property. The common law refuses to recognize at all a conveyance of future property and demands that a fresh conveyance be executed once the property comes into existence.[64] Equity, on the other hand, will treat a purported present conveyance as a binding contract to convey, if consideration has been given for the promise,[65] and (praying in aid the doctrine of specific performance) will automatically convey in equity the property to the transferee once it comes into existence. The importance of this approach cannot be overemphasized for it represents the bedrock upon which companies are able

---

[63] Sections 52 and 85.   [64] *Lunn v Thornton* (1845) 1 CB 379.
[65] *Re Clarke* (1887) 36 Ch D 348; 'Equity does not assist a volunteer'.

to raise general finance on the security of fluctuating assets like stock-in-trade and book debts.[66] A landmark case is the House of Lords decision in *Holroyd v Marshall*.[67] This case concerned the mortgaging of mill machinery, including machinery brought into the mill at a future date in substitution for machinery already there. The question was whether the interest of the mortgagees in respect of that future property prevailed over subsequent execution creditors of the mortgagor. The House of Lords held that it did since, as soon as the new machinery came into the mill, it became encumbered with the mortgagee's equitable interest and the mortgagor held it on the terms of a trust for the mortgagee.

Form

No particular form is exacted in the case of a mortgage of personalty,[68] though if the mortgage is transacted in writing it will probably have to comply with the requirements set down in bills of sale legislation[69] if granted by an individual or other non-corporate entity, such as a trading partnership. This legislation will be considered below. In one particular case, however, a mortgage of personalty will have to be in writing, namely where it is a disposition of a subsisting equitable interest. If, however, the transaction creating the mortgage itself severs the equitable from the legal estate, then the equitable interest will not be a subsisting one and s 53(1)(c) of the Law of Property Act 1925 will not apply. A mortgage of an interest in a trust fund will obviously have to comply with the statutory form since the interest exists already as an equitable one at the time of the mortgage.

Charge

Like a mortgage, a charge will usually permit the grantor to remain in possession of the charged property but, unlike a mortgage, a charge involves no conveyance or assignment of an interest in the property to the grantee.[70] A charge amounts to an appropriation of property by the chargor in favour of the chargee as security for the payment of a debt or performance of another obligation.[71] Salmond writes of a charge casting a

[66] *Tailby v Official Receiver* (1888) 13 App Cas 523.
[67] (1862) 10 HLC 191.   [68] *Flory v Denny* (1852) 7 Ex 581.
[69] Bills of Sale Acts 1878–1891.
[70] *Re Bond Worth Ltd* [1980] Ch 228; *Carreras Rothman v Freeman Mathews Treasure Ltd* [1985] Ch 207.
[71] See *National Provincial Bank v Charnley* [1924] 1 KB 431, *per* Atkin LJ.

shadow over the property in question.[72] Though the debt or obligation need not as such be paid or performed out of the charged property, given that not all charged property generates an income stream to service a debt (but note that payment from the charged property may be contractually required[73]), the chargee has the right of recourse to it in the event of a default by the chargor. There is no such thing as a legal charge properly so called (except in the case of the statutory creation concerning land, a charge by way of legal mortgage)[74] for the common law has always had difficulty carving proprietary interests out of an undifferentiated bulk,[75] and property is charged, that is encumbered, only so far as is necessary to support the relevant obligation.

Evidence of charge

As a matter of evidence, it is more difficult to establish that property has been appropriated by way of charge than to show it has been conveyed by way of mortgage. Difficult issues of construction sometimes arise in the case law. The most important case of this type is the decision of the House of Lords in *Swiss Bank v Lloyds Bank*. Under the now repealed exchange control legislation, a company, IFT, needed the permission of the Bank of England to borrow a sum of Swiss francs required to purchase securities in FIBI, an Israeli company. The Bank of England consent laid down detailed requirements for the loan to be serviced out of the income, and repaid from the eventual resale price, of the FIBI securities. One of the covenants in the agreement between IFT and Swiss Bank, which made the Swiss francs loan, was that IFT should observe all the conditions laid down by the Bank of England. At a later date, IFT granted a charge over its FIBI securities in favour of Lloyds Bank, in order to support a loan made by the bank to IFT's parent company. When IFT got into financial difficulties, a question arose whether IFT had granted a charge over the securities in favour of Swiss Bank, for if it had done, this charge would rank ahead of the charge given to Lloyds Bank. It was clear that the agreement between Swiss Bank and IFT, incorporating as it did the Bank of England conditions, imposed a considerable measure of control over the FIBI securities. But did that add up to a charge? The

---

[72] Fitzgerald, P., *Salmond on Jurisprudence*, 14th edn, London: Sweet & Maxwell, 1966, pp 428–433.

[73] *Cf.* statements in *Swiss Bank v Lloyds Bank* [1982] AC 584; *Rodick v Gandell* (1852) 1 D M & G 763; *Palmer v Carey* [1926] AC 703.

[74] Law of Property Act 1925, ss 85–86.

[75] See *Laurie and Morewood v Dudin and Sons* [1926] 1 KB 223.

House of Lords held that it did not. Swiss Bank was concerned above all that its agreement with IFT remained lawful under UK exchange control legislation; it was stipulating for lawful as opposed to secured repayment of the loan. Consequently, the priority battle was won by Lloyds Bank.

In the Court of Appeal, Buckley LJ put his finger on one vital point relevant in the construction of the agreement for the purpose of discerning a charge:[76]

> [I]f upon the true construction of the relevant documents in the light of any admissible evidence as to surrounding circumstances the parties have entered into a transaction the legal effect of which is to give rise to an equitable charge in favour of one of them over property of the other, the fact that they may not have realised this consequence will not mean that there is no charge. They must be presumed to intend the consequence of their acts.

In construing the agreement, a court may be assisted by evidentiary presumptions. The deposit of documents of title by someone incurring an obligation creates a presumption that a charge was intended (at least in the case of land,[77] and pledges of bills of lading). Even if the advance is given in favour of a third party, the presumption of a charge will be drawn where there is cause and effect between the deposit of the title documents and the making of the advance to the third party.[78] If the parties create a consensual security, it will still be treated as a charge even if they call it an equitable lien, a term associated with securities arising by operation of law and usually seen in the case of sale of land. Thus, in *Re Welsh Irish Ferries Ltd*,[79] a shipowner who took from a time charterer a 'lien upon all cargoes, and upon all sub-freights for any amounts due under this charter . . .' was held to have acquired a charge. This decision has, however, been cogently criticized on the ground that the lien confers merely a right to step in and intercept payment without being able to follow payment into the hands of payees. Hence it is akin to a seller's right of stoppage in transit and is not a property right.[80]

A contractual right to step in and take possession of defined assets does not as such give rise to a charge. It is common for construction contracts to give the employer the right to take over plant on stated events of default committed by the contractor. In *Re Cosslett (Contractors) Ltd*,[81]

---

[76] [1982] AC 584 at pp 595, 596.
[77] *Thames Guaranty v Campbell* [1985] QB 210; *cf. Burdick v Sewell* (1884) 13 QBD 159.
[78] *Re Wallis & Simmons (Builders) Ltd* [1974] 1 WLR 391.
[79] [1986] Ch 471.
[80] See Lord Millett in *Agnew v Commissioner of Inland Revenue* [2001] 2 BCLC 188 (PC).
[81] [1998] Ch 495 (CA).

this right was held not to amount to a charge since the employer was not as such looking to the plant to discharge the contractor's liability. Moreover, the right to take over the plant did not secure the contractor's obligation but rather enabled the employer to carry out performance itself instead of the contractor. In fact, the employer was seeking to minimize a loss flowing from the contractor's breach of contract. In the present case, however, the employer also had the right to sell the plant and apply the proceeds towards discharge of debts owed to it by the contractor. This right was held to be an equitable charge and not a possessory lien coupled with a contractual power of sale. The employer's rights were exclusively contractual and did not derive from the transfer to it of possession of the plant.

In a number of cases, charges have been inferred despite the chargee's attempt to have the relevant contractual clause drafted as a reservation of the property in goods supplied under a sale contract. Where the clause applies to the very goods supplied by the seller, the courts have generally seen no difficulty in giving effect to it in accordance with conventional sale principles,[82] even where the clause reserves the property in the goods until all sums owed to the seller are paid, and not just the contractual price of the goods themselves.[83] Where the seller, however, purports to reserve the property in the money or other proceeds of the original goods, they have in practice interpreted these clauses as creating a charge,[84] though lip service has been paid to the possibility of such clauses satisfying the drafting standard of genuine property reservation clauses.[85]

Mortgage and charge

The line between mortgage and charge is sometimes blurred by statute. Section 205(1)(xvi) of the Law of Property Act 1925, part of the general definition section, gives the following definition of a mortgage:

> 'Mortgage' includes any charge or lien on any property for securing money or money's worth; 'legal mortgage' means a mortgage by demise or sub-demise or a charge by way of legal mortgage . . .

It is common too for the line between mortgages and charges to be blurred in the case law,[86] even where the security is granted over legal as

---

[82] Sale of Goods Act 1979, s 17; see chapter 4.

[83] *Armour v Thyssen Edelstahlwerke AG* [1991] 2 AC 339.

[84] *Re Peachdart Ltd* [1984] Ch 131; *E. Pfeiffer Weinkellerei-Weineinkauf GmbH & Co v Arbuthnot Factors* [1988] 1 WLR 150.

[85] *Clough Mill Ltd v Martin* [1985] 1 WLR 111.

[86] For example, *Garfitt v Allen* (1887) 37 Ch D 48.

opposed to equitable property. Some awareness of this phenomenon is to be seen in the judgment of Buckley LJ in *Swiss Bank v Lloyds Bank* ('an equitable charge may, it is said, take the form either of an equitable mortgage or of an equitable charge not by way of mortgage'). In the case of a binding contract to mortgage property, he asserts that its specific enforceability (*scil.* to convey the legal estate) 'will give rise to an equitable charge on the property by way of mortgage'. Although the remedies differ according to whether the security is a mortgage or a charge, there is a tendency for a blurring of the two to occur where nothing really turns on the difference (as in the judgment of Buckley LJ, above). Nevertheless, a court had to face the difference squarely in *London Country and Westminster Bank v Tompkins*.[87]

The case concerned restrictions contained in a World War I statute (the Increase of Rent and Mortgage Interest (War Restrictions) Act 1915) on the enforcement of the rights of a mortgage under a mortgage.[88] The statute went on to provide in s 2(4) that it did not apply to 'an equitable charge by deposit of title deeds or otherwise'. In 1912, the defendant had deposited with the claimant bank the title deeds of a number of houses as security for an overdraft. The agreement stated: 'I charge all my present and future estate and interest, both legal and equitable, in all the hereditaments and other property comprised in the said deposited deeds and documents . . .'. The agreement went on to provide that the bank 'shall . . . be deemed mortgagees under this deed' and should be entitled to call for 'such further valid legal or other mortgage or mortgages by deed or otherwise . . . as you may require . . .'. It also conferred upon the bank the rights of a mortgagee in respect of the properties charged. The court concluded that the transaction fell outside the statute. One of the judges (Pickford LJ) concluded that it was a charge. The others (Bankes and Scrutton LJJ) concluded that it was an equitable mortgage that amounted to an excluded charge. According to Pickford LJ: '[T]he elaborate and drastic documents by which bankers seek to protect themselves may pass the line between mortgages and charges unintentionally.' He nevertheless concluded that the agreement did not amount to a mortgage for the purpose of the statute, since there had not yet occurred an out-and-out conveyance of the property, though he was troubled by the rather exorbitant language in the agreement. There was therefore no need, in his view, to look to s 2(4). According to Scrutton LJ, the transaction was a mortgage but the excluding words in s 2(4) meant equitable securities in the

---

[87] [1918] 1 KB 515.   [88] Section 1(4).

wide sense (charges and equitable mortgages). There had to be 'some reason why the legislature should stay the enforcement of mortgages during the war and leave unfettered the enforcement of equitable charges'. It probably lay in the desire of the legislature not to hinder borrowers from obtaining temporary loans (such as the overdraft in the present case) from banks on deposit of security. This was reason enough for reading 'equitable charge' in s 2(4) of the statute in the wide sense to mean 'a security not intended to be of a permanent character (*viz*, an equitable mortgage or a charge) and therefore made in an informal way which needs equitable assistance to enforce it in most cases and in most respects'. This degree of judicial control over temporary security complemented the more stringent control laid down by the Act for security of a more permanent character.

Remedies

Both mortgagees and chargees may, where appropriate, sue on the personal covenant of the debtor to pay the agreed sum. Besides this *in personam* action in debt, however, they have certain *in rem* remedies where the debtor is in default. In the case of mortgages, these remedies are four in number. First, there is the remedy of foreclosure. Simply put, this is the lifting of the mortgagor's equity of redemption, the effect of this being that the conveyance or assignment of the property in favour of the mortgagee is given full effect. This remedy is subject to various stringent controls, since it plainly works as a forfeiture. It is significant mainly in the case of mortgages of land and is here noted only in outline. Foreclosure is not a remedy for chargees: a charge involves no conveyance to the chargee so there is no outright transfer held in suspense while the chargor remains in good standing.[89]

The second remedy is to take possession of the property. In principle, a mortgage gives the mortgagee the right to enter immediately upon the property once the mortgage is executed. In practice, an invariable exercise of this right would make the mortgage largely useless as a security device so mortgage agreements will permit the mortgagor to remain in possession. The mortgagor's continuing right to stay, however, will depend upon his remaining in good standing under the mortgage agreement. It therefore follows that a mortgagor who defaults is liable to surrender this right to remain in possession. Where the mortgage is a security bill of sale for the purposes of the Bills of Sale Act 1878

---

[89] *Re Owen* [1894] 3 Ch 220.

(Amendment) Act 1882,[90] there arises an implied remedy of seizure (and sale) which is required by the Act to be exercised within certain limits.[91] These require the personal chattels to be held on the mortgagee's premises for five days before they are sold,[92] in order to give the mortgagor the opportunity to reinstate himself under the bill of sale. The remedy of taking possession is also denied to chargees, again for the reason that there is no conveyance or assignment of property to the chargee. Of course, it is always possible that an agreement will confer on the chargee such added remedies. It will then become a nice question[93] whether the secured creditor is a chargee with enhanced remedies or a mortgagee by another name.

The third remedy of the mortgagee, available also to a chargee, is to sell the property. A mortgagee may take possession prior to sale; a chargee, unable to take possession, will have to apply to court to sell the charged property. An application to the court will also be necessary in all cases where the assistance of the court is needed to effectuate the sale, for example, where the cooperation of the mortgagor is needed for a legal transfer of share certificates made out in the name of the mortgagor. Even if the mortgage is not contained in a deed (where the Law of Property Act 1925, s 101 confers a power of sale), there will be an implied power of sale in the mortgage instrument, exercisable on default.[94] Where the mortgage is a security bill of sale for the purpose of the Bills of Sale Act 1878 (Amendment) Act 1882, we have already seen that a right to sell may be implied under the Act. Any surplus remaining will go to the mortgagor; any deficit may be recouped, if the mortgagor has the assets to do so, by a personal action on the covenant.

The fourth remedy, again available to a chargee too, is to apply to the court for the appointment of a receiver[95] to take possession of the property, though it is almost invariably the case for the agreement giving rise to the mortgage or charge to permit the mortgagee or chargee to appoint a receiver in the name of the mortgagor without having to make a court application (oddly missing in *Cryne v Barclays Bank*[96]). In the case of companies, this receiver, when acting in respect of at least substantially the whole of the company's assets encumbered by a floating charge or by a number of securities that include a floating charge, is known as an

---

[90] See below. [91] *Re Morritt* (1886) 18 QBD 222. [92] Sections 7 and 13.
[93] See *London County and Westminster Bank v Tompkins* [1918] 1 KB 515.
[94] *Deverges v Sandeman Clark & Co* [1902] 1 Ch 579.
[95] Supreme Court Act 1981, s 37(1).
[96] [1987] BCLC 548.

administrative receiver.[97] The administrative receiver, though the agent of the company debtor, acts in the material interests of the secured creditor and pursuant to a mandate that requires the company's indebtedness to be discharged. Because of concerns that the process gives other creditors short shrift, the Enterprise Bill 2002 deprives secured creditors of the power in future to procure the appointment of administrative receivers in new cases falling outside certain statutory exceptions dealing with capital and investment market and project finance transactions. Where the mortgage[98] is in the form of a deed, there is a statutory right to appoint a receiver,[99] whose powers are set out in s 109 of the same Act. There is also a statutory statement of the receiver's powers, presumptively incorporated in the agreement permitting the mortgagee to make the appointment, in the case of certain charges granted by a company.[100] Nevertheless, any well-drawn instrument of mortgage or charge will contain an express power of appointment of a receiver and will set out powers at least as extensive as those contained in s 109 of the Law of Property Act 1925 and Schedule 1 to the Insolvency Act 1986.

Fixed and floating charges

So far, no attempt has been made to distinguish fixed and floating charges. The above discussion is in fact predicated upon the charge being a fixed one that encumbers the assets falling within its grasp. It is in the nature of a fixed charge that the chargor is not at liberty to deal beneficially with the charged asset but must seek the chargee's permission if the asset is to be disposed of or transferred. An unfettered freedom to deal with assets in the ordinary course of business free from the charge is inconsistent with the charge being a fixed one.[101] Lord Millett has vividly demonstrated the limitations of fixed charges:

> [The company chargor] could not give its customers a good title to the goods it sold to them, or make any use of the money they paid for the goods. It could not use such money or the money in its bank account to buy more goods or meet its other commitments. It could not use borrowed money either, not even . . . the money advanced to it by the charge holder. In short, a fixed charge would deprive the company of access to its cash flow, which is the life blood of a business.[102]

---

[97] Insolvency Act 1986, s 29(2).
[98] Or charge: see Law of Property Act 1925, s 205(1)(xvi).
[99] Section 101.
[100] See Insolvency Act 1986, Schedule 1.
[101] *Re Cosslett (Contractors) Ltd* [1998] Ch 495 at pp 509–510 (Millett LJ).
[102] *Agnew v Commissioner of Inland Revenue* [2001] 2 BCLC 188 (PC).

Control of the assets by the chargee is therefore the defining feature of a fixed charge. For reasons that will be explained, however, it is possible to create a charge that in one sense is suspended but is ready to settle in a fixed way upon the assets in the event of this being necessary for the protection of the chargee's interests. This type of charge is known as a floating charge and is regarded as a present security interest[103] though its full force may not, indeed in most cases will not, be fully felt until a future date. There is a certain vagueness about the attachment of even a fixed charge to the assets it includes; this vagueness is necessarily more pronounced in the case of a floating charge.

A floating charge is a 'dormant' security[104] that permits the company debtor to trade beneficially with the charged assets until the occurrence of a default or other prescribed event that causes the charge to 'crystallize'. As Lord Macnaghten later put it in *Illingworth v Houldsworth*:[105]

> A specific [or fixed] charge . . . is one that without more fastens on ascertained and definite property or property capable of being ascertained and defined; a floating charge, on the other hand, is ambulatory and shifting in its nature, hovering over and so to speak floating with the property which it is intended to affect until some event occurs or some act is done which causes it to settle and fasten on the subject of the charge within its reach and grasp.

In a famous passage, Romer LJ once ascribed to a charge three attributes that would give it the character of a floating charge, though he was careful to say that some floating charges would not possess all three attributes. The charge would cover a class of assets present and future; the contents of that class would change from time to time in the ordinary course of business; and the chargor would be at liberty to carry on its business in the ordinary way until the chargee stepped in to prevent it.[106] Of these, the third attribute is the most important;[107] floating charges have been held to exist even in the case of assets that do not fluctuate at all in the

---

[103] *Evans v Rival Granite Quarries Ltd* [1910] 2 KB 979; *Smith v Bridgend Borough Council* [2001] UKHL 58 at [61] (Lord Hoffmann).

[104] Lord Macnaghten in *Government Stock Investment Co v Manila Railway Co* [1897] AC 81.

[105] [1904] AC 355.

[106] *Re Yorkshire Woolcombers Association Ltd* [1903] 2 Ch D 284 at p 295.

[107] *Agnew v Commissioner of Inland Revenue* [2001] 2 BCLC 188 (PC).

ordinary course of business,[108] even a consignment of raw materials with a very short commercial life.[109]

As a matter of construction, if the charge is not clearly expressed to be fixed or floating, there is a tendency for it to be interpreted as a floating one if it covers an extensive range of assets, like the charge on 'all [the] estate, property, and effects' of the chargor.[110] The permission of the chargor is not required for ordinary course dealings with floating charge assets and would not in any case be a practical matter in relation to the trading assets and circulating capital of a company. Any attempt to comply with the requirement of permission which exists in the case of a fixed charge would paralyse the company in its day-to-day activity.[111]

Latterly, the boundary line between fixed and floating charges has been particularly difficult to draw in the case of book debts and their money proceeds. A fixed chargee has a priority advantage over a floating chargee in two major respects. First, a later fixed charge ranks ahead of an earlier floating charge over the same assets, provided that the fixed chargee does not have actual notice of restrictions in the debenture creating the floating charge on the creation of subsequent fixed charges. The presence of some restrictions on dealing with assets is not inconsistent with the nature of a floating charge.[112] Secondly, certain unsecured creditors with a preference ranking, such as employees for back wages, are given a special statutory priority that places them in front of floating chargees but not fixed chargees.[113] These factors have induced banks so far as possible to create fixed charges over book debts and money proceeds which in earlier times would have been encumbered by a floating charge. After the dust has settled on numerous litigated disputes, it is now clear that a charge over book debts will be a fixed charge only if the chargee exercises control over dealings in both the book debts and their money proceeds, such as the contents of the bank account into which they are paid. It is not enough for the chargee to arrogate to itself powers of intervention that it does not in fact exercise.[114] Any attempt to separate the book debt, over which control is exercised, from its money proceeds, over which it is not, so as to take a fixed charge over just the former, will fail. A book debt is only on

---

[108] *Re Atlantic Computers Ltd* [1992] Ch 505 (CA).

[109] *Re Bond Worth Ltd* [1980] Ch 228.

[110] *Re Florence Land and Public Works Co* (1878) 10 Ch D 530.

[111] *Agnew v Commissioner of Inland Revenue* [2001] 2 BCLC 188 (PC).

[112] *Re Cosslett (Contractors) Ltd* [1998] Ch 495 at p 510 (Millett LJ).

[113] Insolvency Act 1986, s 386 and Schedule 6.

[114] *Agnew v Commissioner of Inland Revenue* [2001] 2 BCLC 188 (PC); *Re Brightlife Ltd* [1987] Ch 200.

technical grounds different from its money proceeds: 'the latter are merely the traceable proceeds of the former and represent its entire value'.[115] The book debt will therefore be treated as the subject of a floating charge in view of the freedom given to deal with its money proceeds.

The character of a charge as a floating one, important for priority purposes, is interesting too in conceptual terms.

If a fixed charge is a shadow cast on property,[116] what are we to make of the hovering, ambulatory floating charge? The intrusion of metaphor is some evidence of a legal inability to pin down the essence of an idea that has proved very effective in organizing a security base upon which a company can both provide security to a long-term lender and carry on a normal business activity.

Charge-backs

Floating charges are not the only charges that present conceptual difficulties. These can arise from the practice of banks, indebted to customers holding deposit accounts with them, in taking a fixed charge over their own indebtedness to those customers. This is usually done to secure guarantees given by the customers in respect of advances made by the banks to third-party companies in which the customers have an interest. There are sound practical reasons for banks doing this, but it does seem odd for a bank to take a security over its own obligations, though it might well be said that this is only the mirror image of taking security over the customer's rights. Conceptual difficulties abound. For example, how can the bank enforce the charge when the usual method of enforcement of a charge, over debts owed by third parties to the chargor, involves a demand for payment on the third party? And if the charge is a mortgage rather than a charge, does not the transfer by mortgage to the mortgagee erase by merger the mortgagee's own obligation to the mortgagor? Displaying a certain impatience with theoretical problems of this nature, seen to impede commercial practicalities, the House of Lords has firmly ruled that banks may take a valid charge over their indebtedness to customers.[117]

---

[115] *Agnew v Commissioner of Inland Revenue* [2001] 2 BCLC 188 (PC).

[116] *Salmond, op. cit.*

[117] *Re Bank of Credit and Commerce International SA (No 8)* [1998] AC 214 (HL), disapproving on this point *Re Charge Card Services Ltd* [1987] Ch 150.

Bills of sale legislation

The principal statutes are the Bills of Sale Act 1878 and the Bills of Sale Act 1878 (Amendment) Act 1882. The former statute was enacted to protect creditors misled by the apparent wealth of a debtor in possession of chattels that in reality were owned by or encumbered in favour of someone else.[118] Creditors are protected by a system of registration of bills of sale recording these transactions. The above idea of reputed ownership, extirpated from modern insolvency legislation,[119] seems quite anachronistic in the present credit-based economy. The later statute, driven by the desire to protect needy debtors, deals with those documents (security bills of sale) that record security taken for the repayment of a loan. The creditor must ensure the due observance of certain forms designed to protect the debtor.[120] The later statute, to the extent of its application (only security bills and not all bills), repeals *pro tanto* the earlier statute.[121] It applies to a wide range of security transactions, including mortgages and charges, but does not extend to title-reservation schemes, such as hire purchase.[122]

Scope of legislation

The definition of a bill of sale is to be found in s 4 of the Bill of Sale Act 1878 and covers a wide range of documents, many of whose names no longer possess the currency that they had in Victorian times. Bills of sale of 'personal chattels' can be summarized as either conferring a right of seizure, or conveying or granting legal or equitable interests in such chattels. For our present purposes, such documents have to serve a security function. It is important to stress that the legislation does not apply to the transaction as such but only to the document.[123] In consequence, if the transaction exists in an unwritten form, the legislation does not apply.[124] Hence if an oral agreement has already and effectively been reached, and presumably not merged in a later document, the oral agreement will stand, though it seems that the document may not be adduced as evidence of the oral agreement if it does not comply with the

---

[118] *Manchester, Sheffield and Lincolnshire Railway v North Central Wagon Co* (1888) 13 App Cas 554, *per* Lord Herschell.
[119] See the Insolvency Act 1986 and chapter 2.   [120] Lord Herschell, above.
[121] 1882 Act, s 15.
[122] *McEntire v Crossley Bros* [1895] AC 457.
[123] *Charlesworth v Mills* [1892] AC 231.
[124] *Newlove v Shrewsbury* (1888) 21 QBD 41.

legislation.[125] Similarly, if the only function of a document is to record after the event a transaction fully consummated by conduct, such as a pledge,[126] it will not be struck down simply because the later document does not comply with the legislation. For practical purposes, therefore, bills of sale legislation does not extend to possessory security and would not catch an equitable mortgage arising from the deposit of documentary intangibles. In such a case, possession is given to the mortgagee. Furthermore, the legislation applies only to 'personal chattels'.

Formal requirements

The formal requirements of security bills of sale are as follows. A security bill must be attested and registered in compliance with the Bills of Sale Act 1878 within seven days of its execution or else it is void for all purposes.[127] Attestation has to be made by at least one credible witness.[128] The bill, together with an affidavit of its due execution and attestation and certain personal details concerning the maker of the bill and the witnesses, has to be filed with the registrar.[129] There must be attached to the bill a schedule listing the personal chattels comprised in it.[130] The bill itself is void if it is not made out in the form set out in the Schedule to the 1882 Act,[131] which includes a statement of the consideration for which the bill is granted, though the case law tolerates minor departures from the prescribed form.[132]

Future property

The formal requirements of security bills of sale make it difficult, indeed probably impossible, to comply with the legislation in the case of future property,[133] for it is not easy to see how such items can be listed in the schedule to the bill. For practical purposes, individuals and partnerships cannot therefore give floating charges: the legislation does not extend to security given by a company.[134]

---

[125] *Newlove v Shrewsbury*.
[126] *Ex p Hubbard* (1886) 17 QBD 699; *Johnson v Diprose* [1893] 1 QB 512, *per* Lord Esher.
[127] Bills of Sale Act 1878 (Amendment) Act 1882, s 8.
[128] 1882 Act, s 10.
[129] 1878 Act, s 10.
[130] 1882 Act, s 4.
[131] 1882 Act, s 9.
[132] For example, *Re Morritt* (1886) 18 QBD 222; *Thomas v Kelly* (1888) 13 App Cas 506.
[133] *Thomas v Kelly* (1888) 13 App Cas 506.
[134] Bills of Sale Act 1878 (Amendment) Act 1882, s 17.

Exceptions

It is as well that the legislation does not apply to certain forms of short-term security commonly used in the import-export trade (for example, letters of lien or of hypothecation[135]). The legislation also excludes from the definition of 'bill of sale' certain documents used in the 'ordinary course of business' to represent goods, such as bills of lading and delivery warrants.[136]

Equitable lien

An equitable lien is a non-possessory security conferred by operation of law, the legal incidents of which are similar to a charge. It differs from a charge to the extent that it is non-consensual. It is conferred in limited circumstances. By far the most common case is that of sale of land. The equitable lien of the unpaid vendor for the purchase price continues notwithstanding the purchaser moving into possession of the land. It also acts as a counterpoise to the beneficial interest in the land acquired by the purchaser as soon as contracts are exchanged to conclude a binding contract.

The principal difficulty with equitable liens lies in estimating how far they extend beyond sale of land agreements. Equitable liens have been enforced in a number of cases involving choses in action, but not in cases involving chattels.[137] It is noteworthy that, in sale of goods agreements, there has been strong resistance to the introduction of equitable proprietary ideas.[138] Less resistant to equitable proprietary ideas, Australian courts are more receptive to the role of equitable liens in personal property law.[139] A review of the cases does not indicate very clearly the principles upon which such liens will be imposed.

In *Re Stucley*,[140] a son sold to his father, the sole trustee of a trust fund, his reversionary interest in that fund. The Court of Appeal held that the son had an equitable lien for the unpaid price even though the subject-matter was personalty and not realty. Cozens Hardy LJ thought the lien should apply 'to every case of personal property in which the Court of Equity assumes jurisdiction over the subject-matter of the sale'. Thus

---

[135] Bills of Sale Act 1890, s 1; *Re Hamilton Young & Co* [1905] 2 KB 772.
[136] Bills of Sale Act 1878, s 4.
[137] *Transport and General Credit v Morgan* [1939] 2 All ER 17.
[138] *Re Wait* [1927] 1 Ch 606.
[139] See *Hewett v Court* (1983) 57 ALJR 211; Phillips, J., 'Equitable Liens—A Search for a Unifying Principle', in Palmer, N., and McKendrick, E. (eds), *Interests in Goods*, 2nd edn, London and Hong Kong: LLP, 1998.
[140] [1906] 1 Ch 67.

where the purchaser of property included in a matrimonial settlement paid the price in advance to one of the trustees, he was allowed a lien over the investments purchased with the money when the other trustee later refused to consent to the sale.[141] In another case,[142] a managing director's service agreement required him to assign his shares in the company to certain individuals in the event of his contract being terminated. The price of the shares was to be calculated and paid at a later date when certain accounts were published. He was allowed an equitable lien over the transferred shares so as to secure the eventual payment of the price.

On occasion, a lien has been found where this accorded with the 'intention' of the parties, which comes close to confusing equitable liens and charges. The significance of the distinction is that certain charges (as opposed to liens) granted by companies have to be registered if the chargee's security is to be asserted against creditors of the company or their representatives.[143] The theme of intention was strongly presented in *Dansk Syndikat v Snell*,[144] where the claimants agreed to sell to Snell certain patent rights in return for a cash sum and future royalty payments. Snell sold the patent rights to a company which took them with notice of the agreement with the claimants. When Snell later repudiated his agreement with the claimants, the latter were held to have a lien (or rather an 'analogous right') over the patents for the unpaid royalties as unpaid purchase money.

Finally, an equitable lien may be imposed to give better effect to other equitable rights. In the case of loss insurance, the insurer is subrogated to the rights of the insured against wrongdoers causing the loss. The insurer's right of subrogation is reinforced by an equitable lien over damages payable by the wrongdoer to the insured, which prevents the insured from having the benefit of sums recovered by action without recouping the insurer.[145]

---

[141] *Barker v Cox* (1876) 4 Ch D 464.
[142] *Langen and Wind Ltd v Bell* [1972] Ch 685.
[143] Companies Act 1985, s 395.
[144] [1908] 2 Ch 127.
[145] *Lord Napier and Ettrick v Hunter* [1993] AC 713 (Lord Templeman).

Index

abandonment 18, 22–5
accession of chattels (*accessio*) 75, 106–7,
    109
  meaning 106–7
  ownership 107
action of ejectment 2
actions *in rem*, see *in rem* actions
administrative receivers 188
advancement, presumption of 100–1, 112
agency 44, 97–8
  apparent authority of agent, *see* apparent
      authority
  carriers 89–90
  conversion tort and 58–61
  mercantile, *see* mercantile agents
  tracing and 142
  where goods on sale or return 85
agreed to buy, meaning 135–6
agreement to sell 129–30, 132–3
apparent authority 118–22, 128
  deemed 125, 132, 174
ascertained goods 87–8
asportation
  conversion tort, in 54–5
  trespass, in 54
  unlawful 52
assignments 58
  definition 146
  equitable 97–8, 138, 148–51
  statutory 147, 151–7
  see also choses in action: assignments
attornment 44–6, 91, 95, 133
auctioneers
  conversion tort, liability for 58, 60,
      70

bailment 19, 27, 31, 33–43, 44
  bailees
    attornment by 44–5, 91, 95–6
    conversion tort and 63–4, 117
    involuntary 61–2
    liability of 35, 36–8
    negligence of 37
    nemo dat principle and 117
    possessory interest of 30, 81
    seller as 43

  undertaking by 46
  bailors 64, 70–1
    reversionary interest 76
  banking and 38
  chattel changed during 40
  conversion tort and 59
  definition 33–4
  equivalent quantity of goods to be
      returned 39
  estoppel and 65, 70
  fictitious 24
  for fixed or determinable period 33
  fungible chattels 39
  goods on approval 43
  hire purchase 40–2
  loans for consumption 38–40
  possession and 19, 35
  sale or return, goods on 43, 84
  sub-bailment 34–5
    privity of contract 34
  trespass and 52
  types of 35–6
  wasting 42
  at will 33, 52
    conversion tort and 63, 64, 69–70
  see also pledges
banknotes 10
  transferees for value 165
banks 38
  fixed and floating charges and
      190–1
  no-assignment clauses and 162
bills of exchange 5, 9, 145
  acceptance 166
  assignment 148–9
  bearer 165–6, 167
  definition 165
  forged signatures 167
  gifts 97–8
  holder in due course 137, 165, 167
  negotiability 165
  negotiation 166–7
    restrictions on 166
  payable on demand 166
  sum certain 166
  transfers 145

unconditional order 166
writing 166
see also documentary intangibles
bills of lading 8–9, 46, 74, 92–3, 145
definition 46
document of title, as 128
gifts of 97–8
holders 168
method of transferring rights and
liabilities 167–8
negotiability 165
pledges of 92, 178, 183
possessory lien over 92
trust receipts 178
see also documentary intangibles
bills of sale 192–5
defined 192
document and 192–3
gifts 99
mortgages 41, 181
security bills 186–7
personal chattels, legislation only
applicable to 193
registration of 137, 192
security bills 186–7, 192
formal requirements 193
future property 193
void 193
see also documentary intangibles
body parts 4
bona fide purchaser 12, 46, 116, 137
currency of 165
equitable mortgagee and 180
hire purchase and 41
mercantile agents and 125
motor vehicles 136
recission of contracts and 122, 155
tracing and 143
bona vacantia 23, 112
book debts, charges over 190–1
brokers
conversion tort, liability for 58
bulk cargoes 88–9, 91, 168
business, ordinary course of 127–8, 134, 138
buyers
conditional sale and 135–6
in possession 124–36
deemed authorization of seller 132
deemed consent of owner 135
documents of title 128

carriers 36–8, 44
agents, as 89–90

conversion tort, liability for 46, 58, 59
delivery by 46
misdelivery 62
lien of 171, 172
see also bills of lading
charges 169
assignment, by way of 149, 151, 162, 164
banks and 190–1
book debts 190–1
charge-backs 191
chargees
appointment of receiver by 187–8
control over dealings by 190
notice of restrictions in debentures 190
permission of 188
power of sale 187
taking possession 187
chargors 188
permission of 190
competing creditors with 163
construction contracts and 183–4
construction of document of 183
debts, over 151, 152
defined 181
equitable 184, 186
by deposit of title deeds 185
equitable liens and 183, 194
evidence of 182–4
fixed 188–91
control of assets by chargee 189
meaning 189
fixed and floating charges compared
190
floating 138, 157–8, 187–91
crystallization 189
meaning 189
security bills of sale 193
goods over 91, 140
land of 179, 183
legal 182
mortgages compared 153, 181–6
registration of 195
remedies of chargee 185, 186–8
chattels
abandoned 18, 22–5
accession of, *see* accession of chattels
banknotes 10
coins 10
commingled, *see* commingled chattels
contractual rights in respect of 32–3
conversion of, *see* conversion tort
corpses 4
definition 3

delivery 120–1
detention of 56–7
  unlawful 53
dispositions of 57–8
documentary intangibles not chattels 3–4
documents 8, 9
fungible 39
gifts of, *see* gifts
human body parts 4
improvement to 75–6
law relating to, development of 14–15
leasing of 42
lost 22, 24
ownership of, *see* ownership
personal 3, 193; *see also* choses in action;
    choses in possession
possession of, *see* possession
real 3
seizure of 187, 192
specification of, *see* specification of
    chattels
transfer of interest in 78, 93–4
trespass to, *see* trespass
value of 72–4, 78
  increase in value 75
chattels personal 3, 193 ; *see also* choses in
    action; choses in possession
chattels real, definition 3
cheques 74–5, 148
  definition 166
  see also bills of exchange
choses in action 3, 4–10
  assignments 144–5
    absolute 149, 151–3
    assignees 138, 148
    charge, by way of 149, 151–2, 162, 164
    conditional 149, 151, 153
    consideration 149–51
    debtor's consent to 146, 158–9
    definition 146
    equitable 148–51
    insolvency of assignor 163
    invalid 159
    mortgages 152–3
    no-assignment clauses 158–62
    notice of 159, 162–4
      equitable assignment 148
      statutory assignment 151, 152,
        154–7
    novation 158
    part of debt 153
    priorities between successive transfers
      162–4

    statutory 147, 151–7
    sub-assignments 149
    subject to equities 154–7
    in writing 154
  common law 145
  documentary intangibles 3–4, 6, 8–9
  pure intangibles 6–8, 144–5
choses in possession
  definition 3
  development of 4
  see also chattels
commingled chattels 87, 103
  commixtio (granular mixtures) 107
  confusio (fluid mixtures) 107
  conversion tort 110
  damages 110–11
  fault of a party 110
  ownership 110
  tracing 140
common law
  absolute or true owner 47, 62
  rights at 12
  see also subheading common law *under
    topics*
company shares, *see* shares in a company
computer software 8
conditional sale 41–2, 135–6
  motor vehicles 136
consideration 149–151, 180
constructive trusts 11, 32, 162
contracts
  recission 122–4
  void 114, 122
  voidable 114, 118, 122–4
conversion doctrine 11
conversion tort 12, 47, 115
  accession (*accessio*) and 108
  actionable *per se* 53, 58
    intention, element of 54, 55
    statutory defences 75
  actions for 13
  agents, by 58–61
  asportation as 54–5
  carriers 46, 58, 59
  chattels
    altering nature of 55
    damage to 55
    destruction of 55, 78
    detention of 56–7
    disposition of 57–8
    loss of 55, 73
    using 55
  commingled chattels 110

continuing nature of 78
damages for 68, 71
  consequential 72–3
  measure of 72–4, 75
  nominal 73
date of 72–4
definition 53
delay, effect of 57
documentary intangibles 74–5
entitlement to sue 62–71
forced judicial sale of chattel 72, 76, 78, 141
forfeiture and 56
hire purchase and 73–4
immediate possession 63, 69–71, 141–2
improvements to chattels 75–6
insolvency and 13
interlocutory relief 77
intermediaries, by 58–61
involuntary bailees, by 61–2.
liability in 52–62
lienees, by 172
limitation period 78–9, 135, 141
  when chattel stolen 79, 135
negligence and 55–6, 71, 74, 76
ownership, protection of 54
pledges and 58, 176
possession of chattels without authority 56
restitutionary action, liability for 74
reversionary interests 71
shares in a company 72
skeleton for use of medical students 4
specification and 109
tracing and 78, 141–2
transfer of interest in chattel 78
unsolicited goods 61
value of chattels 72–4, 75, 78
copyright 5, 6, 7, 145
corpses 4

damages 2
assessment of
  in conversion tort 72–4
  in trespass 51
commingled chattels 110–11
conversion tort, in 68, 71, 76
  consequential 72–3
  measure of 72–4, 75
  nominal 73
Dearle v. Hall rule
company shares, successive dealing in 164

tracing, application to 164
debts 5, 6–7, 12
assignment of, *see* choses in action: assignments
book debts, charges over 190
pure intangibles, as 6, 144–5
security for 169; *see also* charges; liens; pledges; mortgages
deeds 93, 96, 180
definition 96
delivery
chattels 120–1
constructive 44–5
deeds 96–7
definition 43
documents 45–6, 120
goods of, *see* goods: delivery
orders 45, 128
warrants 45, 128, 130
detention of chattels 56–7
temporary 66
unlawful 53
detinue 47, 56, 72, 73
abolished 47
conversion tort compared 76–7
documentary intangibles 3, 6, 8–9, 45
conversion tort 74–5
examples 145
gifts 97–8
liens of 170
ownership 15
possession 15
transfer of equitable rights in 145
documents 8
bills of sale 192
delivery 45–6, 120–1
of title 45, 120–1, 125
  definition 128
  deposit of 183, 185
  land to 3, 183
  seller in possession of 129–31
transfer of 145
see also documentary intangibles
donatio mortis causa 80, 93
delivery of gift 102–3
intention of donor 103
pure intangibles 103
double liability 64, 67

ejectment, action of 2
employees 25, 125
employers 25

equitable interests 11–12, 31–2
  immediate possession 63
  competing 138
equitable liens, *see* liens: equitable liens
equity
  choses in action and 5
  conversion, doctrine of 11
  rights 12
  tracing *see* tracing
estoppel 65, 70
  agency, by, *see* apparent authority
  conduct, by 119
  mercantile agents and 124–5
  negligence, by 121–2
  representation, by 119–21
exports 82, 88, 175, 178

finding
  acquisition of possession by 22–5
  finders 59, 66, 69
    duties of 24
  treasure trove 25–6
fixtures 3, 80, 103–6
  examples 105–6
  intention 104, 105–6
  landlord's 104
  meaning 104
  trade 104
foetuses 4
foreclosure 186
foreign law, application of 10
fungible chattels
  bailment of 39
  loan of 39

garnishee orders 130
general property 30–1, 81, 108
  transfer of 93, 122
gifts 80
  advancement, presumption of 100–1
  conditional 99–100
  contract and 93–4
  delivery 99
    completion of 96
    deed by 94
    meaning 94–5
    physical 94, 95, 98
  documentary intangibles 97–8, 100
  donatio mortis causa, see *donatio mortis causa*
  imperfect 97–8, 150–1
  ineffective 99–100
  intention of donor 94, 96

resulting trust, presumption of 100–1
  trusts and 101–2
  unconditional 61
good faith 129, 133
goods 3
  alterations to 83
  altering nature of 55
  approval, sale on 43, 84–6
  ascertained goods 87–8
  ascertaining price 84
  ascertainment, meaning 86–7
  bulk cargoes 88–9, 91, 168
  charges over 91
  commingled 87, 103; *see also* commingled chattels
  conduct of buyer 84–5
  damage to 55
  deliverable state, in 83, 89
  delivery 90, 133
    constructive 133–4
    deliverable state, in 83, 89, 90
    sale or return 86
  destroyed before possession is transferred 81
  destruction of 55, 69
  detention of 53, 56–7
  exports 82, 88, 175, 178
  future goods 82, 86
  general property in 30
  hidden 25–6
  intention of parties 82, 83
    unascertained goods 86, 87, 91
  loss of 24, 55, 135
  notice to buyer 84
  passing of property
    future goods 86
    presumptive rules 82–4, 89–91
    specific goods 82–4
    unascertained goods 86–7
  recovery of 14
  reserving right of disposal 91–3
  retention of title 82–3, 91, 133, 170, 184
  sale or return 84–6
  sale where contract void 81
  specific goods 82–6
  specific property in 30
  stolen 135
  tenancy in common 88–9
  transfer of 80
    intention of parties 80–104
    writing requirement 81
  unascertained goods 82, 86–7, 89–91

unconditionally appropriated to contract 89–91
unlawful interference with 47, 53, 71; *see also* conversion tort; trespass
unpaid seller's lien 83
unsolicited 61
using 55
see also chattels
goodwill
  definition 7
  as pure intangibles 5, 6

hidden goods 25–6
hire purchase 40–2
  apparent authority and 118–19
  assignment of option to purchase 159
  conditional sale and 41–2, 135–6
  conversion tort and 70, 73–4, 122
  failure to register agreement 121–2
  motor vehicles 136
  set off, equitable, and 158
hirers
  hire purchase, in 40–2
  reservation of ownership by 170
  rights of 27–8
holder in due course 137, 165, 167
hypothecation 194

incorporeal property, *see* intangible property
industrial designs, registered 5
information 5–6
in rem actions 2, 12, 13, 15
  mortgagees, by 186–8
  resulting trusts and 113
insolvency 7–8, 13, 15, 87–8
  assignments and 159–60, 163
  bailment and 39
  bills of exchange and 148–9
  charges over goods and 91
  conversion tort and 13
  gifts and 95, 99
  loans and 39
  resulting trusts and 114
  Sale of Goods Act presumptions and 83
  tracing and 140, 141
insurance policy, rights under 5, 195
intangible property 4, 144–5
  computer software 8
  examples 5
  novel types 7
  possession impossible 15

pure intangibles 6–8, 144–5
rights over 4–5
see also choses in action; documentary intangibles
intellectual property 5
interlocutory relief 77
interpleader proceedings 66, 75
intestacy 93
  rules 2
ius tertii 65–8

keys 3
know-how 5, 6

land
  conversion doctrine and 11
  documents of title to 3, 183
  equitable lien of vendor 194
  fixtures, *see* fixtures
  freehold 2
  leasehold 2, 3
  mortgages of, *see* mortgages
  occupier's rights 25
  personal property distinguished 1
land law
  personal property law and 1–2, 14
    restrictive covenants 32
law merchant, choses in action and 5
leasing of chattels 42
  leaseback 45
legal thing in action 154
letters of hypothecation 194
letters of lien 194
liens
  apparent authority 174
  carrier's 171, 172
  common law 173
  conferred by operation of law 174
  definition 170
  detention, right of 171
  entitlement lost 172
  equitable 142, 183
    chattels, involving 194
    choses in action of 194
    compared with charge 194, 195
    defined 194
    insurer's rights of subrogation 195
    land of 194
    personalty of 194–5
  general 171–2
  innkeeper's 171, 173–5
  letters of lien 194
  lienees 69, 171, 173–5

lienors 173–5
limitations of 172–3
non-consensual nature of 170
non-possessory 140
owners 173–5
possessory 169
proceeds, on 142, 194
repairer's 171, 172–4
rights treated as 171
self-help remedy, as 170
solicitor's 171
special 171–2
unpaid seller's 83, 92, 133, 173
   of land 194
loans for consumption 38–40
lost goods 24, 55, 135

market overt 118, 135
abolished 118
mercantile agents 124–36
acting as 134
dealing with goods 127–8
definition 125–6
estoppel and 124–5
ordinary course of business of 127–8
possession by 124–7
   owner's consent to 126–7, 134
milk quota as property 7
misrepresentation 122, 123, 133, 155
fraudulent 156–7
mistake
fundamental 114
recission 155
tracing 142
unilateral 122
money 9–10
had and received, actions for 141
trust terms, held on 11
see also banknotes
mortgages 41, 152, 169
administrative receivers 188
banks and 190–1
bills of sale and 41, 181, 186–7
bona fide purchaser of legal estate 180
charges compared 153, 181–6
deed, in form of 188
defined 179, 184
equitable 180, 185
equity of redemption 179
evidence of 182
foreclosure 186
future property 180–1
land and 179, 186

legal 180
mortgagees
appointment of receiver by 187–8
power of sale 187
remedies of 185, 186–8
taking possession 186, 187
mortgagor continuing in possession 186
personalty and 179, 181
pledges and 177–8
remedies of mortgagee 185, 186–8
seizure 187
share certificate 187
trust funds, interests in 181
motor vehicles 136
repairer's lien 171, 172–4

negligence 50, 61
bailees, of 37
banks, of 74
commingled goods 110
conversion tort and 55–6, 71, 74, 76, 122
by estoppel 121–2
trespass and 76
nemo dat principle 57
exceptions
   buyer in possession 132
   common law 117–24
   good faith, requirement of 125, 133
   motor vehicles 136
   owner's consent to possession 135
   pledgees 177
   statutory 124–36
hire purchase, in 170
meaning 116–17
notice 129–137
assignment of 148, 151, 154–7
Dearle v Hall rule 162–4
constructive 137, 162
in writing 152, 154, 162

owner
absolute or true owner 28–9, 47, 130
liens against 173–5
property interest overridden by
   transferor 115–36
apparent authority of, *see* apparent
   authority
consent to possession by 126–7, 135
definition 29
seller compared 135
ownership 14, 15
abandonment of 22–3, 25
accession of chattels and 107

co-ownership 31, 73; *see also* tenants in common
covenants in respect of chattels 32–3
definition 29–30
documentary intangibles 15
owner, *see* owner
possession, affinity with 29, 62
priority of entitlement paramount 28
protection of 54
registers of 29 n.
reputed 29
reservation of 82–3, 91, 133, 170, 184, 192
specification of chattels and 109
transfer of 43, 80–114

patents 5, 145
pawnbrokers 175–6
personal property (personalty)
definition 1–2
land distinguished 1
law compared with land law 1–2
leases of land 2, 3
pledges 30, 36, 117, 130
bailment
repudiating 177
type of, as 175
bills of lading 92
conversion tort and 58, 63
fiduciary relationship between pledgor and pledgee 176
fraudulent 127
goods on sale or return 85
mercantile agents and 124–5, 127
mortgages by deposit and 177–8
pawnbrokers 175–6
pledgees
liability for conversion tort 176, 177
rights of 27
sale, power of 176
special property in pledge 176
wrongful disposition by 177
pledgor's absolute entitlement to redeem 176
possessory liens compared 169
trust receipts 178
possession
abandonment of chattel 18, 22–5
acquisition by finding 22, 66
actual 51, 52
bailment and 19, 35
consent to, by owner 126–7, 135
constructive 52

control over chattels 17, 18, 25
custody distinguished 20–1, 25
delivery, by 43
definition 16, 51
documentary intangibles 15
document of title
by buyer 132
by seller 129–32
goods, of
by buyer 132–5
by seller 129–32
immediate 51–2, 63, 65, 69–71, 177
tracing 141–2
indivisibility of 19–20
intangible property and 15
legal character 17
lienee, by 171
mercantile agent, by 124–7, 134
mortgagee taking 186, 187
mortgagor continuing in 186
ownership, affinity with 29, 62
priority of entitlement paramount 28
proof of 128
as protected property interest 26–8
protection of 54
purpose of 21–22
surrender of 22, 120
temporary deprivation of 55
transfer of 35, 42, 43–6
constructive 44–5, 91, 95–6
unlawful 66
without authority 56
promissory notes 9, 165
definition 167
see also documentary intangibles
property
common law at 7
future 180–1
general 30–1, 81, 93, 108, 122
retention of 170
immovable 10
incorporeal, *see* intangible property
Insolvency Act 1986, for purposes of 7–8
intangible, *see* intangible property
movable 10
protected interests in 26–8
rights over 12–13, 26
contractual rights compared 26–7
infringements 13
special 30–1, 81
protected property interests 26–8

pure intangibles 6–8, 144–5
  possession impossible 15
  see also choses in action

real actions, *see in rem* actions
realty 1
recaption, *see* self- help
recission 114, 138, 155
registered industrial designs 5
reservation of title 82–3, 91, 133, 170, 184
  security bills of sale 192
restitutionary action 13
  liability for 74
  principles, application of 76
resulting trusts 11, 23, 111
  automatic 112
  constructive trusts compared 113
  gifts 94, 100–1
  intention 112–14
  presumed 112, 113
  void contracts and 114
reversionary interests 71, 194
Romalpa clauses 82–3, 91, 133, 170, 184, 192

Sale of Goods Act 80
  definitions in 81–2
sale on approval 136
sale or return 136
  bailment and 43
security 169
  non-possessory, *see* charges; mortgages
  possessory, *see* liens; pledges
seizure of chattels 187, 192
self-help
  entry onto land of another 77–8
  force, use of 77
  notice to possessor 77
seller
  owner compared 135
  in possession 124
    continuity of possession 131
    deemed 130
  thief as 135
set off 155–5
  common law 157–8
shares in a company 5
  conversion tort and 72
  gifts of 97, 100
  share certificates 74, 145
    deposit of 178
    gifts of 97–8, 103
    mortgage of 187

transfers of 159
  paperless 9
shares in a partnership 145
specific performance 76–7, 88, 180
specific property 30–1
  goods 82–6
specification of chattels (*specificatio*) 108
  meaning 107
  ownership 109
  unlawful 109–110

tenancy in common 88–9, 109
  commingled chattels 110–11
  tracing and 140
third parties 44, 45, 65–8, 75
  apparent authority of owner, *see* apparent authority
  mercantile agents, dealings with 127–8
  owner estopped from denying title to 117–22
  recission of contracts and 122–4
title
  documents of, *see* documents
  indicia of 103, 120–1
  legal interests not overridden by equitable interests 132
  motor vehicles 136
  reservation of 82–3, 91, 133, 170, 184
    security bills of sale 192
  voidable 122–4
    mercantile agency and 127
tracing 13, 78, 109, 111, 132, 134
  bona fide purchaser and 143
  commingled goods 140
  common law 139–41
  Dearle v Hall rule, application of 164
  definition 139
  equitable 139, 140, 141–3
    fiduciary relationship required 141–2
  following and 139
  mixed funds 140, 141
  volunteers and 143
trade marks 5
trade secrets 5
transfers by operation of law 103–114
treasure trove 23, 25–6
trespass 47
  actionable *per se* 49–51
  damages, assessment of 51
  de bonis asportatis 47, 48
  defendant's behaviour 51
  direct 48
  examples 48

indirect 48
inevitable accident 50
mental element 49–51
  wilful act 49–50
mistake, by 50
motive for 50
negligence and 76
to person contrasted 50
possession, protection of 54
self-help 77–8
strict liability for 49–51
who may sue? 51–2
trover 52
trustees 161
change of trustee 162
notice to 162–3
tracing 142; *see also* tracing

trust receipts 178
trusts 11–12, 31–2, 97, 101–2
consent of beneficiary 98
constructive 11, 32, 113
  resulting trusts compared 113
no-assignment clauses and 161–2
resulting, *see* resulting trusts
writing required 102

unjust enrichment 64, 68, 75
unsolicited goods 61

warehouse-keeper's certificate 128
warehousemen 125, 133
wrongful interference with goods 47, 53,
    71; *see also* conversion tort;
    trespass